Beyond the Port City

The Condition of Portuality and the Threshold Concept

Beatrice Moretti

FOREWORD
by Carmen Andriani
AFTERWORD
by Carola Hein

Historic pictoral map: Caribbean, West Indies Exploration Book, "XXXIX. Universalior Cogniti Orbis Tabula ex. ed. Geographiae Ptolemaei, Romae 1508".

Alexander von Humboldt, Aimé Bonpland, 1831, china on paper

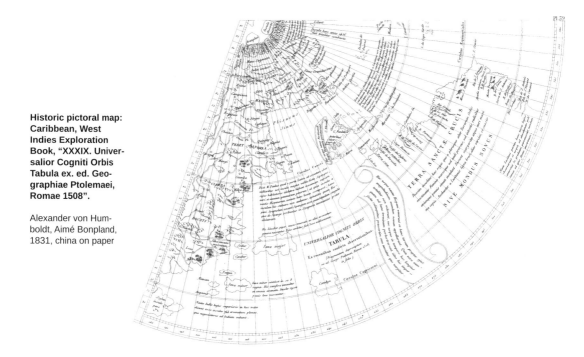

Alexander von Humboldt, *Cosmos: A Sketch of a Physical Description of the Universe*, vol. 1, 1864.

«From the remotest nebulæ and from the revolving double stars, we have descended to the minutest organisms of animal creation, whether manifested in the depths of ocean or on the surface of our globe, and to the delicate vegetable germs which clothe the naked declivity of the ice-crowned mountain summit; and here we have been able to arrange these phenomena according to partially known laws; but other laws of a more mysterious nature rule the higher spheres of the organic world, in which is comprised the human species in all its varied conformation, its creative intellectual power, and the languages to which it has given existence.

A physical delineation of nature terminates at the point where the sphere of intellect begins, and a new world of mind is opened to our view. It marks the limit, but does not pass it.»

Author's Note
This book contains the results of the doctoral research titled "Oltre la Città Portuale. La Condizione di Portualità e il Campo della Soglia" discussed on May 13, 2019 by Beatrice Moretti at dAD, Department Architecture and Design, Polytechnic School of Genoa (Italy). The thesis supervisors were Professor Carmen Andriani (Architecture/Urbanism) and Professor Manuel Gausa Navarro (Landscape/Urbanism).

Table of Contents

6   Abstract, Contribution, and Credits

14   FOREWORD
       Oltre. Metabolisms at the City/Port Border
       by Carmen Andriani

       25   THE PORT CITY
               Infrastructure, Landscape, Borderscape

       41   PORTUALITY
       42   Concept and Condition
       52   Backgrounds
                       Global Phenomena
                       Container and Cluster
                       Criteria and Contexts

       69   THRESHOLD
       70   Nature and Potential
       80   Backgrounds
                       The Concept of Threshold/s
                       The Threshold Heritage
                       From Integration to Coexistence

               105   ATLASES
                       Six Factsheets
                       Six Maps

       147   BEYOND THE PORT CITY
               Models, Strategies, Features, Recurrences

               191   NEW HORIZONS
                       Port Clustering and Governance Patterns
                       The Emergence of the Port City of the Cluster

200   AFTERWORD
        Designing Thresholds in the Port Cityscapes
        by Carola Hein

210   Bibliography

Abstract, Contribution, and Credits

The port city is the result of a relationship — that of the port and the city — so that its very definition is derived from the degree of intimacy or conflict that the two entities have established over the years. Since ancient times, ports have been both peculiar and generic places: made of the same constitutive elements even at distant latitudes, they combine their language with the urban one, making port cities universal categories, mirrors of each other.

Over the twentieth century, the city-port relationship has evolved, making it ever more contentious when it comes to defining its nature. Global phenomena and local alterations make research call into question the cataloguing of the port city: thus, it sets out to ascertain if the ambivalent dimension that today characterizes the city-port link is reflected in this cataloguing or if, instead, it serves to identify tools for taking it further, towards an extension of its original meanings.

It should be noted that most of the current studies on the port city still focus on the decommissioning and reconversion for urban uses of the areas between the city and the port. The waterfront projects, conceived overseas and then exported to Europe in the 1980s, were based on a standardized approach: they grafted new districts that leaned toward tourist-based commerce in place of port areas whose ownership had shifted to the municipality, delocalizing the port and occupying free stretches of coastline. Although in some cases, these projects re-established the connection between the historical centers and the sea, they negated the figure of the port within the city, contributing to the development of cloned seafronts all over the world.

As the years passed, this mentality solidified, often replicating itself even in the absence of major port decommissioning. It is as if this plan had fueled the belief that, in order to intervene in urban spaces in proximity to the port, it was always essential to replace and/or remove the port instead of imagining a different project between the two entities. Nonetheless, with the end of the great waves of port decommissioning, this approach has been surpassed, and it is now possible to note that new formulas for intervention and new fields of work are emerging.

These ideas are implemented out by supporting the recognition of *portuality* as a specific condition and by believing that the city-port *threshold* could emerge as the main symbolic field of exploration. The city-port threshold materializes in the space along the margin between the two authorities, in that recurring landscape in which the city and the port are side by side. This heterogeneous but unique system is originated by an administrative boundary that becomes an accumulator of change and transit, a space fragmented into parts where the juxtapositions take sufficient shape to be recognizable.

According to this approach, it is possible to update the old city-port dichotomy by outlining a new vision in which the port city is a *forma urbis* in progress, a plural figure influenced by the speed of changing processes and affected by the many factors that every day are embodied in its territorial palimpsest. By studying several contexts in Europe, however, it can be noted that some of these are behaving in an unprecedented way in relation to the design of the threshold between city and port. A small selection of city-port authorities, in fact, seems to have gone beyond the past practices of port substitution, instead designing and implementing alternative strategies based on the idea of coexistence.

In light of these assumptions, the condition of portuality is an alternative approach to the subject of the port city. By investigating portuality within the field of the city-port threshold, in fact, the study developed below aims to define interpretative and design tools using an inductive technique that from the finding of particular facts dates back to general statements and formulations.

During the three years of work, several interviews and dialogues with institutions, researchers and professionals from the world of architecture and urban planning but also from the port planning sector have allowed the construction and development of the research line. The most important exchanges are listed below in the form of acknowledgements.

Institutions/Public Bodies

Italian Ministry of Infrastructure, Superior Council of Public Works

Port System Authority of the Western Ligurian Sea (Genoa, Italy)

Municipality of Genoa (Italy), Urbanism Department

Delft University of Technology, Department of Public Building (the Netherlands)

The Worldwide Network of Port Cities — AIVP

Professors/Researchers/Professionals

Martin Aarts
    Senior Advisor and Head of Urban Planning,
    Municipality of Rotterdam (the Netherlands)

Maurizio Carta
    Architect and Professor, University of Palermo (Italy)

Sergio Crotti
    Architect and Professor, Polytechnic University of Milan (Italy)

Tom Daamen
    Construction Engineer, Building Project Manager, and Professor,
    Department of Urban Development and Management, TU Delft (the Netherlands)

Matteo di Venosa
    Architect and Professor, University of Chieti-Pescara (Italy)

Giuliano Gallanti
    Former president of the Port Authority of Livorno (Italy), Vice President of
    the Association of European Ports — ESPO

Francesco Garofalo
    Landscape Architect, Openfabric, Rotterdam (the Netherlands)

Franck Geiling
    Euroméditerranée, Marseille (France)

Francesco Karrer
    Architect, former President of the Superior Council of Public Works (Italy)

Carlo Prati
    Architect and Professor, University of Chieti-Pescara (Italy)
    Design Consultant and Project Manager, Società Valle 3.0, Rome

Mark Schoonderbeek
    Architect and Professor,
    Department of Public Building, Border Condition Research Group,
    TU Delft (the Netherlands)

Dirk Schubert
    HafenCity Universität Hamburg — HCU (Germany)

«The original configuration of the eighteenth century urban port edge, a restricted space overlooked majestically by the city, where various civic activities, with their institutional representations, coexisted with the commercial activities involving maritime or river traffic, was structurally modified by the creation of a new artificial terrain. The great extension of artificial terrain, in many cases reaching dozens of hectares, led to the creation of a new territory grafted onto the coastal edge of the consolidated city that acquired a distinctive shape, following totally different rules of formation that had nothing to do with the rules and traditions of urban construction.

[...]

In planning port basins, the design categories of street, square, route and street alignment, height-width relationship were no longer pertinent, and the rules of composition referring to visual perspectives, archetypal figures and metaphorical or allegorical development lost all meaning; the new port territory generated and developed throughout the nineteenth century in Europe was conceptually closer to a support mechanism than to a district of the city.»

Alessandro Rosselli

Alessandro Rosselli, "The Port as Structure and Meaning", *Portus*, no. 10 (Venice: RETE Publisher, 2005).

«The threshold must be carefully distinguished from the boundary. A Schwelle ‹threshold› is a zone. Transformation, passage, wave action. […] Whereas a boundary is a line that separates, a threshold is a zone of transition.

[…]

These gateways – the entrances to the arcades – are thresholds. No stone step serves to mark them.
But this marking is accomplished by the expectant posture of the handful of people. Tightly measured paces reflect the fact, altogether unknowingly, that a decision lies ahead.

[…]

Threshold magic. At the entrance to the skating rink, to the pub, to the tennis court, to resort locations: penates. The hen that lays the golden praline eggs, the machine that stamps our names on nameplates, slot machines, fortunetelling devices, and above all weighing devices […] these guard the threshold.»

Walter Benjamin

Walter Benjamin,
The Arcades Project
(Cambridge, MA and London: The Belknap Press of Harvard University Press, 1982).

Oltre.
Metabolisms at the City/Port Border

Carmen Andriani is an architect, full professor of architectural and urban design at the dAD, Polytechnic School of Genoa since 2014 and at the University of Chieti-Pescara (1992–2014). She deals with complex projects, in particular abandoned industrial heritage sites, trans-formations of port areas, relationships between infrastructure and landscape, and regeneration of frag-ile territories in the Mediterranean area. Being a member of numerous scientific committees, she has been visiting professor and guest critic at various schools including Waterloo University in Canada, Faculty of Architecture of the Universidad de la República (UdelaR), Tongji University, Cornell University in Rome, and Florida International University. Her writings and projects are published in numerous catalogs and magazines. Invited to various editions of the Milan Triennale and the Venice Biennale, she curated the volume *Patrimonio e Abitare* (2010). In recent years, Andriani has been scientific director of research agreed with the port authorities and municipalities. In 2014, she founded the Coastal Design Lab, an integrated architecture and urban planning project of the master degree course, dAD UniGE, working on the complex and inclusive design of the coastline (*costaldesignlab. wordpress.com*).

Carmen Andriani

Oltre means *beyond* or *on the other side*. If you go back to the San-skrit prefix "ut," root of the Latin etymology "ultra," it also means outside. The immediate meaning of the word is therefore that of going beyond one's real or conceptual sphere. Going beyond a field also means going beyond a limit, entering an unregulated, ambiguous, uncertain, and, in some ways, indecipherable zone.

"Out There: Architecture Beyond Building," for example, was the motto of an edition of the Venice Biennale[1] where, through this title, a shift in the terms became clear: affirming that architecture was beyond the building or that it could be learned from sectors external to those within the discipline denounced the insufficiency of traditional design tools and at the same time encouraged experimental and visionary models.

Beyond the Port City (*Oltre la città portuale*), the title of this book and the result of a doctoral research project, describes the going beyond the field and at the same time the exploration of a current, urgent, and highly debated topic: the interface between city and port. It is an ambiguous state between urbanity and portuality, an ancient dichotomy to be understood as the two sides of the same coin, a residual field with unclear contours and a fluid and interstitial breadth, an exemplary site of the postmodern project.

The nature of these areas has to do, first and foremost, with the decom-missioning process. We could say that it is the articulation — on the water-front, whether that of the sea or a river — of a phenomenon that marked the transition from the industrial to the post-industrial era in the past decades of the short century and the structural erosion of an economic, social, and thus also territorial, organizational system. When, as early as the 1960s, entire production-based, industrial, and logistical ensembles were expelled from

1
The Venice Biennale,
11th International
Architecture Exhi-
bition, Out There:
Architecture Beyond
Building, curator:
Aaron Betsky; see
also: Aaron Betsky,
"Breve introduzio-
ne all'architettura
sperimentale", in Exh.
Cat., vol. 3 (Venice:
Marsilio, 2008).

and moved outside the consolidated city, this led to large sores — empty spaces and abandoned artifacts — within the urban fabric.

A sudden detachment that returned immense areas, or brownfields as they were universally called in the heated urban and architectural debate that characterized the last decades of the twentieth century, to many European cities. It was an extraordinary opportunity to complete entire parts of the city, to rethink models and methods of growth, no longer expanding towards the *outside* but *on the inside*, in that middle ground or interface between the consolidated fragments of the city all around it. It was necessary to understand how those suddenly freed-up areas should or could accommodate the strains activated by the pre-existing structures along their perimeter, and to question what to do with the traces and the artifacts no longer in use and sedimented within those areas over time. Every design strategy seemed possible: from that of stitching together to that of *damnatio memoriae*, from the encounter with the pre-existing structures and the accumulation of meaning that the

recent past had deposited (the IBA experience gained in Berlin over the course of the 1980s being an exemplary case) to the idea of a completely new project, like what occurred in Paris or at the Barcelona seafront through projects powered by the ambition of steering the destiny of the part of the city in which they would have been established.

Fig. 1
Elevator 5 B1,
Montréal, 2017.

In port cities, the phenomenon of dismantling has taken roughly the same course: delocalization, which began in the late 1960s first in North America and then in Europe following the decline in activities related to trade and, to some extent, to tourism, also had inevitable consequences on the urban evolution of the individual cities. In the case of Montreal, for example, one of the most flourishing river ports in North America until the middle of the last century,[2] a progressive dismantling of large areas and related artifacts began in the 1970s. In 1978, the famous *élévateur à grain n.2* was demolished, which Le Corbusier used in the second chapter of *Vers une architecture* (1923) to explain, through the barren and monumental

2
For further details,
see: Carmen Andria-
ni, "Metamorfosi dei
Paesaggi Infrastruttu-
rali, dal Canal Lachine
al Silo n.5 del Porto di
Montreal", in *Portus
Revista de la RETE
— Asociacion entre
puertes y ciudades 8*
(2004).

3
It is said that, admiring the monumental simplicity of North American silos, Le Corbusier pronounced the famous phrase: "L'architecture est le jeu savant, correct et magnifique des volumes assemblés sous la lumière," adding that engineers thus definitively declared the end of architecture.

4
Walter Gropius, "Die Entwicklung moderner Industriebaukunst", in *Die Kunst in Industrie und Handel. Jahrbuch des Deutschen Werkbundes 1913*, Jena (1913).

5
Reyner Banham, "Catacombs of the Modern Movement: Grain Elevators in Myth and Reality", *Archetype*, vol. 1, no. 4 (1980).

image of the silo, how "architecture has nothing to do with styles"[3] and how the iconic value of those great grain machines already celebrated by Gropius was a symbol of modernity capable of upending somnolent academic architecture.

In the case of Montreal, the reconversion followed a complex trajectory: the planning of the enormous property, extending over 53 hectares of land, was legally asserted by various public and private entities. The 1990 *Plan d'Aménagement* essentially identified three issues: the iconic value of the port resulting from its most significant artifacts, the theme of the historical place as the recognized heritage of a community, and the creation of a multipurpose public space. The city seemed to reconquer spaces they had lost, leaving port buildings deprived of their original function with the task of representing, via a dismal scenography, the "Catacombs of the Modern Movement," as Banham affirmed in a provocative and empathic article published in 1980.[5]

In fact, over the decades, redevelopment processes have impacted ports all over the world. Technological advances in logistical and commercial systems, new units of measurement for the storage of goods, the computerization of their movement, and above all the new logics of the global market have created an extremely competitive context that requires continuous updating, both in technical-operational and spatial terms. The maritime transport of consumer goods has continuously revised its routes on the basis of an economy measured on a global scale. In the West, the North Sea and the Mediterranean are the nerve centers of trade. Rotterdam, Hamburg, and Antwerp in Northern Europe, and Genoa, Marseille, Trieste, Palermo, and the Port of Piraeus in the Mediterranean are just some of the main ports of call for these routes.

The port is therefore essentially a complex infrastructure, a site of production, operational activities, shipbuilding, and the storage of goods: a variable landscape on the water's edge that is measured by the large size of port machines, cranes, logistics platforms, and the maneuvers of ever larger ships. It is therefore easy to understand how the port system comes into conflict with the city system, especially when these two entities exist one within the other or otherwise border on each other, as is the case in most European ports. It is a clear conflict of functions, missions, instruments, government principles and rules, and administrations that oversee their development. The delocalization of some key activities or entire port areas — as was the case for the old port of Trieste, now protected as an example of valuable industrial archeology; or the decommissioning of some artifacts such as the former Hennebique grain silo in Genoa; and, more generally, of operational port buildings in most Italian ports — has gradually made this borderline, once distinctly delineated, more porous and now rendered it discontinuous through the dismantling processes.

For a long time, this phenomenon was intended as restitution to the city of a view of the water that had been denied until then: a sort of mandatory act, a kind of compensation through the creation of uniform urban waterfronts (with the spirit of the original model in particular still prevailing, i.e., the reconversion of Baltimore's Inner Harbor between the 1950s and 1980s, the prototype of many urban and real estate redevelopment projects). In reality, the hypothesis supported by this book turns this conception upside down and extends it.

Beyond the Port City carries the reasoning beyond this interpretation and makes a conceptual leap: from the notion of "restitution" to that of "coexistence." It is therefore not a question of denying the condition of portuality, if this is an integral part of the urban identity and history of the city and of its economy. Nor is it a question of disguising its presence or relocating its activities to a foreign elsewhere but of recognizing its existence and redefining its perimeter each time. The line that marks the administrative border between city and port — in fact distinguishing them — extends into a field with variable depth in which conditions, functions, uses, artifacts, and destinies all persist. It is beneficial to include them in a single vision capable of working with the synergies of the differences by transforming them into added value.

On the contrary, the notion of a limit or border in the postmodern era is no longer univocal. Material and immaterial barriers create fields of separation, overlapping, and interference. Non-permanent contexts fluctuate within continuously variable perimeters. The multiplication of borders corresponds to their weakening and renders them permeable. Marseille, Rotterdam, Genoa, Palermo, Hamburg, and Copenhagen are useful cases for describing the phenomenon and for drawing an effective comparison in order to demonstrate the reasoning that this book establishes. The field of the city-port interface — defined in the book as *threshold* — follows the developments of the administrative border: it is therefore a linear field, parallel to the silhouette of the coast in the case of seaports or spirally wound along the sinuous course of a river, as in the case of Rotterdam. They are pixels in sequence, pieces of a mosaic that mark the varying intensities along a hybrid border with soft edges.

This exploration outlines a third area, neither city nor port, but with the characteristics and materials of both. It brings together the long list of abandoned architectural artifacts, underutilized infrastructures, and defunct machinery. It is an area of silence. It is a void waiting to be repopulated with new functions, uses, people, and movement. It is a new area that stretches out like a spine between two defined identities of the city: the urban one towards the land and the port one towards the water. It presents the opportunity for innovative and experimental planning, founded on the valorization of both elements, on the hybridization of functions, and, above all, on the fabric of connections. The relational aspect is the principal mission of the interface: specializing the functions and creating short routes to and from the city, towards the water as well as towards the land, but also towards the territory to which it belongs, are among the most important expected outcomes.

Creating the conditions for establishing not so much an inert set of buildings and open spaces frozen in a master plan but rather a relational and multidirectional field with mixed functions is another challenge: more closely resembling an infrastructure than an urban project, the interface between the city and the port could function as a sort of large magnet, active on two fronts, both that of proximity, to benefit the neighboring areas, and the longer distance, in a broader territorial system.

This perspective would end up being, for example, more functional for the new reform of ports launched in Italy in 2016. The merging of several

port authorities into a single cluster (15 system authorities replacing the 24 individual port authorities) has eroded the two-way connection between city and port, necessarily projecting it into a wider territorial context. Genoa, for example, is part of the Western Ligurian Sea Port Authority, just as Trieste is part of that of the Eastern Adriatic Sea, Palermo of the Western Sicilian Sea, and so on.

Fig. 2
Former Hennebique Silo in Genoa (Italy), Gian Luca Porcile, 2016.

This new structure, technically inspired by an administrative and logistical simplification, is in fact a powerful device to break down a consolidated (and depressed) system of single, unrelated units and to give them a new form. *Beyond the Port City* therefore also means: shifting the point of view

6
Carmen Andriani, Beatrice Moretti, Davide Servente, "Patrimonio di confine tra Città e Porto. Il caso di Genova", PAESAGGIO URBANO, no. 3 (2018), 29–39; to further explore the notion of "heritage," see: Carmen Andriani, ed., *Il patrimonio e l'abitare* (Rome: Donzelli editore, 2010). See also: Carmen Andriani, "Patrimonio ed Abitare", in *Progetto per l'Identità dell'Architettura del XX sec.*, Pierfranco Galliani, ed. (2014), 75–89.

7
As an active part in the debate on land management, these issues are addressed at the permanent laboratory of the Coastal Design Lab of the Master of Science in Architecture course at the Polytechnic School of the University of Genoa. The Coastal Design Lab (conceived and coordinated by Prof. Arch. Carmen Andriani and active since 2014) studies experimental and research-based solutions, putting forward different scenarios in close dialogue with local institutions and associations. Starting from these assumptions, it initiates autonomous projects in parallel with educational activities, editing publications, and organizing conferences and exhibitions. The research activity of the CDL is aimed at formulating new methodologies of analysis and intervention for the reclamation and regeneration of abandoned or underutilized port areas and buildings in nodal contexts on the city/port borderline.

anew, moving on to a further dimension of the issue, putting the entire system of city-port thresholds up for discussion and connecting them in a relationship of mutual synergy, valorizing the potential of each of them in relation to environmental, cultural, logistical, urban, port, and infrastructural systems.

Coastal landscapes bring out a different and at the same time recognizable urbanity. It is the laboratory of the hybrid city measured by the large scale of the horizon, infrastructures, and topography: it is no coincidence that the first plates of Barbieri's *Forma Genuae* dating from 1938 represents planimetrically the breadth of the gulf and the compressed geography of the contours overlooking the sea. Italy has 8,000 kilometers of coastline. For over thirty years, dismantling and redevelopment processes have been taking place in port cities, many of which have been characterized by a substantial elimination of port activities, especially in the completed projects at the end of the last century.

In Genoa, along the 22 kilometers of coastal port development, founded on docks and piers often removed from the sea through repeated excavations and filling over time, three redevelopment processes are underway that inspire hope: the former Hennebique Silo,[6] the Enel thermoelectric power plant decommissioned in 2017, and the Levante Waterfront, a project by the Renzo Piano Building Workshop – RPBW that was donated to the city during a collaboration between the region, the municipality, and the port authority. In the latter case, shipyards, workshops, and recreational boating coexist with urban functions, public spaces, and provided services, while a new system of connections links the waterfront to the rest of the city both by sea with the opening of internal canals and overland, thereby overcoming the difference in altitude of the Carignano hill.

The transformation processes of these border areas, prompted by contrasting pressures as in the cases presented, are subject to temporary conditions of fragility. The city/port metabolism must be able to absorb and manage the enormous amount of data, traces, and sediments that affect the dynamic modification processes, but it must also be able to grasp the broad spectrum of literary, aesthetic, and artistic implications that these contexts have generated over time.

The presence of water and ports, specifically, represents the added value of cities; they have made their identities diverse, flowing, and inclusive; and, in this perspective, the temporary border that oscillates between the dual city and port condition will preserve both, not through exceptional actions in the form of individual objects, but rather in a revolutionary way through the spatial relationships it is able to activate.

Fig. 3
Port of Genoa,
Roberto Merlo, 2015.

THE PORT CITY

Infrastructure, Landscape, Borderscape

THE PORT CITY

Infrastructure,
Landscape,
Borderscape

As points of intersection between land and water, port cities emerge and develop according to a dual nature: the terrestrial one linked to the stability and possession of solid ground, and the marine one connected instead to the desire and need for discovery and encounters across the sea.

Since ancient times, ports have played an important role in socio-economic development but also in the identity of coastal landscapes. Ports are one of the oldest built structures whose formation, in many cases, developed in parallel with the founding of an urban settlement. For this reason, speaking about a port city means speaking in a comprehensive way about cities, since it is a truly interesting example of an urban synecdoche.[1]

At the outset of maritime trade and for many centuries thereafter, ports appeared within the urban layout as real public works of architecture: in the emporium port, the spaces of commerce were those of collective life, sales took place in squares and city streets, merchants carried out their trades within particular building types combined with private residences. Even the port infrastructures, like protective seawalls, were nothing other than the continuation into the water of the idea of defensive walls. An example of this model is the port of Halicarnassus which Cesare Cesariano reconstructs and depicts based on the descriptions of Vitruvius' *De architectura*: a system of cavea-like semicircular docks that translates the port city into a seamless design in which it is not possible to distinguish (and ultimately would not have meant distinguishing) one entity from the other.[2]

An eternal dualism, in short, that corresponds with a delicate balance. A physical, symbolic kind of cohesion but also an economic and cultural one, which gave rise to a complex organism commonly known as a port city. The port city is the result of a relationship between two territories and two entities: its very definition depends on the intensity of this linkage and the degree of intimacy, or conflict, that the two sides have established over the years.

1
Rinio Bruttomesso, Città-Porto. *Mappe per nuove rotte urbane* (Venice: X Mostra Internazionale di Architettura, la Biennale di Venezia, Marsilio Editore, 2006).

2
Rosario Pavia, Matteo Di Venosa, *Waterfront, dal conflitto all'integrazione* (Trento: BABEL, LISTLab, 2012).

3
Cesar Ducruet, Wouter Jacobs, Jason Monios, Theo Notteboom, Jean-Paul Rodrigue, Brian Slack, Tam Ka-chai, Gordon Wilmsmeier, "Port geography at the crossroads with human geography: between flows and spaces", *Journal of Transport Geography*, no. 41 (2010), 84–96, Amsterdam: Elsevier.

4
Rinio Bruttomesso, Jean Alemany, eds., *The Port City of the XXIst Century. New Challenges in the Relationship Between Port and City* (Venice: RETE Publisher, 2011).

5
Carola Hein, ed., *Port Cities: Dynamic Landscapes and Global Networks* (London: Routledge, 2010).

6
Reyner Banham, *A Concrete Atlantis: U.S. Industrial Building and European Modern Architecture 1900–1925* (Cambridge, MA and London: The MIT Press, 1986).

César Ducruet believes that the evolution of commercial logic and the gradual dismantling and restructuring of port areas since the end of the twentieth century have gradually made the concept of a port city increasingly confused.[3] Due to actions at the end of the twentieth century that reconverted disused port areas, in many cases re-establishing the link between the historic centers and the sea (but not the port), the idea solidified that in order to transform urban spaces near the port it was essential to replace and/or remove the port. These practices, in fact, contributed to fueling the dichotomy between port and city, instead of imagining a different project between the two entities: this actually negated any potential interaction and denied the figure of the port within the city.[4]

It is evident how these (and other) metamorphoses have steered the evolution of the city-port organism. Maritime geography, more than other disciplines, has dealt with the evolution of the port city by cataloguing the variety of configurations using morphological diagrams that provided a universally understandable interpretation tool, at least in Europe. Through this cataloguing, the characteristics of an identity were also traced, supporting the specific idea according to which port cities are useful models for exploring the modifications of contemporary space and that, however dissimilar, "resemble one another," becoming mirrors for one another.[5] Because of analogous evolutionary phases (especially in the nineteenth and twentieth centuries), each port actually does have a list of similar elements that, when combined with urban morphology, makes it a place that is simultaneously particular and generic. These are characteristics that recur in industrial buildings and produce a "vocabulary of forms" that can respond to the logic of production and ever-changing and growing operational needs.[6]

Like all classifications, however, even that of a port city is not impervious to time nor, above all, to the evolution of the relationship that defines it. Especially between the twentieth and twenty-first centuries the dynamism and uncertainty of the commercial world, combined with the effects of the global economy, profoundly changed the relationship between city and port, shifting the balance and, in essence, creating a rift in the combined development of the two poles.

Then, in more recent times, the clustering phenomenon again revolutionized the features of this relationship: by bringing together different scales within vast territorial systems, this process provided a different perspective not only for the infrastructural works but also for the cities of these ports, potentially reunited in coastal conurbations on a scale that was regional at minimum.

The impact of these metamorphoses, some of which are still ongoing, motivates the research undertaken here to question the effectiveness of the concept of a port city and to assess whether the current manifold and ambivalent dimension between city and port is still reflected in this cataloguing. Even more, it prompts an assessment of the state of interpretive and design tools with which the city-port issue has been managed in recent decades.

To set up this investigation, an invariant is called into question: namely, venturing to move beyond the port city by proposing a conceptual overcoming of this cataloguing, in order to both measure its terminological incisiveness and to test its value on a design level. The initial step of this process is establishing a privileged observation point, that is, one that is able to recognize the existence of a specific city-port mixture, a product of the meeting (or clash) between the city and the port. Already in long-ago eras, in fact, the dominant presence of the port generated a particular dimension in the environment around it that sparked fascinating narratives. It is the image of a city, or rather of the vast basins of a port city, that Paul Valéry describes as a "gigantic construction," a "semi-natural establishment," an artifice that is the meeting point between natural power and human ingenuity.[7] In this narrative, which depicts the port city as a fusion of culture and nature, complementary parts of the same structure, the first traces of an alternative reasoning on the port city were outlined. A perspective that would be able to overcome the antithetical approach in which the port component emerged as a harmful and sector-specific mechanism and, on the contrary, grasp the complexity of the contemporary city-port relationship.

With this positioning, especially in the area of planning and territorial transformations, the areas dedicated to port activities cannot be considered merely functional sectors attached to the city, but instead are vital components of a single apparatus, structural parts of an evolving organism. In order to position the new point of view — theoretical and strategic — the assumptions from which the investigation departs are laid out below.

Infrastructure

Ports are sophisticated infrastructures that contribute to alterate the original state of places according to a mechanism that leads from an alteration (territorial, environmental, economic etc.) to the project, first disrupting territories and then reestablishing them, enriched with new uses and meanings. In this process, the port component adds a "structural" character to urban settlements, making it possible to maintain that cities with a port are extraordinary urban infrastructures with a dual identity.

7
Paul Valéry, *Eupalino o Dell'Architettura* (Pordenone: Edizioni biblioteca dell'Immagine, 1988).

Ports possess infrastructural characteristics. Literally, they are facilities located "in the middle" that not only connect distant places but, even more so, mediate between forces that are often antithetical and guarantee the cohesion of the territories by building a unified appearance.

In terms of the relationship between urban planning and infrastructure, Stan Allen maintains that the idea of *infrastructural urbanism* can offer a new model that, by attributing a renewed meaning to the potential of architecture, aids in understanding and addressing the spatial transformations of cities and territories.[8] Issues such as mobility and transport have in general always been part of traditional architectural skills (before the separation of planning disciplines) and, over the years, have been employed to deal with problems on a large scale. These specialities, Allen continues, can (and must) be demanded in the scope of architecture and implemented with the available new technologies. In other words, Allen proposes the idea of strategically making use of the typical characteristics of infrastructures (detailed design, standard elements, structures repeated among the principal ones), thus facilitating "an architectural approach to urbanism."[9]

Infrastructures have a fundamental role in the constituting of functioning systems that can establish relationships and at the same time modify the spatial component. Following this reasoning, Allen introduces other qualities — for example, flexibility, forecasting, and adaptability — that contribute to enriching the vision of ports as infrastructural complexes:

> ——— Infrastructures are flexible and anticipatory. They work with time and are open to change. By specifying what must be fixed and what is subject to change, they can be precise and indeterminate at the same time. They work through management and cultivation, changing slowly to adjust to shifting conditions. They do not progress toward a predominated state (as with master planning strategies), but are always evolving within a loose envelope of constraints.[10]

In this "urban" vision of infrastructure, port systems are complex groups of flows of goods and people that acquire the typical attributes of the infrastructure. Among them, for example, it can bring to mind a certain "degree of play," that is a sort of indefiniteness or rather of elasticity given to the structures in order to foresee future technological adaptations. This lines up particularly well with the uncertainty and instability of the port world:

8
Stan Allen, "Infrastructural Urbanism", in *Points + Lines: Diagrams and Projects for the City* (New York: Princeton Architectural Press, 1999), 46–59.

9
Ibid., 51.

10
Ibid., 55.

——— Although static in and of themselves, infrastructures organize and manage complex systems of flow, movement, and exchange. Not only do they provide a network of pathways, they also work through systems of locks, gates and valves — a series of checks that control and regulate flow. […] What seems crucial is the degree of play designed into the system, slots left unoccupied, space left free for unanticipated development.[11]

11
Ibid.

The port is a complex infrastructure that influences the transformations of its surroundings in many respects, physical and otherwise. In this sense, Rhoads Murphey broadens the vision from infrastructure to the territories surrounding it. According to his thinking, the port city is a distinct organism within the field of urban settlements, a bearer of universal characteristics and plural meanings: a magnet whose validity as a hub for exchanges between land and sea is as undeniable as the awareness that it is because of this infrastructure that very large territories work efficiently.[12]

12
Rhoads Murphey, "On the Evolution of the Port City", in *Brides of the Sea: Port Cities of Asia from the 16th–20th Centuries*, Frank Broeze (Randwick, Australia: NSWU — New South Wales University Press, 1989), 223–247.

What takes a city with a port and renders it a port city, Murphey further argues, is therefore the entirety of networks of exchange and services that are located inland, that extended space (maritime or terrestrial) all around the port, where the infrastructures conquer space and materialize their impact on the territory. This is how the so-called inland is identified, i.e., the "place behind" that area that is blurred and for which it is difficult to determine its perimeters, where all the facilities that allow cities (and the port) to exist are concentrated and referred to:

——— No city can be simply a port but must be involved in a variety of other activities, including additional basic as well as service functions beyond the handling of water-borne trade and its integration with land transport. It also provides other goods and services, related to or growing out of its port functions, to a wider tributary area […].[13]

13
Ibid., 246.

Landscape

Thinking of port cities as particular forms of landscape legitimizes the idea that the port is an out-of-the-ordinary spatial and relational form, a device that is relevant not only in economic-commercial terms but also in terms of the definition of an urban identity. This assumption fits into the progression that, in recent decades, has involved the concept of landscape and its applications in urban matters. At the turn of the twenty-first century, the crisis of the concept of territory as an analytical and measurable space led to a radical shift in studies to the territorial scale, attributing new strategic meanings to the notion of landscape. With the digital-technological revolution, built spaces lost their precise physical connotation and became fields of relations: due to new global communication networks, there was no longer any need for the territory to meet and communicate, but the need for landscapes and for places to live and to be recognized increased appreciably.[14]

In this framework, landscape was subjected to a process of semantic stress, and not only its definition but also its identity was enriched: it replaced architecture as a model of construction of contemporary urban planning by becoming "both the lens through which the contemporary city is represented and the medium through which it is constructed."[15]

These ideas are part of a broader and more complex reasoning that transformed the landscape from a predominantly aesthetic or aestheticizing notion, natural beauty or a panorama to "a universe of existing things, therefore that can neither be touched nor seen: again, but in an unreflective way, it no longer takes on the appearance of a complex of objects but the nature of a way of seeing."[16] Using this meaning, landscape, made artificial through human intervention, is a candidate for becoming a preferential means of interpreting and representing not only spaces, but the relationships, the histories and the performativity of places. To use Andreas Kipar's words in defining the new conceptual potential of the term:

> ———— The landscape as a living mirror of our being finds its origin in the term land (in Italian the relation is between the words paese and paesaggio A/N) [...] and reminds us of the divergence between a portion of a territory that is aesthetically neutral and the landscape that has changed in standing, through a historical-artistic elaboration that is anything but neutral. [...] The landscape is an infrastructure because it is the medium that allows us to relate to the space that surrounds us, from every point of view, and that allows us to carry out activities. This is the task of infrastructure, that is, to be in-between, and indeed the landscape is between us and nature.[17]

From this moment on, the meanings for the concept of landscape become innumerable. In his studies, Michael Jakob, for example, theorizes "omni-landscape" as an epochal theme. An international "non-verbal phe-

14
Franco Farinelli, *La crisi della ragione cartografica* (Bologna: Piccola Biblioteca Einaudi, 2009).

15
Charles Waldheim, eds., *The Landscape Urbanism Reader* (New York: Princeton Architectural Press, 2006).

16
Franco Farinelli, "L'arguzia del paesaggio", *Casabella*, no. 575–576 (1991), 10–12.

17
Andreas Kipar, "Infrastrutture e paesaggio", *Ce.S.E.T., Atti del XXXIX Incontro di Studio* (2010), 47–53.

nomenon" that goes beyond traditional linguistic and disciplinary boundaries. According to Jacob, the recent role of landscape as an instrument and expression of the world arises through contrast in the specific attempt by the city to invent and define its "other."[18]

The urban disorder of the late twentieth century, the crisis of planning and the growing illegibility of territories, in fact, prompted a push to identify new references with which to interpret the transformations: they fueled the desire to comprehend the spatial forms that continued to generate, indeed defining them as "other" compared to the commonly understood city. This led to the need to speak about, map out or even exhibit the landscape, or rather the new forms in which the landscape was being modeled.

Among the numerous examples, it makes sense to call to mind the DATAR photographic mission for which Gabriele Basilico documented the transformations of the northern French coast, revisiting the variations of a stretch of coastline marked by large landings, infrastructures, and industrial centers in continuous evolution.[19]

Those immortalized by the Italian photographer are derived landscapes, influenced by continuous technological and commercial adaptations that determined the development of an analytical dimension. It is the presence and continuous expansion of large infrastructural complexes, such as ports or airports, in fact, that motivate the production of new forms of landscape disposed (and subjected) to change and to the progressive evolution of their structures.

These configurations have been the subject of Charles Waldheim's *Landscape Urbanism* for at least two decades.[20] The theory, already developed at the end of the nineties, investigates the landscape by positioning it as the primary interpretative tool of the space in which we live and of the relationships we establish.

According to this thought, the landscape is, through planning, a palimpsest of the histories and processes that are memorized and settled in it, "an apparent form of a cultural, economic, and social context, even before being a physical one."[21]

The objective of *Landscape Urbanism* is to interpret and transform urban settings through the lens, or the many lenses, of the landscape. From this important research so many adjectivizations and potential uses of the term have been derived that, in this way, it becomes both indefinite and promiscuous, acquiring significant conceptual value. In Waldheim's vision, landscape is the "medium of urbanism,"[22] especially in those contexts where the architectural and urban orders have been ren-

18
Michael Jakob, *Il paesaggio* (Bologna: Universale Paperbacks Il Mulino, 2009).

19
The "Mission Photographique de la DATAR" (Délégation à l'Aménagement du Territoire et à l'Action Régionale) was a project that, between 1984 and 1985, involved an international group of photographers engaged by the French government to interpret the transformations of the national landscape. Basilico was the only Italian involved and decided to document the coasts, with over 200 images collected in the volume Bord de mer: mission *photographique de la Datar 1984–85*, published by Art & Udine in 1992.

20
Landscape Urbanism is an urban planning discipline that claims that the best way to organize cities is through landscape design rather than architecture. LU emerges for the first time in the mid nineties as a branch of Landscape Ecology that studies the organization of human activities in the natural landscape. Since that time, LU has taken on very different uses as a tool for reorganizing cities in post-industrial decline and highly infrastructured

territories. Cf. Charles Waldheim, *The Landscape Urbanism Reader* (New York, USA: Princeton Architectural Press, 2006) and Gareth Doherty, Charles Waldheim, eds., *Is Landscape...? Essays on the Identity of Landscape* (Abingdon and New York, USA: Routledge, 2015).

21
Mosè Ricci, "Pi(C)ity", in Manuel Gausa, Mosè Ricci, Nicola Canessa, Mathilde Marengo, Emanuela Nan, eds., *MED.NET. IT.01* (Trento: LISt Lab, 2011).

22
Charles Waldheim, *Landscape as Urbanism: A General Theory* (Princeton and Oxford: Princeton University Press, 2016).

23
Ibid.

24
Vicente Guallart, Manuel Gausa, Willy Muller, *Diccionario Metapolis Arquitectura Avanzada* (Barcelona: Actar, 2000).

25
Susan Nigra Snyder, Alex Wall, "Emerging Landscapes of Movement and Logistics", *Architectural Design Profile*, no. 134 (1998), 16–21.

26
Ibid.

dered obsolete and inadequate by the presence of large infrastructures, such as airports and ports:

> ———— Landscape has been found relevant for sites in which a strictly architectural order of the city has been rendered obsolete or inadequate through social, technological or environmental change. The discourse and practices of landscape urbanism have been found particularly useful for thinking through large infrastructural arrays such as ports and transportation corridors. Airports, in particular, have been central to the discourse and practices of landscape urbanism as sites whose scale, infrastructural connectivity, and environmental impacts outstrip a strictly architectonic model of city making.[23]

Landscape Urbanism undertakes an important revolution in the way of thinking about and seeing anthropic space and, above all, highly infrastructured areas. It contributes to highlighting issues that are not discussed very much in the contemporary context, such as, for example, the forms of landscape generated by the complex set of traffic and logistic flows that support and serve territories and cities. These are distinct spatial conformations that have been defined over the years through concepts like *paisajes operativos* or *distribution landscapes*.[24] Referring to the latter, for example, the potential of these spaces as areas of contemporary research can be understood:[25]

> ———— Will this discontinuous urban landscape of flow and interchange become, as Manuel Castells has asked, 'the most representative urban face of the 21st century?' Beyond understanding the locational logic of these new developments, we believe the distribution landscape is a testing ground for new kinds of settlements, spatial patterns and possibly an architecture where the shape of urban life is free to take on a new form.[26]

Charles Waldheim also contributed to these reflections by defining them as *logistics landscapes*, that is, products of logistics or rather of the transformations that the logistics system had imposed on the built environment. Logistics landscapes are artificial territories characterized by new industrial forms structured around global trade networks and vast areas destined to accommodate the import/export process and the transport and delivery of goods:[27]

27
Charles Waldheim, Alan Berger, "Logistic Landscape", *Landscape Journal*, vol. 27, no. 2. (Madison, USA: Harvard Graduate School, Board of Regents of the University of Wisconsin System, 2008), 219–246.

———— By describing this logistics landscape in spatial and economic terms, it may be possible to apprehend the forms that it takes, to anticipate the priorities that it pursues, to understand the hyper-rationality behind its seemingly unconscious construction, and to acknowledge our embeddedness in the culture it represents. The case of logistics infrastructures also reinforces the role of landscape in relation to the cultural conditions of advanced capital.[28]

28
Ibid., 232.

What is crucial at this point is that Waldheim introduces ports as among the most emblematic examples of logistics landscapes:

———— Among the clearest example of these sites are the ports that accept, redirect, and stream the contemporary flow of consumer culture. [...] This transition [from a Fordist regime of mass consumer goods to a post-Fordist regime of flexible accumulation] has also revealed new forms of urbanization. Each of these transformations bears distinct implications for the landscape medium.[29]

29
Charles Waldheim, "Four: Post-Fordist Economies and Logistics Landscape", in *Landscape as Urbanism. A General Theory* (Princeton and Oxford: Princeton University Press, 2016).

Through this interpretation, the port landscape therefore becomes associated with those spatial configurations that saw long periods of disuse, segregation, and sedimentation and that were confronted with the need to totally reform themselves. Thus, the port, and the city with which it has developed over the centuries, can be considered a system genetically structured to change and inclined to structural and linguistic hybridization, where outdated technologies give way to new logics, and industrial machines provide opportunities for reuse. It is an analytical space, the result of operational activity that derives its principal approach from the infrastructural dimension. After all, the scale of the landscape is precisely that of the port since it is itself "a strategic area where the city becomes landscape."[30]

30
Michelangelo Russo, "Harbourscape: Between Specialization and Public Space", in *The Fluid City Paradigm. Waterfront Regeneration as an Urban Renewal Strategy*, Maurizio Carta, Daniele Ronsivalle, eds. (Palermo: UNIPA Springer Series, 2016), 31–44.

Borderscape

The city-port territories are distinguished by a particular condition that is liminal, border-like and intrinsic. This dimension, which originated in large part for functional and administrative reasons, describes a recurring picture in contemporary ports and brings to the fore issues of management, the transformation of border spaces, but also of the legitimization of the two institutional realities.

Anthropized spaces reflect the effects of political-administrative management and the political ideologies of a single place; this dependence sets conditions for urban and territorial planning. Arjan Harbers maintains that for the exploration of discontinuous and jagged contexts in different political and normative systems, traditions, and local alliances, it is necessary to make use of new classifications that can bring new areas of research to light, above all those that are emblematic of such conditions.[31]

However, to facilitate a critical rethinking of the relationships between forms of power, citizenship, and identity in the age of globalization, it makes sense to take into account the crucial transition from the concept of border to that of bordering. This transition dates back to the nineties and is one that made it possible to understand borders as dynamic processes of spatial differentiation. Also, according to Harbers, the places chosen for the study of spatial themes are precisely borders, or rather borderscapes, those liminal organisms that, positioned between different political-administrative entities, represent today's territorial complexity:

> ———— Spatial planning has always had to follow the existing landscape. Settlements grew up at places where conditions for economic gain were at their best. [...] Today fast rail links, airports, and motorways are what make towns and cities grow. 'Magnets' like these shape and solidify the urban field into one of a number of -scapes. We shall describe the distortions borders bring to the built environment or nature as 'border solidifications' or borderscapes. [...] Borderscapes can find expression in various ways.[32]

The formulation of the term borderscape is part of a widespread practice of using the suffix "-scape," which attributes both complexity and a certain degree of indefiniteness. As in the case of the word "landscape," this suffix confers not only cultural, aesthetic, and symbolic values but, above all, connects its original meaning to the term "shape," referring back to the act of giving shape to anthropized spaces. This semantic process is only one part of the wider evolutionary trajectory of the concept of landscape that takes on renewed value in design, being combined with urbanism-related language on the one hand and with the contrary,

31
Arjan Harbers,
"Borderscapes,
The Influence of
National Borders on
Spatial Planning", in
Robert Broesi, Pieter
Jannink, Wouter Veld-
huis, Ivan Nio, eds.,
*Euroscapes – Forum
2003* (Amsterdam:
MUST Publishers and
AetA, 2005), 143–166.

32
Ibid., 143.

overlapping, sometimes replacing, concept of architecture on the other. The terminological extension introduces new settings and narratives for territorial borders: no longer just lines on a map, but landscapes in an extended sense, dynamic devices and border infrastructures.

With this signification, the border becomes a figure capable of representing a condition, a status, a property. Depending on its function and position, it is either a *limes* (an exclusive place, i.e., a limit or a demarcation) or a *limen* (a threshold that, instead of isolating, is inclusive).[33] Referencing the research of Michael Foucault with regard to the relationship between power and space, Piero Zanini affirms that precisely the border is the place where juxtapositions and discrepancies manifest themselves explicitly. For this reason, investigating and conceptualizing the liminal condition makes it possible to explore all the contradictions and conflicts and "to comprehend different aspects of the same reality as parts of a single complexity."

Liminality, originating from the fragmentations and discontinuities of cities and territories, thus often corresponds to an absence of a discipline in which it is possible to explore the contradictions but also the boundless vivacity of the border. This recalls the ideas of "figurability" of urban spaces and of the "mental image" of places which reveals that the personality of places is made more explicit and clearer precisely by the presence of a liminal condition. In his manifesto on discarded spaces, Alan Berger maintains that the liminal dimension often overlaps with and responds to the residual one. A dimension that is frequently found in the in-between landscapes of the contemporary city:

——— Much of the landscape surface left in the wake of rapid horizontal urbanization is not a clearly defined, stable, and fixed entity. It is between occupancies and uses, successional phases, and (dis)investment cycles. The term *in-between* describes a state of liminality, something that lives in transition and eludes classification, something that resists new stability and reincorporation. The in-between landscapes of the horizontal city are liminal because they remain at the margins (or *limen*, "threshold" in Latin), awaiting a societal desire to inscribe them with value and status.[34]

The liminality of some contemporary spaces therefore is a necessary prerequisite for the project, a temporary regime that, almost like a rite

33
In Latin, the term *līmĕn* (*liminis*) is the threshold: that element of the house that "translates" from the inside to the outside and vice versa. The *līmĕs* (*limitis*), on the other hand, has another meaning: it contains a place and, at the same time, ends with a place.

34
Alan Berger, *Drosscape: Wasting Land in Urban America* (Princeton: Princeton Architectural Press, 2006), 29.

of passage, eludes any classification by continually instigating change, in search of a status, of a new equilibrium between the parts.

From this point of view, the contemporary port city — especially its "promiscuous" condition generated by the meeting of civil and operational structures along the edge of the city — makes it possible to explore a particular case of the liminal landscape, that is, the border. A borderscape in which an "otherness" of the port in relation to the city is recognized, a symbolic regime, but also a spatial one, which characterizes coastal organisms by outlining the contours of a new urbanity.

PORTUALITY

Concept and Condition
Backgrounds

Global Phenomena
Container and Cluster
Criteria and Contexts

PORTUALITY

Concept and Condition
Backgrounds
Global Phenomena
Container and Cluster
Criteria and Contexts

Concept and Condition
Relationship

Much has been written about the evolution of port cities and the transformation of operational areas in contact with the city since the last decades of the twentieth century. First in post-Fordist America and then in Europe (in London, Barcelona, and Glasgow, among the first cases), the obsolescence and abandonment of many port infrastructures were the origin of profound alterations of the urban fabric and its overall equilibrium. In particular, the processes of dismantling operational and industrial properties triggered the redevelopment of large parts of the seafront freed from their port function, developing a model of regeneration over the years that was tried out all over the world.[1]

In more recent times, this process has been combined with the reduction of heavy-duty production close to urban areas, the progressive expansion of the logistics sector in the field of maritime trade, and the aggravation of environmental issues. These phenomena, among others, have exacerbated the differences between the city and the port, altering, for example, the evolutionary temporalities of the respective structures and requiring a profound rethinking of the port's role, especially in the presence of complex and high-density urban areas.

Brian Hoyle, who along with other maritime geographers contributed to defining the concept of a port city by studying its evolution, acknowledges that in the interdependence between port and city there is an interface space (physical and mental) that is often the source of management-related problems and of a controversial debate at the planning level. This playing field takes the form of a "zone" that marks the border and is often characterized by a non-organic system of disused areas, highly specialized port functions, urban activities of the advanced tertiary sec-

1
First of all, we can mention the case of the Inner Harbor in Baltimore (Maryland, USA). The redevelopment took place after the dismantling in the 1950s; in fact, it gave rise to the so-called "Baltimore Model," a scheme of intervention replicated in numerous ports around the world. The "Baltimore Model" is recognized as the first international example of the conversion of a post-industrial waterfront.

2
Brian S. Hoyle, "Identity and Interdependence: Transport and Transformation at the Port-City Interface", Fourth Intermediate Meeting, Koper (March 2006), 13–23.

tor, city segments and green areas, archaeological areas and more.[2] It is precisely in light of this complexity that a new investigation on the subject of port cities today questions the effectiveness of this definition within the current framework, seeking to develop a new line of reasoning. A line of reasoning in which the dynamic and plural nature of the city-port organism emerges and in which the particular attributes of the relationship that structures it can be seen.

Milieu

The city and the port are different but complementary realities that exist in an inescapable synergy, merged in a liminal bond that carries the characteristics of one situation into the other and represents the relationship of convergence/divergence between the city and its "invisible double."[3]

3
Carlo Bertelli refers to the port as a reality separated from the city but still experienced as an "indivisible double." Cf. Carlo Bertelli, "Culture locali e modelli internazionali", in Nove opere del porto vecchio. La costruzione del porto di Genova tra Otto e Novecento (Genoa: Facoltà di Architettura, Istituto di Storia dell'Architettura, Sagep Editori, 1988), 17–22.

Moreover, it can be recognized that the encounter between city and port produces a dimension in its own right, in which the specificity of port cities with respect to other types of cities is highlighted and those qualities that make a "general city" into a "port city" are identified.[4] This alternative approach to the city-port bond shows right from the start a conceptual potential, and it orients itself towards the definition of a "third" dimension, positioned between the city and the port and capable of representing the degree of dependence of the two parts. In this sense, Frank Broeze has sketched out a new perspective:

4
Frank Broeze, "Port Cities: The Search for an Identity", Journal of Urban History, vol. 11 (1985), 209–225.

———— What is necessary, therefore, in order to properly understand the nature, functioning, and significance of port cities, is a dynamic multidisciplinary synthesis of port and city. The starting point must be that […] the port creates in the urban community that surrounds it a "distinctive form of environment," a *milieu* that derives its uniqueness from the physical and economic dominance of the port. Hence the analysis must take its start at the places where goods and passengers are transferred between ship and shore, the ultimate rationale of the port […].[5]

5
Ibid., 213.

Broeze maintains that the port creates "a distinct environmental and formal system" in the urban context that surrounds it, which derives its uniqueness from the dominant presence of the port infrastructure. Precisely for these reasons, an investigation of the port city must start in the place where goods and passengers meet: in this special space, Broeze continues, lies the intrinsic logic of the port city.

Evolution

The evolution of the existing relationships between a city and its port is a long process, the subject of an act of synthesis conducted, first and foremost, by maritime geography beginning in the 1960s. Through the elaboration of necessarily conceptual models, it is possible to comprehend the transitions and the causes that led to the current stage.

From the beginning, the city and the port lived in a symbiotic spatial amalgamation and functional cohesion. As Rosario Pavia writes, "In the past, urban identity, like its form, included that of the port," and this organic unity was clearly traceable not only in the plans and views from the Middle Ages to the nineteenth century, but also in the classical treatise writer who, starting from Leon Battista Alberti, included the port among the public buildings of the city.[6]

It was only between the eighteenth and nineteenth centuries that the growth of maritime traffic and the establishment of industries brought about the first clear separation of the two nuclei, whereupon Pavia claims that it is more appropriate to speak of "ports of a city" rather than "port cities" or "port-city."

The constant evolution of the dimensions of docking and shipping facilities and the complexity, speed, and automation of the goods transhipment processes rendered the port infrastructure more and more autonomous and ill-suited to contact with the urban fabric, accelerating the process of exodus of ports from the center to the city suburbs. During this phase, the port stopped being an emporium: silos and warehouses for the storage and processing of goods lost their *raison d'être*, just as knowledge and cultures accrued over time.

In modern times, the port was no longer a part of the city but took on a territorial dimension and developed a personal language made up of spatial codes, forms, and proportions that generated an exclusively port-related and operational grammar. This detachment increased further in the twentieth century with the proliferation of containerized trade on a global scale: this profound revolution had an effect on the size and organization of the ports, transforming the coastal territory so as to adapt it to the logic of the market, the needs of navigation safety, and production performance standards. The container, introduced in the fifties thanks to an insight by the entrepreneur Malcolm McLean, is perhaps one of the first and most viral global phenomena, as "it puts an end to the very concept of quayside warehouses, because the container itself is the construction."[7]

6
Rosario Pavia, Matteo Di Venosa, *Waterfront, dal conflitto all'integrazione* (Trento: BABEL, LISTLab, 2012).

7
Marinke Steenhuis, ed., *The Port of Rotterdam – A World Between City and Sea* (Rotterdam: nai010 Publishers, 2015).

In this context, new laws imposed further delineations between the port and the city with the objective of governing trade more efficiently and guaranteeing competitiveness at the port. In the last forty years of the twentieth century, a definitive break occurred: every relationship fractured and even the original port nucleus, still within the urban fabric, was abandoned since it remained inactive in light of the new port logics.

The last phase theorized by Hoyle concerned the redevelopment of the waterfront, or rather the abandoned primitive facilities. However, this last stage has not been reached everywhere and, in some cases, docks and port facilities still have no function or identity today.

Detachment

It is possible to recognize the process just described in many European contexts characterized by evolutionary dynamics and often similar historical events. This makes it possible to understand why, for some decades now, the relationship between a city and its port has become conflictual, especially in terms of planning and the management of processes.

It is a kind of detachment that, originating from the fracture between urban planning policies and port policies, is often unable to grasp the new nexus between the port economy and that of the city, between the identity of the port and that of the city. In addition, the dismantling of large port areas connected to the city at the end of the twentieth century brought the waterfront to the fore along with its potential to be reconverted for an urban purpose. If, on the one hand, the measures initiated encouraged the regeneration of abandoned areas, on the other hand, however, they also offered substantial compensation for the city.

Today, it is evident that this widespread approach might have fueled a negative and sector-specific perception of the port: more than thirty years later, it is clear that these practices not only standardized waterfronts all over the world, but above all they did not allow for the recognition of city-port situation in its entirety and complexity. Moreover, this fed a sense of insufficient awareness of the narrow port landscape between the city property border and the sea. These considerations are confirmed in much of the city-port literature of the last fifty years, in which the theme of port cities is addressed in a unidirectional way:

——— The widespread concern over environmental quality issues tends to portray the port as an important negative impact factor. [...] Another generalized idea, particularly in cities with ports right in their inner-city areas is to project the port as an element of instability, disorganization and urban discontinuity (Cau, 1996). Current planning policies in favor of inner-city regeneration tend to devaluate the importance of the port as an element of the city's competitive advantage. And yet, the symbolic function of the port image has usually been recognized as a strong point of reference of the cities' identity (Mathé, 1992).[8]

Character

Moving beyond this sector-specific conception of the port means recognizing the particularities of cities with a port. One priority is developing an awareness about what Claude Prelorenzo defines as the "cultural dimension of the port landscape," in other words, a point of view that conceives of the landscape produced by the presence of the port as an organic component above all of urban culture.[9] Cities and ports, today as in the past, produce a dimension in which they not only share spaces and a strategic potential but contribute to the construction of a new identity for the port city:

———— Art is no longer the opposite of industry or commerce, recreation is a leader market, images are important for both the identity of the city and the notoriety of the port. These converging factors have already created shared vocabularies that can help, perhaps not to blend the port and urban landscapes entirely, but at least to soften the heterogeneity which, for a century, had separated the city and the port. The "new frontier", so dear to Rinio Bruttomesso, is succeeded by the spatial, cultural and economic community.[10]

The port city possesses a multiplicity of characteristics that differentiate it from "other types" of cities, but engaging with them is a complex task and, perhaps for this very reason, they are dealt with only sporadically in the European literature on cities and ports. And yet, this angle, almost completely unexplored, often returns in slightly different forms in the research of authors who contribute to generating a guiding vision.

Carola Hein, for example, takes up Broeze's work, making it the foundation of her investigations into the particularity of port landscapes.[11] In her thoughts, the characterizing aspect that the port component infuses into urban territories emerges, breathing life into particular forms of landscape:

[8] Paulo Pinho, Filipa Malafaya, Luísa Mendes, "Urban Planning and Port Management: The Changing Nature of City-Port Interactions", Littoral 2002, *The Changing Coast. EUROCOAST/EUCC* (Porto: EUROCOAST, Portugal, 2002), 567–575.

[9] Claude Prelorenzo, "The Cultures of Port Landscapes. Differences and Similarities between Port and City", *Portus*, no. 18 (Venice: RETE Publisher, 2009), 50–55.

[10] Ibid., 55.

[11] Hein Carola, ed., *Port Cities: Dynamic Landscapes and Global Networks* (London: Routledge, 2010).

[...] maritime and associated networks create dynamic, multi-scaled, and interconnected cityscapes. I call them "port city-scapes," and they exist around the world. [...] As a result of the various flows between port cities, specific elements of their respective urban environment are related through a range of factors such as funding, technology, style, concept or building material.[12]

12
Ibid., 5.

For this reason, port cities are not only particular and unique places, but also universal models for thinking about global dynamics and their effects on contemporary spaces. They are at once peculiar and generic landscapes that, influenced by recurring local and global factors, become elements of comparison even at very distant latitudes.

——— As global and local factors add up differently and distinctively, they make each port city a particular place. There is no single urban form, pattern, or dynamic that characterizes them. Yet port cities show common traits, making them faraway mirrors of each other. The combination of difference and similarities makes port cities uniquely valuable for thinking about changes in these networks and their reflection in built form, and for thinking about changes in these networks and their influence on the urban environment.[13]

13
Ibid., 10.

Ambivalence

In addition to producing a special morphology of recurring landscapes, the meeting between city and port gives rise to an indefiniteness, or rather an ambivalence, which for years has been propelling urban planners, historians, and geographers to elaborate theories and tools to clarify it or, if nothing else, to outline its principal contours.

Rhoads Murphey, for example, states that the distinction between what is (or is not) a port city is to be found in a multi-pronged and, above all, broadened vision in terms of dynamics and spaces.[14] A perspective according to which a city cannot exist without supplying goods and services to an extended area connected to it under an administrative aegis. This ensemble of spaces and resources is the hinterland that the port puts at the service of the city and that is projected onto the neighboring territories, bringing them into a single system; in the case of ports, this area also includes bodies of water belonging to the same jurisdiction.

14
Rhoads Murphey, "On the Evolution of the Port City", in Frank Broeze, *Brides of the Sea: Port Cities of Asia from the 16th–20th Centuries* (Randwick, Australia: NSWU — New South Wales University Press, 1989), 223–247.

As long as city and port share the same hinterland, says Murphey, together with the necessary facilities, it is not possible to talk about their existence separately. In this sense, it is truly difficult to define what is and what is not a port, to draw a demarcation line establishing which elements are placed within certain limits and distinguishing it from other types of built systems.

Thinking about the definition of a port city, Michelangelo Russo maintains that the port of today cannot be understood without recognizing its dual nature as a public space and, at the same time, a landscape:[15]

15
Michelangelo Russo, "Harbourscape: Between Special- ization and Public Space", in *The Fluid City Paradigm: Water- front Regeneration as an Urban Renewal Strategy*, Maurizio Carta, Daniele Ron- sivalle, eds. (Palermo: UNIPA Springer Series, 2016), 31–44.

――――― [The port] is a strategic area where the city becomes landscape. The port infrastructure arises following the natural morphology of the waterfront and remodeling a space that is not only an access device, but also a place where it is possible to perceive the territory-landscape, the shoreline and the urban front. A line with different dimensions but, at the same time, an incredible depth that defines the city identity, strengthened by ar- chitectural elements […] improving its magnet role, an attractor for common economics and urban activities.[16]

16
Ibid., 31.

This multifaceted identity, however, seems to no longer exist once the port has become an independent infrastructure governed within a specific territorial enclave through dedicated laws. In spite of this, the port remains a fundamental part of the city as an extension of its fabric and of the con- tours that shape its spatial form: this is why Russo proposes a two-dimen- sional reading (longitudinal and transversal), in order to interpret the space of transition between land and water as a single territorial sequence; he defines it as:

――――― […] an uncertain space, with an identity that changes in the course of time leaving the prosperity of the landscape and growing in a closed, unfathomable, and supervised envelope […]. An area in transition, an urban dividing line that, thank to flows and functions density, increased its attractiveness and its ability to receive its symbolic and representative value […].[17]

17
Ibid., 35.

Superstructure
In light of the most recent transformations, the relationship between city and port has in a certain sense been upended, where two entities that

once functioned only if closely connected, today, on the contrary, need autonomous spaces and independence to guarantee their operation and security. This new relational dimension raises the question of whether the port of the coming decades will have to completely break away from the city, becoming a sophisticated and alien infrastructure where goods pass almost without stopping, large commercial arteries direct products to distant destinations, and human presence is reduced to a minimum. According to this vision, which in fact is already present at Asian ports and in the largest European ports, the apparent divergence of the two components nevertheless produces a powerful image, which expresses the logistical-infrastructural dimension of these places.

In support of an overall definition of the port city, Peter Reeves adds that it is essential to take into account the size of this "superstructure," conferred principally through the export radius of goods and people on land and sea.[18] The nature of the contemporary city-port organism is indeed strongly conditioned by the mechanisms that surround it and the modifications that determine its operational and social structure:

18
Peter Reeves, "Studying the Asian Port City", in *Brides of the Sea: Port Cities of Asia from the 16th–20th Centuries*, Frank Broeze, ed. (Randwick, Australia: NSWU — New South Wales University Press, 1989), 29–30.

———— Around the physical heart of the port city [there are] a series of conceptually concentric circles representing the economic, social, cultural and political life of the human community constituting its population; all of this is firmly set within the port city's spatial and architectural configuration and appearance. Only in this way [...] can both the inner functioning and the organic evolution of the port city be understood.[19]

19
Ibid., 29.

Specificity

The considerable evolution undergone by port cities in recent decades is of interest to various disciplines, certainly historical studies and, as previously described, numerous maritime geography studies in Europe. In this context, urban planning in the realm of the port seems to be positioned at a distance, since looking at plans and projects mostly neglects the particularity of these issues.

As the studies of César Ducruet testify[20] the literature on city-port areas of the last thirty years has continued to produce case studies focused on the urban redevelopment of the abandoned areas from the port, failing to completely capture the specificity of city-port organisms. The increase in such studies has therefore contributed to blurring the strategic potential of the matter:

20
Cesar Ducruet, "The port city in multidisciplinary analysis", in *The Port City of the 21st Century: New Challenges in the Relationship between Port and City*, Bruttomesso Rinio, Jean Alemany, eds. (Venice: RETE Publisher, 2011), 32–48.

21
Ibid., 32.

———— Over the last five decades, the literature on port cities has continuously and rapidly been growing. Research in this field became paradoxically more intense as many port cities were actually losing their port activities and maritime identity. The concept of port city itself has thus become blurred. Despite the number of models and case studies available in the literature, there is still very little evidence about the specificity of nowadays port cities compared with "other cities" [...].[21]

The specificity of port cities compared to other urban forms, therefore, is consolidated into a new idea, a distinct concept, bearer of universal elements and plural meanings: neither city nor port alone, the port city is a hub of exchange between land and sea where international characteristics have been joined with local factors over time, bringing a unique, unparalleled organism to life.

In this perspective, port cities are particular urban forms that do not respond to the habits of growth of other types of cities because they have their own. They may even constitute an urban category in their own right since, as Ducruet states in the same essay, "port cities have sufficient particularities to form a distinct urban category, implicitly claiming that every port city is governed by identical mechanisms."[22]

22
Ibid., 33.

Condition

Recognizing the specificity of port cities with respect to other urban forms fosters new ways of thinking, like wondering if this particularity might not be decisive in understanding the current nature of the relationship between urban and operational territories. If, in other words, it is possible to affirm that there is an intermediate and alternative dimension between city and port produced by the encounter or better by the clash between a city and its port.

It is once again Broeze who offers the tools for the complex and ambiguous definition of the identity of the contemporary port city, especially in light of the complications brought about by the multi-functionality now attained by most of the world's ports.[23] This trend has often turned many port cities into general cities, overlooking all the specific economic, social, political, and cultural factors on which the life of the city hinges and which is defined by the presence of the port. In short, Broeze confers on the concept of the "port city" a non-generic meaning and, above all, confirms its promiscuous nature:

23
Frank Broeze, "Gateways of Asia: Port Cities of Asia in the 13th-20th Centuries", Asian Studies Association of Australia, Comparative Asian Studies Series, vol. 2 (1997), 1–17.

24
Ibid., 3–4.

———— Explicitly or implicitly, with all the fuzziness around the edges and all the dilemmas that no precise definition or conceptualization can ever avoid, there is a clearly distinct semi-maritime semi-terrestrial urban structure on the physical border between land and sea. As such, this concept of port city can surely be used as a heuristic tool, both geographically and historically, for an analysis of its historical development.[24]

Rinio Bruttomesso had already grasped this issue by putting forward the hypothesis of replacing the idea of a "port city" with that of a "port-city": a new "type" of city that, already at the beginning of the twenty-first century, had some distinctive and particular traits, which materialized in the urban utilization of significant port areas and in the more incisive role of the port in the city economy.

However, in the current framework, rather than finding a new expression to articulate the city-port binomial, recognizing the "other," almost alien, dimension is considered a priority, one that describes the specific conditions of port cities compared to other urban configurations. Different but recognizable conditions put into play through the commingling of the maritime port landscape and the urban landscape. To explain this status and grasp its strategic potential, the idea of *portuality*[25] is being introduced, attributing new meanings to a term used thus far in a generic and haphazard way.

25
Literally, the term portuality describes the ensemble of elements that combine to give the port its particular character or to characterize a port with respect to another. Also, it is the set of various activities (organizational, management, operational, etc.) that, governed by specific laws and regulations, are carried out by one or more port systems. Cf. Università Cattolica del Sacro Cuore di Milano. *Glossario della Logistica*.

Portuality

Portuality is a concept but also a derived condition. It represents a new urbanity capable of embodying the inescapable bond that often places an entity (city or port) in co-dependence or in opposition to the other. This is a condition that presupposes the existence of an otherness with respect to the city and the port as simply understood. It outlines the contours of a hybrid and heterogeneous dimension that, as the result of diverse and juxtaposed components, embodies the complexity of the current city-port relationship.

Studied in different and even very dissimilar contexts, portuality is a category that makes it possible to compare city-port contexts, transforming them into particular and, at the same time, general research areas. Recognizing portuality enables the development of an investigation in ontological terms but also in operational terms: through its definition, not only do the potentials of symbolizing the city-port relationship actually emerge, but also the potentials of providing strategic direction in the context of the border project between city and port.

The territory that today divides (and at the same time connects) the port and the city represents a real separation but also an overlap (a physical one, and also one of interests and competencies) that acquires a key role in the relational system between the two landscapes. Moreover, the recurring presence of this border space in various contexts makes it a privileged field of investigation. Within its sphere, traffic and flows from land and sea are concentrated and, above all, the potentials for sharing between city-port territories are represented.

The border between city and port is a heterogeneous but compact one, emerging as a powerful space of intermediation and transition, a place where a sense of suspension and the frequent absence of discipline correspond with richness, liveliness, and authentic characteristics. Precisely for this reason, where port and city flank each other, the condition of portuality manifests itself more explicitly. Its materialization gives rise to a logistics landscape, an interface that is continually subjected to transits and modifications, a place where the personality and temperament of the port city itself are represented. This suggests that the border represents not only the nature of the city-port relationship but above all becomes the preferential investigation area of the conditions of portuality.

Employing the concept of portuality in urban studies, then is an early attempt to extend the cataloguing of port cities, that is, to redefine the nature of the contemporary city-port relationship by recognizing the existence of the specific conditions of port cities compared to other urban forms.

Backgrounds
Global Phenomena

In order to study the contemporary port city and outline the characteristics of the condition that develop in border spaces, it is fundamental to investigate the specific phenomena that have contributed to altering the characteristic features of the relationship between the city and the port. These are complex and constantly evolving processes that must be considered on a global scale, since it is exclusively at this scale that it is possible to grasp the extent of the effects on the functioning and structure of the operational infrastructures and the spaces attached to them.

The most recent studies on the subject of world cities come from the work of the *Globalization and World Cities Group* (*GaWC*) and focus for the

26
For further informa-
tion, refer to the *Glo-*
balization and World
Cities Research
Network. GaWC is a
think tank founded in
1998 that studies the
relationship between
world cities in the
context of global-
ization. It is located
in the Geography
Department of Lough-
borough University
in Leicestershire,
England (*lboro.ac.uk*).

27
Ann Verhetsel, Steve
Sel, "World Maritime
Cities: From Which
Cities Do Container
Shipping Companies
Make Decisions?",
Transport Policy, no.
16 (2009), 240–250.

28
Manuel Castells, *La*
nascita della società
in rete (Milan: UBE
Paperback, 1996).

29
Saskia Sassen, *Le*
città nell'economia
globale (Bologna:
Saggi, Il Mulino,
1991).

most part on the effects that the advent of the global economy, and more generally globalization, have brought to urban and territorial structures.[26]

Despite the important contributions of these surveys, the studies of Verhetsel and Sel find a gap in the work of the GaWC relating to the issue of the global city in the maritime and port sector (world maritime city). However, in no sector are the processes of globalization and its effects on the morphology of society, production, and trade as profound as in the city-port area.

The research of Verhetsel and Sel therefore fills this disciplinary gap, and their results enable us to affirm that many of the hubs classified as global cities actually have a decisive maritime port focus.[27] After all, ports are the culmination of innovation in terms of economy, society, and culture: places where the phenomena of modernization manifest themselves first, to then become common and extended globally. Globalization, indeed, permeates the maritime port sector and is the basis of many other developments in the city-port setting, in logistical-managerial terms but also in physical-spatial terms.

Network

At the end of the second millennium, the technological revolution based on information and on a new digital and universal language transformed society in every sphere of human activity. The economy became a global one, and world society shaped its morphology accordingly, giving rise to a variable geometry system based on the concept of the network.

In his trilogy *The Information Age,*[28] Manuel Castells thoroughly explores these phenomena, claiming that the emergence and progressive proliferation of the new social structure has had significant repercussions on the concept of space. In particular, he affirms that the global and information economy of the new millennium creates the so-called "space of flows" (which replaces the "space of places"), an unprecedented spatial configuration determined by new logics and structured by the networked system. The space of flows is the dominant spatial incarnation of the power and function of the new global society. Precisely from this dialectical opposition ("flows" versus "places"), important factors of change for the architectural and urban disciplines emerge, and interesting points of observation for large cities are consolidated.

Saskia Sassen[29] had already argued that the concept of cities in the global era was not as much linked to the location of the large corporate headquarters in the cities as it was to the presence of advanced production services around them. These services (production centers, single markets, logistical-infrastructural complexes) pervade the entire geography of the planet, and the architecture of the global network is structured on them, which is repeated on a regional and local scale in a dynamic system. In this perspective, the global city loses its physical dimension to become a diffuse and increasingly virtual entity:

> ———— The global city is not a place but a process. A process through which the centers of production and consumption of advanced services [...] are connected via a global network on the basis of information flows, which, at the same time, reduce the importance of the links of global cities with their hinterlands.[30]

30
Manuel Castells, "Lo Spazio dei Flussi", in *La nascita della società in rete*, Manuel Castells, ed. (Milan: UBE Paperback), 435–491.

Not all cities defined by Sassen as "global" are, in effect, port cities. However, what is interesting about this study is understanding how the process of globalization and the idea of the network change spatiality and how they alter the logic of commerce, especially in large infrastructural hubs such as ports.

These phenomena then not only gave rise to the informational city but threw the concepts of geographical specificity, physical contiguity and, more generally, territory into crisis. The advent of digital technology enabled the introduction of automation and delocalization into production and exchange processes and, since each phase of the process could be split and completed in different places and times, there was a real dissociation between spatial proximity and the performance of functions. Thus defined, the "space of flows" influenced the physical and logistical transformations of the spaces intended for production. Places for living and work are concrete and real entities (infrastructural hubs, airports, ports, and rear ports) that continue to exist but subject their dynamics to the network structure that operates through the flows.

There is no doubt that the changes described above affect above all those spheres of human activity connected to the system of mobility of goods and people. For this reason, the maritime port sector, which has always been organized around a network logic, was more impacted by the innovations introduced by globalization starting in the second half of the twentieth century.

Logistics
In the global era, the maritime port sector experienced a significant increase in the volume of traffic sustained by the continuous growth of the

general cargo sector. The advent of the container, already in the middle of the twentieth century, was a revolution that permeated worldwide traffic, imposing a total restructuring of the commercial scheme. These changes had an influence on the structure of ports and cities, as they required the construction of an infrastructural network capable of sustaining the required speed and accessibility and produced substantial transformations in terms of operating equipment on both the land and sea sides.

Following the unrestrained globalization of the last decade, new processes were thus affirmed, such as the transfer of productive seafront activities to logistical ones. Furthermore, the development of advanced technologies in terms of the management model for ports led to the formulation of increasingly sophisticated exchange systems: advanced services to optimize transit times for goods and vehicles, virtual customs clearance practices, and strategic and digital support among the various components.

All this contributed to a progressively intense dematerialization of production and commercial activities that involved the majority of ports. Today, in fact, goods are stored briefly on the docks of the port to then leave by sea on smaller ships or travel rapidly on dedicated arteries towards platforms located in inland areas positioned far from the water's edge. The terminals are in constant telematics interaction with other ports and rear-port zones for the forwarding of products via instantaneous and increasingly immaterial dialogue networks. At the most advanced ports, terminals are equipped with electrification systems, and the handling equipment is controlled remotely almost without the need for on-site personnel; the railway networks reach the dockside and allow fast transport of cargo towards its final destination.

In short, logistics is replacing industry, introducing new solutions for coexistence with the edge of the city. At the same time, the city is discovering unexplored horizons of investment for relocating creative and manufacturing activities principally linked to the tertiary sector and design to disused industrial warehouses. This makes logistics a new field of experimentation for the architectural project. As stated in *Aesthetics and Politics of Logistics*,[31] with this specialization even architecture of logistics exists that transfers phenomena of a political-economic nature to the topography. This turns logistics from being merely functional into a tool for reading the most abstract mechanisms of our world. Its rules produce architectures: multidimensional and multifunctional spatial devices that, interwoven between city and port, are genetically responsible for change, mediation, and breaking with the ordinary.

31
Hamed Khosravi, Taneha Kuzniecow Bacchin, Filippo LaFleur, *Aesthetics and Politics of Logistics* (Venice and Rotterdam: Humboldt Books, 2019).

Gateway

The restructuring of the equilibrium between the urban, the economic, and production as a result of global phenomena has reshaped ports in terms of services and spaces, transforming them into rings of an ever more articulated network at an international level, the gateways to oceanic maritime traffic with strong connections to the overall logistics system.

These changes translate into the relocation of port functions away from the port limits and, even more so, into the transition from the emporium port model to the gateway port model, which represents the ports as the origin or destination of the great transoceanic trade routes.

In the emporium port model, goods were stored for days in dedicated warehouses in order to be handled, processed, and then sold and forwarded to other destinations. The gateway, on the other hand, is a hub that moves millions of containers every year and where the goods transit invisibly on dedicated infrastructures almost without stopping; the products are not processed by local companies but move towards inland logistics platforms.

The expansion of port trade into a wider geographical scale that goes beyond the port perimeter is then exacerbated by the shifting of heavy-duty port functions to areas that are further and further away from urban core, both to get away from road congestion in the city center and to avoid having large carriers get too close to the city. This is certainly also influenced by the pressure of environmental issues, generated by new standards of quality imposed by protocols on an international scale and by the growing demand for real estate in central areas of the city.

Metamorphoses of this caliber restructure the city-port relationship in a substantial way. If, on the one hand, the transfer of port areas away from the city minimizes frictions on the city-port axis, on the other, it shifts the equilibrium between them and envisages new scenarios especially for the intermediate areas between port and city.

Container and Cluster

The global perspective is fundamental in order to grasp the nature of a trans-scalar object of the contemporary port. Ducruet[32] already argued that the port was an exemplary laboratory for the study of the transformations brought about by global phenomena. In his studies, he affirms that the relationship between the port and the city should be investigated in a sufficiently broad context so as to fully grasp the implications and potential for transformation on a local scale:

32
Cesar Ducruet, "The Port City in Multidisciplinary Analysis", in *The Port City of the XXIst Century: New Challenges in the Relationship between Port and City*, Bruttomesso Rinio, Jean Alemany, eds. (Venice: RETE Publisher, 2011), 32–48.

33
Ibid., 41.

——— [The] primary context for this relationship must be found in a scale much larger than the local scale, which for the level of performance and competitiveness of the most important ports must be a global scale.[33]

Globalization has entered into the mechanisms of the port world, influencing its evolutionary factors and producing a vast catalogue of contexts. And yet, in the various models of port cities, there are common traits through which it is possible to appreciate the capability of technological innovations and regulatory reforms and, finally, to frame local transformations within a global perspective.

Models

34
The work of James Bird contributed to theorizing the development of seaports, in particular, by identifying technology as one of the main factors in the growth of the port. In parallel to the spatial approach represented by Anyport, Bird has recognized the existence of other approaches able to communicate the city-port evolution over the centuries. In these terms, it is interesting to recall the so-called "behavioral approach," which emerged in the 1980s, trying to evaluate the relationships from the point of view of port users. Cf. Tom Daamen, "Sustainable Development of the European Port-City Interface", *Paper ENHR Conference, Sustainable Urban Areas* (2007), 1–20.

In this context, a starting point is certainly the *Anyport Model* developed by James Bird in 1963.[34] The model describes the evolution of the port through a predominantly spatial approach that, divided into five phases, conceives the port space through a direct relationship between form and function.

Bird's conceptualization endeavored to formulate a model valid for "every port": a universal interpretive tool for all the particular morphological-structural changes that affect ports (and their cities) and that generate similar reactions even at great distances. These evolutionary similarities have been shared by port cities for years and, putting aside unequivocal local details, are the origin of permanent and collective characteristics.

Anyport was not a model to which all ports had to conform but a basis for comparing very different contexts. For at least four decades, it provided maritime geography with morphological data relating to the city-port relationship. Only in the light of technological innovation and the modernization of ports in the mid-twentieth century was it updated and superseded by the Brian Hoyle's diagram published in 1989. This scheme proposes five phases that cover a very vast period (from the early Middle Ages to the early 2000s) and that synthesize the evolutionary dynamics that have been established between the urban territory and the port area.

In the long initial phase, which lasted for about fourteen centuries, city and port lived in a symbiotic spatial amalgamation and functional cohesion, producing mutual benefits and results. At that time, the form and identity of cities included the port within the city fabric as public architecture. Beginning in the nineteenth century, cities and ports began to grow simultaneously and along diverging trajectories: the transition from sailing ships to steamships and the progressive modernization of goods handling processes accelerated the exodus of ports from the center to the city suburbs. Along the port's edge, there was a dense fabric made up of warehouses, commercial offices, and dock equipment that supported the management of cargo. In addition, the specialization of goods guided the evolution of a veritable legacy of operational structures that, together with the multiple modes of transport and labor, contributed to the formation of the port landscape of that time:

——— The original layout of the eighteenth-century urban-port border, [...] in the nineteenth century, is structurally modified by the creation of new artificial land. [...] The considerable extension of artificial land shapes the emergence of a new territory that is grafted onto the coastal edge of the consolidated city, assuming a distinct form, whose principle of formation is totally different and independent of the rules and customs of urban construction. [...] The new port area is closer to being a support to a mechanism than a part of the city.[35]

35
Alessandro Rosselli, "Il porto come struttura e significato", *Portus*, no. 10 (2005), 4–5.

Containerization

The process of expansion and updating of the port infrastructure increased further during the twentieth century, following the industrial boom and above all the proliferation of the container. The use of standardized loading units enabled the standardization, automation, and speed-up of the processes (also through the introduction of mechanical cranes for loading and unloading); all this contributed to an agile transhipment of goods by land and by sea and to an increase in productivity that, in fact, radically transformed the relationship with the city and the neighboring territories.

This global phenomenon caused ports to engage in a larger scale of interactions, rendering the technological apparatus and the production and efficiency ambitions of these infrastructures increasingly complex. In this phase formulated by Hoyle new market logics and laws emerge that impose specific boundaries between port and city territories with the aim of efficiently governing exchanges, but above all guaranteeing security and autonomy to both. During these years, new "artificial land" of several hectares emerged, which was grafted onto the coastal edge of the city following rules of development independent of the norms of urban construction. In this dimension, the same aqueous medium was aimed at productive efficiency and modified its connotation as a natural element to assume that of an infrastructural surface.

The rules of commerce governed not only exchanges and routes but also shaped ports by deriving factors that characterized the overall system and the individual artifacts:

> ——— Ports are literally shaped by the necessary commonalities of measurement. [...] Not only the goods that were shipped have to be standardized, but also the harbor facilities had to offer similar wharves, docks, and tools for loading and discharging to accommodate the same vessels across the world. The form of the cargo and its particular needs, from spices to coffee or carpets, shaped the buildings that accommodate them.[36]

36
Carola Hein, ed., *Port Cities: Dynamic Landscapes and Global Networks* (London: Routledge, 2010).

Within a few decades, containerized trade was spreading to ports all over the world, rendering the architecture and technological apparatus of the early port obsolete. The last two phases indeed describe the transformations that, at the end of the twentieth century, led to the port and the city being permanently separated through an irreversible process that also affected cities. In these circumstances, the historical port hub was abandoned, as it was no longer used given the new port logics and, in the following decades, it became the object of urban redevelopment. The so-called *waterfront projects* proposed as acts of regeneration of the abandoned original structures often aimed at compensating the city for the many years of disconnection from the sea.

On this subject, Edoardo Benvenuto argued (referring in particular to the conversion of the Old Port of Genoa in Italy) that the spaces that had at one time been ports had been "betrayed by the functional transformation that sees them obligated to accept within themselves the exact opposite of the reason that brought them into being."[37] Once the port function ceased, these projects tried to return the areas to the city through the inclusion of speculative activities connected to leisure, consumption, and the self-image of the city, though it generated a substantial displacement, if not a veritable betrayal, of the location's identity.

37
Edoardo Benvenuto was one of the most complex and important figures of the Genoese context of the late twentieth century, especially in the field of construction history and science. He combined the technical activity with important philosophical and theological knowledge. He was dean of the Faculty of Architecture of Genoa from 1980 until his sudden death in 1997. Cf. Edoardo Benvenuto, "La ricerca d'identità", in *Osservatorio: Waterfront Portuali. GB progetti*, supplement to no. 8 (Genoa: EDITRICE PROGETTI s.r.l, 1992), 8–12.

An update of Hoyle's model, presented by Dirk Schubert in 2011, proposes a sixth phase in which Schubert gives an account of the transformations that, at the turn of the millennium, further changed the city-port relationship, propelling contemporary seaports into a larger territorial dimension.

Gigantism

Globalization and intermodal traffic in internal territories redefine the role and functioning of ports, renewing the alliance with the city in terms of strategies and developing the figure of the port authorities as active subjects of planning and project processes. In this sense, naval gigantism, i.e., the evolution of ships in terms of size, is an effect of globalization that exerts considerable pressure on the infrastructure, defining new structures and declaring the marginality of seaports not capable of accommodating the new carriers.[38]

The increase in the size of ships, which had already begun in the early 2000s, was due to the need to reduce transport costs, from which the choice of maximizing loads on increasingly larger ships was derived. Thus, naval gigantism is associated with the continuing tendency toward the concentration of the market in the hands of an ever smaller number of operators, which additionally direct the use of the fleet toward specific commercial areas that are equipped and more favorable to the new rules of the sector.

Finally, the growth in the size of ships also influences maritime trade in terms of distances: new carriers, in fact, prefer the *pendulum* routes[39] that cross the Mediterranean Sea through the Suez Canal.[40] This scenario places the ports of the Mediterranean coasts in a strategic position so as to intercept the principal flows and become fundamental hubs in the transhipment system.[41]

Regionalization

The shift in development perspectives towards a broader geographical scale that involves land traffic (on rail and road) and that goes beyond the physical perimeter of the port reflects the process of port regionalization, postulated by Notteboom and Rodrigue in 2006. This reasoning adds a new phase to the Bird scheme (articulated in the phases of Setting, Expansion, Specialization, Regionalization) and configures the "port-city-territory" model, whose potential resides in the conception of a networked system connected on a global scale through material and immaterial relations.[42]

The current evolution of ports actually depends more and more on new phenomena not included in the twentieth-century diagrams already described. To be noted among them are the growth of so-called seaport terminals that function as large transhipment hubs within the global maritime system and the proliferation of distribution by land. The latter, for example, holds an increasingly important role in the overall framework,

---

38
Michele Acciaro, *Gigantismo navale: rationale e limiti* (Rome: Assagenti, 2015).

39
The three *pendulum* routes (South China Express — SCX, European Union Mediterranean — EUM, Atlantic Express — ATX) provide a round-trip on the same route. With the development of containerized traffic, continuous growth in the size of ships has been seen. Since, until 2016, ships of particularly high capacity could not cross the Panama Canal, intercontinental traffic has progressively relocated to these routes that exploit the Far East-Europe-North America commercial axis, following the Suez Canal — Strait of Gibraltar route in the direction of the Northern Range and/or Atlantic route ports.

40
On August 6, 2015, the New Suez Canal was inaugurated. The project added a second 35-km lane to the existing canal, allowing ships to pass in opposite directions. The inter-

vention increased the depth of 37 meters. Thanks to this expansion, there are no dimensional limits on the passage of ships. On February 24, 2016, the Suez Canal Authority officially opened the new side channel that serves the East Terminal for berthing and unberthing vessels from the terminal. This should allow an increase in the convenience of the passage through Suez for some Asian routes that currently use the passage through the Panama Canal (also expanded in 2016) as well.

41
Transhipment is the transfer of cargo from one ship to another, usually through unloading in the port and reloading. The phenomenon is typical of container transport but has also spread to air transport. It has a scheme, also called Hub-and-Spoke, which consists of the transfer of containers from large container ships onto smaller vessels called feeder ships. With these systems, goods are transported from large international ports (called hub transhipment) either on trains or on feeder ship networks to other ports.

42
Theo Notteboom, Jean-Paul Rodrigue, "Port Regionalization: Towards a New Phase in Port Development", *Maritime Policy and Management*, vol. 32, no. 3 (2005), 297–313.

43
For further information (*ec.europa.eu/transport/themes/infrastructure_en*).

since it acts as an effective element in the configuration of logistics platforms within or near the port area.

Each of these processes is well described by the regionalization phase that, moreover, contributes to reducing distribution costs by favoring the integration of the different transport systems in the logistical chain (hubs, ports, railways or roads, airports, platforms, and processing and sorting centers). Regionalization responds to the rules of contemporary logistics: it contributes to the delocalization of production and commerce, since it attracts companies that do not require localization right at the dock but are more easily located in inland areas.

Corridors

The aspect through which today's competition is played out is no longer the local market but the system of services and infrastructure: in this sense, the spaces and the network of corridors that link the port node to the other territorial nodes take on importance. The regionalization process transforms the trinomial "port-city-industrial areas" into the new formula "port-city-logistical rear port" thanks to the development of an intermodal network and an efficient virtual communications scheme.

In Europe, the development of these theories takes shape in the TEN-T project (Trans-European Networks – Transport), which is still being completed. The program involves the construction of a network of infrastructures aimed at supporting the single market and guaranteeing the free movement of goods and people and strengthening growth, employment, and the competitiveness of the European Union. The system of connections by sea via the "Motorways of the Sea" is combined with the land corridors. This network represents an alternative and complementary solution to road transport and is aimed at making trucks, containers, and vehicles travel on ships, enhancing maritime transport.[43]

Clusterization

The most interesting and decisive development in the current context, however, is represented by the push towards clusterization that some port entities had already been trying out since the 1980s.

In Europe, the clearest examples are the hubs of the Copenhagen and Malmö ports, which together constitute a single port authority in the Baltic region (beginning in 2000), and the alliance formed in 2012 between the ports of Paris, Rouen, and Le Havre (HAROPA), which provides an Atlantic outlet to the logistical structures aligned along the axis of the Seine. In both recently instituted cases, it can be noted that the formalization of the new model of government has preceded spatial and organizational transformations that in fact require several decades to be configured.

In Italy, the concept of a port system and the need to involve the hinterland areas in the overall structure were already present in the first legislation in the sector enacted in 1994. Law No. 84, in fact, spoke of the port as a system capable of thinking outside the state-owned port property towards areas functionally connected to maritime traffic. However, it is only through the 2016 Port Reform that the 24 port authorities were merged into 15 port system authorities.[44]

44
This refers to Legislative Decree No. 169 (August 4, 2016): "Riorganizzazione, razionalizzazione e semplificazione della disciplina concernente le Autorità Portuali di cui alla legge 28 gennaio 1994, n. 84".

In addition, the clusterization of Italian ports runs parallel to the formalization of ten metropolitan cities in 2014 (Law No. 56) that eliminated the figure of the provinces and proposed a coordinated structure of several nuclei and several territories. Even if the consequences of the regulations are not yet tangible due to their recent entry into force, it is clear that their formalization modifies the equilibria and introduces new scenarios not only in territorial or port logics, but also (or above all) for cities.

In fact, beyond the complex process of administrative adaptation, the Port Reform of the Italian ports highlights a latent potential not so much of the consortium of ports but of the territories that connect them, also united in the cluster. This aggregation potentially produces a new city-port entity extended along the coast and depth-wise towards the hinterland. A heterogeneous and polycentric conurbation, a sort of "city of the cluster" made up of several ports and several cities that becomes responsible for a territory in which new possibilities for the interaction of complex systems will materialize in the decades to come.

Criteria and Contexts

There are vastly diverse port landscapes on the global stage, characterized by economic and morphological conditions that make them unique cases. However, in the recent past, global phenomena have influenced the evolution of ports, contributing to generating similar reactions and similar territorial structures.

Some processes, such as divestments, technological adaptations, and economic-commercial logics, thus guided local urban planning that, supported by public initiatives and/or private contributions, is transforming the areas between the city and the port, generating a varied collection of examples and a significant number of projects and strategies.

Selection

In order to make the study contexts more comparable, this study is positioned in the European context, having selected a group of port cities that have gone through the same macro-transformations in historical, economic, environmental, and social terms.

First of all, the study has delimited a set of criteria by which to guide the selection. Initially, the group of ports that were candidates for the investigation was broader; subsequently, by refining the selection technique, the list was reduced to six study contexts. The first act of selection concerned the choice of the European area so as to guarantee a homogenous backdrop to the study. Subsequently, the type of port was taken into consideration, selecting only multi-purpose ports, i.e., those equipped with a full range of operational functions (commercial, industrial, shipbuilding, petrochemical, and passenger-based). However, as the cargo sector is leading in contemporary maritime trade and establishes the port's performance, the selection favored ports with predominantly commercial activities. Functional variety, however, is an important prerequisite because it gives rise to a broad and heterogeneous range of city-port relationships.

Finally, the selection traced the form of the administrative border between city and port, conducting a preliminary exploration based on site inspections and the in-depth study of urban planning instruments. The border emerged thanks to a predominantly inductive approach, one that is aimed at evaluating the reciprocal position of city and port fabrics and, consequently, at highlighting the existence of a more or less profound physical-spatial interaction, a mirror of the economic, social, and figurative-symbolic ties between the two realities.

To clarify this last step, it is useful to provide an example. In the first layer of filtering, there was a decision to also include the port of Gioia Tauro in Calabria in the selection, which is a large container terminal and transshipment hub in the southern Mediterranean. However, the overall configuration of the port, with the built-up area to the south and the port in the north in a clearly detached position, did not allow for the development of a study consistent with the fundamental principles of the research.

Although the physical distance between the two entities does not preclude the existence of relations between the two parts, it nonetheless inhibits the physical proximity between the two areas, thus preventing the formation and recognition of a city-port border, the preferential object of the study.

The final criterion that guided the selection was the identification of an interesting set of design approaches within each context. Only in a small group of ports was it actually possible to identify sites specifically dedicated to the modifications of the city-port border. These are strategies that aspire to overcome the port dismantling/urban redevelopment scheme common in the late twentieth century, experimenting instead with actions inspired by an unprecedented awareness according to which the port does not abandon the field but, on the contrary, assumes a central role in the regeneration of territories. This design approach is common to all the selected study contexts, since it makes it possible not to renounce the port (from a functional, economic, but also figurative-symbolic point of view) but to make use of its dominant presence, employing its dynamism as the ingredient of a common project.

Distinct from this last and essential criterion, the city-port border is a figure that exists and is also evident in many other contexts: it is a heterogeneous area in Barcelona, rich in contrasts and contradictions in Naples, and highly infrastructured in Le Havre. This observation makes the study of the border between city and port particularly significant because it introduces an experimental perspective in many other European and non-European contexts.

Families

The six ports selected for the study refer to two systems connected in multiple perspectives but that indeed exhibit many differences. Northern Ports of the Northern Range (Rotterdam, Hamburg, and Copenhagen) are river ports located at long, medium or short distances from the mouth of the river. The Mediterranean ones (Marseilles, Genoa, Palermo), on the other hand, are open sea ports with high coastlines, very deep seabeds, and sea protection structures of significant dimensions.

A further difference is the scale of the port in terms of size but also in terms of commercial performance, i.e., annual production volume. Last but not least, the great variety of port management governing schemes, from which different programs for the treatment of the city-port border are derived, represents an element of interest and fundamental comparison for the whole study. In fact, four of the six study contexts are part of a recently formalized port system consortium: Copenhagen and Malmö (since 2001), Marseille, Martigues, Port-de-Bouc, Fos-sur-Mer, Port-Saint-Louis-du-Rhône (since 2008/2009), Genoa and Savona-Vado Ligure, Palermo, Termini Imerese, Trapani, and Porto Empedocle (all from 2016).

In the case of port consortiums of two or more ports, the research takes the particularity of this structure into consideration, especially from a management standpoint, and evaluates the main consequences in terms of planning, depending on the varied timing of the mergers entering into force. However, the investigation focuses exclusively on the principal port of the port grouping, i.e., the one of the greatest size and complexity in morphological-territorial terms, with a variety of established functions, and with a strategic role within the cluster. This clearly does not exclude that in the other system hubs, of smaller size and impact, a city-port border capable of defining a potential field of future research exists and could be recognized.

Research

The method of exploration is based on complementary tools employed in each context. First of all, all port cities were the object of a site inspection, making the most of the possibilities offered by the context in terms of accessibility of spaces and availability of local authorities.

With regard to the sources, it is necessary to underscore how obtaining written documentation did not always correspond to their actual possibility of being used. In some cases, in fact, the materials found were only in the original language (Danish, German, or French), which made some data difficult to access. Nevertheless, the research was able to take advantage of numerous scientific contributions both from the study and from meetings and interviews with public and private entities.

Due to the mutability of the subject matter, the research sought to maintain direct contact, one as up to date as possible, with the contemporary framework in the belief that this would make it possible to reach conclusions that were equally dynamic and open. Such a methodology, i.e., one based on the study of preferential contexts, is appropriate for this type of research, since it unites the different cases by developing a wide-ranging line of reasoning on the situation of port facilities found in the various port cities.

Subsequently, through the factsheets (see: *ATLASES*), the aim is to establish an early potentially expandable overview of projects and strategies. In this way, the uniqueness of each individual context is valid not only for constructing critical images of the specific place but for restoring the complexity of the contemporary port city.

THRESHOLD

Nature and Potential
Backgrounds
The Concept of Threshold/s
The Threshold Heritage
From Integration
to Coexistence

THRESHOLD

Nature and Potential

Backgrounds
The Concept of Threshold/s
The Threshold Heritage
From Integration to Coexistence

Nature and Potential

Power

Much of the literature on so-called "border studies" shares the view that the renewed interest in the subject in the new millennium has emerged in conjunction with the implementation of borders and territorial frictions. The formation of new barriers, largely resulting from acts of violence and the consequent defense, extends the examination of borders in such a way as to broaden the field of investigation to different types of spatial divisions.

This line of reasoning involves many disciplines, those related to both space and others, and it brings together authority and territories by reflecting on the effects of what Foucault called the "mechanism of power."[1] The issue of borders, above all military and political, has been present in the spatial disciplines since the second postwar period, demonstrating that scientific research on this subject had not disappeared at all; on the contrary, it had become so widespread that it had transformed entire nations into "borderlands."[2]

The circulation of these theories triggered a change: if originally the border in architecture referred to the fundamental gesture of marking a boundary between the known and the unknown, giving a human order to the chaos of nature, today the argument emerges in an exemplary way, since contested spaces, and the resulting borders, have now been extended on a global scale. For this reason, it can be said that contemporary spatiality is increasingly determined by the geometry of many types of borders and their variations.

Along this line of thinking, Piero Zanini asserts that man tends to live within a limited space because he needs a kind of barrier (not only a physical one) that protects him and at the same time defines him. Along the border, the feeling of disorientation increases, references are lost, and as

[1]
Michel Foucault, *Security, Territory, Population*, Lectures at the Collège de France, 1977–1978 (New York: Davidson, Arnold I. Editions, 2007).

[2]
Anssi Paasi, "A Border Theory: An Unattainable Dream or a Realistic Aim for Border Scholars?", in *The Ashgate Research Companion to Border Studies*, Doris Wastl-Walter, ed. (London: Taylor & Francis Group), 11–33.

a consequence the need for possession, legitimacy, and belonging grows. According to Franco La Cecla, differences are exacerbated along the margins, and it is possible to encounter the true authenticity of places.[3]

These reflections reveal that the theme of borders has a lot to do not only with the security or regulation of spaces but also with the construction of spatial identity and the personality of inhabitants and places.

Space

The interest of urban studies in the multiple types of borders is principally owed to Sharon Zukin who, at the end of the twentieth century, introduced the fundamental idea of liminal space, extending the concept of "liminality" that Victor Turner had proposed in the temporal realm into the realm of spatiality.[4] Zukin maintains that the border spaces, or liminal spaces, are figures that are increasingly placed "at the center" of cities (and not in the suburbs) where they are formed as a result of forces that modify the structure of territories. These are territorial alterations that don't remain separated from the central hub of life and work in the city, but that manifest themselves clearly, soliciting the development of tools suited to study them.

The increasing focus on mobility and commerce in the field of sociology and the increasingly concrete emergence of the network society thus produced irreversible changes: the transition to a global scale and the crisis of the concept of territory, for example, accentuated social and political differences and expanded the range of contemporary conditions and practices. Along this line of thinking, the expansion of the concept of "space," which is asserted in the architectural sphere especially in postmodernism, renews the interest in borders, producing a fragmentation of accepted meanings through which space is described and conceptualized. This turning point — called the "spatial turn" — expands the concept, transforming space into a powerful contemporary metaphor, a constitutive paradigm of political and social relations.[5]

The "spatial turn" offers an opportunity to develop alternative approaches to certain disciplines that were previously "de-spatialized" (geography, for example) and, at the same time, to produce multiple forms of space; interstitial, residual, or liminal spaces that guide research and design toward the discontinuities and demarcation lines of cities and territories, encouraging exploration of the borders in their stable and crystallized nature.

In this re-evaluation of the concept of space, the effects of globalization again exert their impact: indeed, with the proliferation of digital tools, new technologies, and the virtual dimension, there was no longer a need

3
For further information, refer to Piero Zanini's and Franco La Cecla's studies about border spatiality and the effects it causes in terms of the orientation, perception, and personality of places. Cf. Piero Zanini, *Significati del confine. I limiti naturali, storici, mentali* (Milan: Bruno Mondadori Editore, 2000), and Franco La Cecla, *Perdersi. L'uomo senza ambiente* (Rome and Bari: Laterza, 1988).

4
Susan Zukin, *Landscapes of Power* (Berkeley, CA: University of California Press, 1991), and Victor Turner, *La Foresta dei Simboli* (Brescia: Morcelliana, 1967).

5
Chiara Brambilla, Jussi Laine, James W. Scott, Gianluca Bocchi, *Borderscaping: Imaginations and Practices of Border Making* (London: Routledge, 2015).

for physical space in order to establish relationships, but rather the need for places in which to recognize oneself, for cultural and symbolic landscapes capable of representing bonds, and for telling stories and portraying personal images.

Borders

The impact of global dynamics on territoriality has manifested itself in theoretical terms but even more so in terms of the transformation and management of built spaces. The contemporary world has been "de-solidified," asserting its "liquid" complexity, and has assumed an increasingly "de-bordered" form, i.e., one without limits, which casts doubt on national hierarchies and the concepts of center and periphery.

Nevertheless, and paradoxically in this precise context, the issue of borders has come back to forcefully assert itself: "The border, seen as sur-passed, as by-passed by globalization, returns in reality magnified to a tendentially worldwide scale. Globalization is the shifting of the border to its conceivable limits [...]."[6]

6
Pasquale Ferrara, "Limes. Il confine nell'era postglobale", *Sophia*, vol. 3, no. 2 (2011), 183–194.

Straddling the twentieth century and the new millennium, an unprecedented explosion of various forms of borders can be indeed seen: static or naturalized lines that mark the limits of the authorities and that arise largely for reasons of surveillance, regulation, and fear. The association between the phenomena of globalization and "bordering" (literally, the production of borders) confirm the thinking that "borders are everywhere,"[7] recognizing their unstoppable multiplication but also the ability for them to become lenses through which to interpret societies and territories. Thanks to this rediscovery, the notion of the border was enriched with meanings and operativity: it used liminal spaces as objects of study to describe a new spatiality in which the relationship between forms of power and constructed systems is interwoven and, at the same time, the concepts of citizenship, belonging, and identity take shape.

7
Anssi Paasi, "A Border Theory: An unattainable dream or a realistic aim for border scholars?", in *The Ashgate Research Companion to Border Studies*, Doris Wastl-Walter, ed. (London: Taylor&-Francis Group), 22.

With the "bordering" process, borders became devices of spatial differentiation integrated into a framework that was no longer immobile but in the process of becoming. This freed up their critical potential and highlighted the urgency of identifying a more articulate and contemporary notion to describe them. In this sense, the idea of a *borderscape*, theorized by Arjan Harbers in the early 2000s, undoubtedly furnishes an effective notion from both an ontological and a methodological point of view.

Borderscapes, especially those produced by the presence of large infrastructural complexes are indeed preferential places for understanding the spatial fragmentation and the political-institutional relations that animate territories:

——— Political ideologies have affected architecture since earliest times. Government buildings and urban ensembles reflect not only the *zeitgeist* but also the political climate at the time of building. [...] An attempt to make sense of this patchwork [...] with different political systems, traditions and alliances requires case studies, new classifications and recommendations on a continental scale. The best places to carry out such research are border areas, the fault lines between political entities.[8]

8
Arjan Harbers, "Borderscapes: The Influence of National Borders on Spatial Planning", in *Euroscapes – Forum 2003*, Robert Broesi, Pieter Jannink, Wouter Veldhuis, Ivan Nio, eds. (Amsterdam: MUST Publishers and AetA, 2005), 143–166.

Definitions

The plurality and dynamism of borders are often a source of ambiguity. The absence of unambiguous meanings announces a conflict, also physical, that spills out along the edges, turning them into places of separation and confrontation. Borders are territorial solidifications, at times marked by clear and continuous lines, at other times by complex, blurred, and multilayered sequences. Spaces where one does not dwell, but where distance is created with barriers and filter areas; areas where projects don't see the light of day and where the specifications for urban plans are blurred.

The proliferation of terms coined to represent the diversification of borders (in numerous European languages) somehow seems to confirm the richness and disorder of this subject. Border, boundary, limit, edge but also barrier, frontier, interface, threshold: each of these terms more or less alludes to the same basic concept. It describes an element that is "between" other things, that divides, that confirms the end of one situation or status and the beginning of another, implicitly marking a decisive structural variation. It is something that connects by separating (or vice versa) and produces around itself a certain condition — or more concretely an area — onto which it transfers its own genetic characteristics. In this sense, it is worth talking about "border space" but even more of "border as space" in order to assess its full weight and size.[9]

9
Piero Zanini, *Significati del confine. I limiti naturali, storici, mentali* (Milan: Bruno Mondadori Editore, 2000).

The routes that can potentially be taken with these lines of reasoning are many and lead to the complex interweaving of disciplines. Thus, the terms quoted above are not synonymous, but, with minor or major nuances they allow for variations in meaning that are by no means negligible.

What matters in this context is the isolation of two key ideas. The border, the subject of this study, is an element of variable thickness and intensity, whose form is difficult to describe in a finite way and therefore requires dedicated codes and languages.

Secondly, this border is an intermediate space, a "unifying suture" rather than an "isolating barrier."[10] It is an interface that takes the instability and mutability of urban organisms into consideration and presupposes transition and movement. A field in which, as flows and forces converge and diverge, the identity and character of communities and places condense.

Place

The border is an element that identifies, or better yet, gives rise to a place imbued with a boundary-defined spatial dimension. A dimension capable of being articulated in numerous syntheses and of transforming the border into a means for comprehending the contemporary modifications of the so-called spatial disciplines.[11] The production of borders, after all, is a continuous practice in the contemporary city (and not only), and this proliferation has modified the original role of the border:

——— The spatio-temporal limits fixed by today's transformations of the established form define new thresholds, understood as gravitational lessons of the physical, cultural, and functional components given for discreet surroundings.[12]

The contemporary concept of the border has therefore abandoned its classic identity as a separating object in order to take on a new configuration, becoming not only more heterogeneous but above all more extensive and dynamic. It has become a structural element of urban systems, a spatial but also mental, cultural, and ideological border. Nevertheless, the exploration in urban planning matters conveys a quite different picture, especially when it comes to territorial planning, where the question of borders is almost non-existent, or rather it is treated in a haphazard and non-specific way.

Certainly, these are territories for which it is not easy to formulate guidelines for development and that, as a result, often remain unexplored, literally on the margins.

Yet, in some particular cases — for example, the borders that divide cities and ports from a legal standpoint — there are intriguing possibilities generating new synergies that benefit both sides.

10
Kevin Lynch, *L'immagine della città* (Milan: Marsilio Editore, 1964, 2006).

11
For further information, refer to the studies and publications of the "Border Conditions" research group, directed by Marc Schoonderbeek. Formed in the Faculty of Architecture of the Delft University of Technology in 2002, the research group works in the field of international border studies.

12
Sergio Crotti, *Figure architettoniche: soglia* (Milan: Edizioni Unicopli, 2000).

Threshold

The port dimension has always assumed a certain aptitude for change. Due to the incessant technological and infrastructural evolutions and the global maritime-commercial dynamics, the structure and syntax of the port city are often asked to undergo profound cycles of transformation and updating. Each phase of the process has been confronted not only with physical precedents but above all with traces of urban and human memory accumulated through overlapping actions. These are mostly decommissionings of obsolete areas and artifacts, renovation and assimilation of instruments and mechanisms, and the linguistic alteration of building codes.

In this complex framework, the most evident intermingling condenses along functional and administrative borders: although they are often perceived as contested spaces, in reality the border landscapes between city and port are responsive interfaces, endowed with a receptive potential and, first and foremost, inclined and/or subject to change.

Thanks to maritime geography studies, it is possible to evaluate the spatial conformations taken on by port cities over the centuries. Between the nineteenth and twentieth centuries, in particular, the emergence of a border that divides and simultaneously connects the port and the city can be observed: a real and perceptible figure in the everyday movement of people and goods, a physical and effective front. Thus understood, the city-port border is a liminal space, a third state with respect to the city or the port as usually understood: a dynamic threshold.

The idea that there is a threshold capable of separating and, simultaneously, connecting urban and operational areas is a concept that would never have been understood in past eras when the city and the port lived in a state of substantial spatial and symbolic cohesion. In fact, it is only following the expansion and specialization of port infrastructures that external actions have modified the areas of connection between city and port and transformed ports into autonomous entities both administratively and physically.

——— The port-city interface is a phrase that would not have been understood in past times when an interdependent city and port shared a common identity. [...] As ports and cities have developed new roles within contrasted but interrelated and interdependent systems at local, regional and global scales, a new interface between port and city has emerged [...] as a major concern of many people and organizations over the past fifty years.[13]

13
Brian S. Hoyle, "Identity and Interdependence: Transport and Transformation at the Port-City Interface", in *Fourth Intermediate Meeting*, Koper (March 2006), 13–23.

Medium

Using the concept of threshold, an indefinite formulation of a variable and arbitrary breadth, represents a crucial step in overcoming the ideas of the border, boundary, and limit, since it makes possible the evolution of a legal border into a design border.

Conceptually, a threshold is a precarious and discontinuous filtering space, fragmented into parts in which juxtapositions and antinomies take on concrete form so as to conquer space and become recognizable. Literally, the city-port threshold is that strip of variable thickness produced by the presence of the administrative limit that divides the territory of the city from that of the port. It is a physical element but also a system in which the entirety of interactions and dependencies is concentrated that irreversibly link a city to its port. It is a place that expands in breadth according to the transformations of neighboring spaces, whether it be dismantling, reconversion, or, on the contrary, expansions in operational terms. In its liminal state, flows from land and sea converge, and the potential for contact, sharing, and design of city-port territories is characterized.

The notion of threshold is meant to signify a territory subjected to continuous overlaps that balance opposing forces, guaranteeing its constancy.

———— [It is] a medium of interscalar communication, a condenser of multiple relationships, a dynamic attractor of the involved areas that can therefore be considered the generating nucleus of transformations.[14]

The transition to the concept of threshold is therefore not accidental but a precise choice. In such a way, the meaning of the idea of the border (or limit, margin, or edge) is actually enriched by acquiring the sense of movement and change.

Figure

The city-port threshold is an architectural figure that varies according to the context and multiple other factors. Its form, in fact, has no general structure or standard typology, but it can find its articulation in different models largely due to the variation of aspects linked to the morphology of the specific places, the planning tools in force, and the territories' government. In this sense, the management aspect almost always appears to be the most appropriate filter through which to explore the current nature of the city-port dimension in different study contexts:

14
Sergio Crotti, *Figure architettoniche: soglia* (Milan: Edizioni Unicopli, 2000).

———— [Today] the forces that shape geographical shifts in the port-city interface have become much more complex, and are better explained from an institutionalist point of view: a view that attends to the rules, norms, and beliefs that govern the policies and plans for city and port, without neglecting the ever-changing behavior and capabilities of those affected by the port and port-related projects.[15]

15
Tom Daamen, Erik Louw, "The Challenge of the Dutch Port-City Interface", *Tijdschrift voor Economische en Sociale Geografie*, vol. 107, no. 5 (2016), 642–651.

The port border (with the city) is thus a system of separation that translates into a line drawn on the map and to which plural meanings are attributed. It marks the beginning and the end of the jurisdiction of the port authority, but, even more than that, its liminal regime, the ensemble of flows and forces that offset and restrain each other, and it generates the creation of a symbolic place that represents the temperament of the port city itself.

Alteration

The formation of the city-port threshold derives from an alteration of space, which represents the many ways in which power is reflected in social and spatial configurations.[16] The city-port threshold is a political construction; although its administrative function is often dominant, what matters in this context is knowing how to recognize its potential ability to become a dynamic organism and a design framework.

16
Mark Schoonderbeek, "The Border as Threshold Space of Simultaneities", *Archimaera*, vol. 5 (2013), 151–165.

The landscape of the threshold is legitimated through an encounter (or a clash), and, unsurprisingly, it exists from the moment the relationship between city and port becomes controversial:

———— The port-city interface may be described as a system, or as a concept, or as a series of mechanisms that, collectively and individually, link port and city, closely or tenuously. [...] In spatial terms, on land and water, an interface zone exists between urban activities and maritime activities. Through this zone there may run a line of demarcation between urban and port administrations. The zone may be an area of cooperation or of conflict, and may present a scene of degeneration and decay, or may be characterized by regeneration and lively growth.[17]

17
Ibid.

Paradigm

While the economic, commercial, and cultural interactions that structure the connection between the two territories are condensed in the territory of the threshold, the city-port condition is defined. It is for this reason that the threshold becomes the primary field of investigation and the paradigm through which (and in which) to explore the features of the contemporary city-port intermingling, the specific condition that this book has already named *portuality*.

After all, the threshold between city and port is capable of acquiring significant value also in symbolic terms: it is indeed the opinion of many that the identity of a port city is an idea that plays out right along the border and defines itself through the type of interactions that are detectable along the shared interface.[18]

18
For further information, refer to Yehuda Hayuth, "The Port-Urban Interface: An Area in Transition", *The Royal Geographical Society Stable*, vol. 14, no. 3 (1982), 219–224, and Brian S. Hoyle, "Tomorrow's World? Divergence and Reconvergence at the Port-City interface", in *The Port City of the XXIst Century: New Challenges in the Relationship between Port and City*, Bruttomesso Rinio, Jean Alemany, eds. (Venice: RETE Publisher, 2011), 15–28.

Fragment

The study of the city-port threshold aims to investigate in a unified way the set of artifacts, infrastructures, and facilities that have arisen over time and that have been developed along the border of the port area, considering them as a heterogeneous but compact system. Between a city and its port there are in fact points or rather entire zones of potential contact that wind along and across the state-owned property border. What defines the intensity of this possible dialogue is the nature of the port and the urban activities that are facing one another.

Despite the differences derived from individual contexts, the threshold can indeed be investigated as a significant fragment of a broader, more general complexity.

Maps

There are many thresholds in the contemporary city (not only between city and port) that can be explored along the discontinuous edges of territories. Natural or artificial fractures along which a change of status occurs.

In the city-port case, depicting and conveying these liminal figures requires the construction of a longitudinal narrative in which the rhythm of the relationship between port and city is marked. Such a representation process must thus take into account the different geometries in which the threshold is formed and develop a dedicated interpretive methodology. With the aim of developing maps of city-port thresholds the objective therefore is to restore the ambivalence and plurality provoked by external agents or intentionally introduced through the project (see: *ATLASES*).

The construction of a map is an exercise that, according to Mohsen Mostafavi, presupposes a cartographic imagination, a sort of new ability

19
Mohsen Mostafavi,
Foreword to *Is
Landscape...? Essays
on the Identity of
Landscape*, Gareth
Doherty, Charles
Waldheim, eds.
(Abingdon, NY: Rout-
ledge, 2015).

20
The verisimilar nar-
rative and theory are
very specific and well
investigated in the
architectural field.
For further infor-
mation, among
others, refer to
Charles Baudelaire,
"Oeuvres", vol. 2,
in Benjamin Walter,
Eiland Howard, eds.,
*Selected Writings:
1938–1940* (Harvard
University Press,
2006), 341, and to
Nicola Braghieri,
"L'impossibile veri-
simile e il possibile
incredibile", in
*Sull'arte, Terza lettura
del ciclo "Avanti non
si torna"* (1995–2002)
(*ex-m.eu*).

to "see reality" and to portray it in its "imaginative components" through a set of conventional signs.[19]

A map is the representation of a social construct within a spatial frame-work and offers a means of navigating the space it depicts. In addition, in its structuring a lot depends on the purpose and on the history that the map pro-poses to recount in that particular situation. The decision to use conventions to represent places and their qualities therefore involves a symbolic language rich in abstraction that can communicate relevant characteristic contents. A cartography of this type is closer not to a real but rather to a *verisimilar* kind of narrative.[20] Tending toward the verisimilar provides valuable weap-ons since it builds a message that goes beyond measurements, propor-tions, and canonical time sequences: it seeks to depict not what it is or what it was, but what it could be. By using this approach to map the city-port threshold, it is possible to transmit the dynamism of the landscape, its variations, and the inseparable relationship between what is given as a starting point (topography) and what happens afterward (the project).

However, the representation of borders, and the spaces generated by them, is controversial since it poses the problem of the relationship between space and rules and of depicting a contradictory and paradoxical situation — but not only that. It is a matter of mapping something that is there but not seen, which establishes an institutional regime and produces a binding status but is often completely invisible. Placing a border in space, has to do with the awareness that people have of their existence. It con-cerns the processes, not at all stable, that determine their form and nature, and it depends on the practices of constructing the concept of the border.

Specifically speaking, the city-port threshold describes a blocked sit-uation in which, in most cases, the physical border between the two terri-tories coincides with the administrative limit. All of this is exacerbated by the planning that continues to work on contoured spaces beyond which another world begins and other rules apply. The threshold is a spatial sequence in which different characteristics are recognized, ones that make openings, interferences, and transitions possible (or impossible). This type of map is therefore intended to take into account the fragility and tension related to the changes of these spaces, with the purpose of giving form to "the imaginary power of borders as a concept."[21]

Interpretation

A map has always been a simplified representation that involves degrees of inaccuracy and approximation. After all, the more technology

21
James D. Sidaway,
"The Poetry of
Boundaries", in
*Borderscapes: Hidden
Geographies and
Politics at Territory's
Edge* (Borderlines
series), Prem Kumar
Rajaram, Carl Grundy-
Warr, eds. (University
of Minnesota Press),
161–181.

has provided accurate and realistic aids to describe the world (satellite images, shots from space stations, parametric surveys), the more the search for languages capable of expressing links, impressions, and even feelings have expanded. Maps were enriched with signs that put physical objects less and less in focus, so as to focus instead on spatial phenomena, on stories derived from experiences, on the landscapes produced. Although this evolution has required an updating in terms of representation, it has nevertheless not changed the original ambiguous nature of maps: imperfect images that render a never definitive reality but rather a fluctuating and dynamic one.

These qualities seem to fit well with the nature of borders: they are in tune with their ability to interpret the variations of contemporary spaces, to systemize the project's scales, enhancing the heterogeneity of urban and human cultural heritage. For this reason, the process of conceptualizing borders requires that these landscapes are interpreted and understood as "places in the world that become, through their evocative power, metaphors of existential situations, keys of comparison between cultures."[22]

The following maps of the city-port threshold constitute a first atlas of non-neutral images intended to give voice to the discontinuity of territories. Perhaps the idea of representing a border verges on impracticability, since its purpose is to give shape to something intangible and to grasp a meaning where one would be tempted to see only things and facts. Therefore, maps are useful tools not only for locating the geometry of the threshold, but above all for rendering its breadth and spatial impact in terms of relationships and the potential design consistence.

The richness and plurality of the threshold, in any case, can also produce a sense of disorientation, almost of vertigo. Experiencing the border means dealing with its energy, but also accepting the contradiction that it inadvertently generates. Remaining displaced in an attempt to represent the landscapes of the threshold, therefore, is a fundamental part of the process of constructing tools capable of understanding and conveying its complexity.

Backgrounds
The Concept of Threshold/s

"A liminal figure, a space of transition, a place of distinction, the threshold is a term whose conceptual extension goes from origin myths to the foundational rites, spanning historical periods and traversing multiple domains of knowledge."[23] To understand the concept of threshold from the

22
Franco La Cecla, Piero Zanini, *Lo stretto indispensabile. Le terre divise da un piccolo pezzo di terra* (Milan: Bruno Mondadori, 2004).

23
Sergio Crotti, *Figure architettoniche: soglia* (Milan: Edizioni Unicopli, 2000).

standpoint of the architectural disciplines, it may at first be useful to go beyond disciplines by extending the reasoning and transferring it to territories in which the meaning of borders is compromised and unexplored concretizations of the border issue are produced.

First, for example, it is possible to refer to some aspects of the myth of the cave recounted by Plato in the seventh book of *La Repubblica*.[24] According to one of the many interpretations of this text, universally recognized as fundamental for the history of Western thought and culture, the cave metaphorically represents a threshold, i.e., a world placed in a middle position between the condition of mortality and that of immortality.

It is no coincidence that the threshold (from the Latin sŏlea, sole of the foot, sole) corresponds to the entrance (and exit) of a place, in this case the cave, and coincides with the area that connects the terrestrial world and its projection on the rear wall. According to Plato, between the internal dimension (limited and reflected) and the external dimension (complete and real) lies the attainment of pure knowledge, but above all a zone of transition, full of contradictions and differences, which becomes an incubator of powerful and multiple innovations.

Moving beyond the mythical narrative, the concept of liminality, as related in Victor Turner's research, describes a condition in the process of transformation and considers this provisional state a window of exchange and observation, a threshold in temporal terms.

Turner made the liminal regime correspond to a timeless, perturbatory, and revolutionary interval: "In liminality, profane social relations can be interrupted, previous rights and obligations are suspended, and it may seem like the social order has been subverted [...]."[25] According to this perspective, thresholds are times (or places) on the verge of change, where a neutralization of the prearranged relations occurs. They are *intermezzi* in which a suspension of ordinary regimes is tried out, and a degree of freedom arises in which something extraordinary can happen.

Doorway

Another eloquent interpretation of the concept of threshold is found in the work *Disegno di una porta per entrare nell'ombra* (*Design of a Door to Enter the Darkness*) created by Ettore Sottsass in 1973.[26]

The project consisted of several portals made of slats of wood, rope, and palm leaves, which were placed in a desert plain right on the border between a sunny area and a shadowy area. While these were modest creations, the works were not mere installations but works of architecture that

24
Raoul Bunschoten states that, "The cave is a perfect liminal body: a threshold space of life and its border between mortality and immortality. [...] The Neo-Platonists uses the cave as a concept – a model of the hybrid nature of a threshold space [...]." Cf. Raul Bunschoten, "Liminal Bodies and Urban Incubators", in *Border Conditions*, Mark Schoonderbeek, ed. (Amsterdam: Architectura & Natura, first edition), 278.

25
Victor Turner, *Dal rito al teatro* (Bologna: Il Mulino, 2014), 26, 27.

26
Between 1972/1974, Ettore Sottsass created "Metaphors," a series of installations which reduce architecture to a fragile outline that alludes to the presence of man, but what appears is instead the immutable background of the landscape, in its multiple variations: residual, relational, and sometimes liminal. The linguistic figure of the metaphor therefore connects man to the landscape, reconstructing the broken link between the two. Cf. Ettore Sottsass, *There Is a Planet*, exhibition curated by Barbara Radice (Milan: Triennale Design Museum, 2017).

marked the passage from light to darkness. Their function was to explore the spatiality of the border by changing the perception of the landscape and influencing the mood of the users. Each portal erected a barrier and divided a unified space by shifting attention to a discontinuity, the one between light and shadow, otherwise not very evident in three-dimensional terms. By creating an opening in this front, the possibility of a crossing over was guaranteed, which in a tacit but insistent way gave rise to an invitation or a challenge. Going beyond the portal caused a feeling of excitement and even fear, almost as if something unexpected and incredible could happen once on the other side.

The work generated an intermediate field, a space full of liminal qualities that evoked trepidation and expectation towards a "beyond" to be reached and experienced.

Genesis

Like its nature, the genesis of the threshold is as open as it is ambiguous; it is revealed through contrast and contains some revelations.

Firstly, the threshold is a related notion but substantially different from the boundary, border, limit or margin. The border emerges from the need to establish fixed points, lines of force useful for recognizing a difference and consecrating the existence of a sort of alterity or otherness. Secondly, the threshold is an inclusive device, not simply a line, but a zone with territorial proportions that is defined by drawing legitimacy from its middle and composite position.

In line with Sottsass' vision, Unwin argues that a barrier serves to hold things, people, and places on one side, while the existence of openings offers the possibility to move from one side to the other, creating a threshold that spurs interaction.[27] For this reason, Unwin continues, thresholds are formed before borders because they already exist in the form of promises, in the awareness that, beyond the barriers, there is another world to be accessed.

The genesis of the threshold is therefore configured as a foundational gesture that not only produces a clear separation but lays the foundations for the search for a future connection. In other words, it is the perception of detachment that renders the subsequent contact natural; as Georg Simmel maintained:

——— [We] can only sense those things to be related which we have previously somehow isolated from one another; things must first be separated from one another in order to be together. [28]

27
Simon Unwin,
Doorway (Oxon: Routledge, 2007).

28
Georg Simmel, "Bridge and Door", *Theory, Culture & Society Journal*, vol. 11.1 (1994), 5–10.

After all, the construction of barriers and simultaneously of openings falls within the sphere of great human conquests. It demonstrates the ability to counter nature by cutting out a portion of finite space from the rest of the continuous and infinite world and underscores the possibility of getting out of it at any moment by going beyond the limit.

Globalization

The geographer Franco Farinelli has asserted that the phenomenon of globalization has forced us to recognize the world for what it really is: a globe and not a map.[29]

29
For further information, refer to Franco Farinelli, *La crisi della ragione cartografica* (Bologna: Piccola Biblioteca Einaudi, 2009), and Franco Farinelli, *Geografia. Un'introduzione ai modelli del mondo* (Bologna: Piccola Biblioteca Einaudi, 2003).

As anticipated, the mechanisms of the man-made world have been upended by dynamics that, having an effect on spatial forms, have contributed to strengthening the concept of borders. The phenomenon of bordering (i.e., the production of borders) actually runs concurrently to that of globalization, even if the former theorizes the multiplication of borders and the latter proposes a world without limits. According to this perspective, the space of the border is manifested as the formal result of decision-making processes of a cultural kind but above all of mechanisms of power.

Spatial divisions are a dominant theme in the research of Michel Foucault, who pays particular attention to the contemporary condition of borders by distinguishing some aspects that influence their configuration more than others.[30] According to his approach, sovereignty, discipline, and security generate a territorial fragmentation in which the border functions as a physical element of control, as a means for recognizing the presence of an elsewhere.

30
For further information, refer to Michel Foucault, *Security, Territory, Population: Lectures at the Collège de France, 1977–1978* (New York: Davidson, Arnold I. Editions, 2007), and Michel Foucault, *Spazi altri. I luoghi delle eterotopie*, Salvo Vaccaro, ed. (Milan: Mimesis Edizioni, 1985).

Depending on the dynamics that act upon territories it can therefore be argued that there are several possible spatial conceptualizations of the border to which a great many potential applicative variations of this element correspond.

Liminality

Although today the definition of a border refers largely to political and social limitations, the border remains an element in which the ambiguity of meaning is a mirror of its capacity to become an investigative tool in the field of urban studies. Looking at borders as central subjects of research and projects concerns an increasingly broader catalogue of spatial situations that are no longer peripheral but located in the center of cities.

To describe the rapid reversal of the categories of space, Sharon Zukin used the term liminality, thereby connecting again to Victor Turn-

31
Susan Zukin, *Land-scapes of Power* (Berkeley, CA: University of California Press, 1991).

er's definition with regard to liminal experience and its repercussions on the formation of new urban spaces.[31] According to Zukin, liminality is a way of looking at the marginal and intermediate areas of cities that have a decisive influence on the human perception of places in terms of orientation, localization, and territorial belonging, since it destabilizes identity by imposing new hierarchies.

Going toward the edge and experiencing liminality helps in the understanding of the nature of borders. Their accounts lead us to practice tolerance, to stand side by side despite respective particularities, accepting to be part of a single reality. The concept of liminality is therefore applicable not only to time but also to space. It is an idea that, from a representation of an interval "outside of time," the form of thresholds can materialize "within" territories and cities.

Organism

32
Marc Schoonderbeek, *Border Conditions* (Amsterdam: Architectura & Natura, 2010).

Spatiality, power, and borders are linked through a close relationship of reciprocal conditioning. As Schoonderbeek asserts, the imposition of a border within a territory generates a spatial condition full of design potential. Thresholds take on a two-dimensional consistency and reveal a distance and a breadth.[32] The threshold is a concept only understood by developing a progressive process of broadening its meanings. From a linear element, it can be conceived first and foremost as a space, or rather as a derived spatial environment on which it transfers its own characteristics. Attributing an areal dimension to boundary lines also gives them a sort of density and physical consistency. In this way, borders materialize; they literally take shape and become "liminal bodies." In the form of bodies or organisms, borders are transformed into urban incubators, i.e., elements that generate solutions and varied spatial contexts.[33]

33
Raul Bunschoten, "Liminal Bodies and Urban Incubators", in *Border Conditions*, Marc Schoonderbeek, ed. (Amsterdam: Architectura & Natura, 2010), 278–282.

Field

Along this line of reasoning, the threshold progressively evolves from a linear concept to an element with a surface (space, place) and even a three-dimensionality (body, organism).

34
Stan Allen, "From Object to Field", in *Architectural Design*, no. 5–6 (1997), 24–31.

According to Stan Allen, however, it is possible to take a further step and replace the notion of "space" with that of "field." The field, or rather the "field condition,"[34] expresses the form of geometric relations that literally stand between things. It is a material condition, not a theoretical practice, which produces a horizontal phenomenon that can be represented mainly through flat diagrams.[35]

35
To describe the "field condition," Allen borrowed Sanford Kwinter's studies: "This notion of 'the field' expresses the

complete immanence of forces and events while supplanting the old concept of space identified with the Cartesian substratum and ether theory... The field describes a space of propagation, of effects, it contains no matter or material points, rather functions, vectors and speeds. [...]." From "La Città Nuova: Modernity and Continuity", *Zone*, no. 1/2 (1986), 88–89.

The transition proposed by Allen, "from object to field," brings out the potential of the concept of field above all in relation to the world of logistics or in terms of measuring the impact of flows and forces that animate urban contexts and make them function. The notion of field is proposed as a critical tool in the complexity of the urban context, where both architecture and urban planning have had difficulties defining their roles and bringing order to the chaos of cities and territories.

If this does not entirely clarify the operational possibilities of the notion of "field," it nevertheless allows for an enrichment of the discussion by asking whether the threshold, as described thus far, can also be considered a field. That is, if from some angle the liminal condition that it generates and which permeates it cannot be read, as Allen claims, according to its abilities as a foreign element but at the same time in relation with all the others.

The Threshold Heritage

The concept of threshold is particularly elusive: paradoxically, it appears clearer in the conceptualizations just seen than in the spatiality of the contemporary city. And yet, using the concept of threshold to explore certain rigid and constrained spaces introduces an untapped potential and opens up new horizons, especially in the field of urban and architectural design.

The city-port threshold, for example, is an exemplary case of a border that offsets and restrains forces and flows that are often opposing. In the majority of cases, this threshold winds along the route of the administrative border, where two different territories sit side by side, becoming a common category of port cities even at very distant latitudes. Despite being the stage for much of the evolution of the city-port nucleus, it remains an indecipherable place.

The city-port threshold is made up of various types of elements, some of them are in disuse, others belong to the variety of facilities that make the contemporary port active and functional. This sedimentation is a mirror of the exploitation of these spaces and testifies, just like a physical chronology, to the functions assumed by the border during the lifetime of each port.

In the early days, the threshold rose as a demarcation indicating the limits of certain areas, such as free zones or customs areas, which were legally detached from the city. In those days, one could not deny the existence of a border between the city and the port, but its role could not be compared to that taken on following the expansion of the port beginning in the nineteenth century. In modern times, this border indeed marked the relevant area of the port authority and consequently that of the municipal authority: this genesis "by contrast" endowed it with a regime of simultaneous closeness and hostility, of an intrinsic but increasingly perceptible dichotomy along its entire trajectory.

Analogies

The European context offers a disparate series of port cities in which it is nevertheless possible to recognize analogous and recurring phases of evolution. The imposing extension of the port territory throughout the nineteenth century, for example, is certainly a significant analogy both in Nordic and Mediterranean ports. The new territory that originated along the coasts in order to multiply landings and stretches of water indeed shifted the balance, establishing city-port relationships that are still in evidence today.

Since the arrival of globally driven phenomena, cities and ports have thus increasingly seen their primary needs and fields of interest diverge. Ports, on the one hand, have been confronted with the rules of worldwide maritime transport and of the principal operators that drive the market. Cities, on the other hand, have become places of production in constant evolution, where connections on a territorial scale play an increasingly important role. Also for this reason, there are port cities today in which a degree of interaction is maintained between the consolidated urban area and the operational one and, instead elsewhere, ports that became complex hubs of traffic for several decades ago. In these, the existence of a homonymous urban core makes it impossible to detect either a city-port mix based on a physical, symbolic, or cultural relationship, or the presence of a shared threshold.

Autonomy

Despite indisputable similarities among European port cities, the origin of the city-port threshold is in reality extremely varied and not always contemporaneous in different contexts.

As already mentioned, starting from the nineteenth-century expansion of ports, port and city have gradually become more and more detached. In the majority of cases, this transformation coincided with the formalization of an administrative status that made the port an autonomous political subject.

From that moment on, multiple port governance models came into being: different management plans and variable interdependencies between parties and stakeholders that reflected local balances of power and generated independent and distinct threshold configurations.

Atlantic

In the ports of the Northern Range that are the subject of this study (Rotterdam, Hamburg, and Copenhagen), the port has been constituted as an autonomous authority only in relatively recent times, mostly at the turn of the new millennium. Originally, these ports had a predominantly urban style of management, i.e., they were guided by the municipality or, in some cases, by the State. Exemples of this model are the Municipal Port Authority established in Rotterdam in 1923 or the Bureau of Hamburg Port Authority that, beginning in the 1950s, managed the Hanseatic port within the department of the Authority of Economy and Labour.

In the second half of the twentieth century, when the infrastructure was confronted with important developments and needed new tools in terms of planning and governance, the ports faced a complete restructuring, developing potentialities similar to those of a private individual (or a corporation), especially in relation to direct investments and financial autonomy.

Today, in these ports of the Northern Range, the port authority is a public company with limited liability, i.e., an organism in which public bodies, such as the State, the regional authority, or the municipality itself, have a stake, thus provide front-line support in the operation of the port infrastructure.

Mediterranean

In the ports of Marseille, Genoa, and Palermo, on the other hand, the port has been administered by port authorities for some decades now, public bodies whose organization varies according to national regulations. These are entities subordinate to the State whose governing bodies are composed of representatives of the authorities (region(s), province(s), or municipality(ies)).

The Italian port system, however, has specific features that make it scarcely comparable with that of other countries in the Mediterranean context. Many ports spread out over an extended coastline and a critical morphological configuration have made it difficult to concentrate a diversity of functions in a few centers. Italian ports are thus almost all located near the ancient nucleus of cities, and this has an effect on their functioning.

Looking more specifically at the Italian cases, it can be noted that, already by the beginning of the twentieth century, urban land was divided from the port by means of rings and that, in the following decades, the State recognized the establishment of autonomous port organizations.

With this process, the port broke away from municipal control and became managed by independent bodies, such as consortia, superintendencies, and mechanical equipment companies.

This situation persisted until the end of the twentieth century, when the continuous expansion of the port and the need to upgrade the ground network and increase the speed of processes made the drafting of a dedicated national regulation inevitable. Law No. 84 of 1994[36] developed guidelines for both planning and administration. With the entry into force of this law, the major ports received a new perspective in which the Port Regulatory Plans (P.R.P.) were no longer just simple programs of maritime and infrastructural works but complex planning and management processes. Therefore, at the most important ports, Port Authorities (AP) were set up, public bodies of a judicial nature to which tasks of control, management, and guidance were entrusted. With this directive, the port separated from the municipal territory by establishing an administrative border: according to the law, the limits of the district were actually established by the Ministry of Transport and Navigation, defining the overall structure of the port within the guidelines of the Port Regulatory Plan.

Another innovation of 84/94 was the involvement of other entities in the drafting of the planning tool; however, despite this push for interaction, throughout the period of activity of the regulation, a certain fragmentation remained that was not even overcome by the entry into force of the Legislative Decree No. 169 of 2016.[37] The Reform of the Italian Ports does not propose changes in terms of limitation of areas or specific management of boundaries, but entirely replaces the law 84/94 through a restructuring of the port facility that introduces the notion of a system. The Reform, in fact, establishes the Port System Authorities (AdSP) that group the individual entities together into territorial clusters: with this in mind, not only does a new relationship between the ports and the cities solidify, but the equilibrium that structures the governing model changes profoundly. Nevertheless, the requirements of the regulatory update do not change the role of the border, which remains as a demarcation element in legal, functional, and urban planning terms.

Heritage

A linear sequence of operating machines in various states of abandonment and use snake along the city-port threshold. They are the residue of the emporium port or are still functioning artifacts that define a recurring

36
Reference is to Law No. 84/1994 and further modifications: "Riordino della legislazione in materia portuale."

37
Reference is to Decree No. 169/2016: "Riorganizzazione, razionalizzazione e semplificazione della disciplina concernente le Autorità Portuali di cui alla legge 28 gennaio 1994, n. 84."

landscape: no longer simply isolated objects but fragments of a single system, a specific architectural, industrial, and urban heritage anchored on the border line between city and port.

The compactness of this single system manifests itself through the widespread homogeneity of building characteristics that contributes to defining a new architectural typology. Indeed, the buildings that make up the city-port border "are no longer simple square volumes softened by applied decorative elements, but organisms possessing entirely new formal values, governed not by external rules but by their own industrial function."[38]

Since the twentieth century, the term heritage has acquired a broader remit, up to including entire systems, both material and immaterial, in its definition, along with architectural works that are not necessarily bearers of high artistic value and/or responding to a salient aesthetic principle. With this in mind, heritage is not an inert but an "active" concept that transforms into an essential tool capable of moving through everyday life: not so much in terms of its absolute value as for its ability to establish links between different places and times in cities and, even further, to bring them together by creating a common denominator of the processes of transformation.[39]

According to Carlo Olmo, heritage equals "a set of inheritances, which in turn are sets of ideas, values, and political and cultural strategies that are often in conflict."[40] Thus understood, even the catalogue of artifacts that make up the city-port threshold is an exemplary case of heritage that starts from the front of the port and involves pieces of the city further inland. In this heterogeneous but compact system, warehouses, silos, bunkers, and dockside equipment become the crucial ingredients of a strategic map in which their regeneration triggers a coordinated and comprehensive project of actualization.

From Integration to Coexistence

The contemporary project of the city-port areas reveals some new approaches that modify the relationship between the two components and generate a different model of a port city. In these approaches, it is the threshold that becomes the center of theoretical reasoning and strategic projects. Its liminal landscape, located between a practically invisible line that remains nonetheless regularly marked within planning tools, is a reflection of the continuous structural transformations that affect ports.

Along the way, the reorganizing actions of the vast port heritage are concentrated, and, unlike in the past decades, the most recent design experiments are recorded.

38
Mauro Moriconi, Francesco Rosadini, "Genova 900. L'architettura del Movimento Moderno", *Universale di Architettura*, no. 154 (2004), 5–18.

39
Carmen Andriani, "Introduzione. Ricordo al futuro", in *Il patrimonio e l'abitare*, Carmen Andriani, ed. (Rome: Donzelli Editore, 2010), xiii–xxiv.

40
Carlo Olmo, "Conservare le storie", in *Il patrimonio e l'abitare*, Carmen Andriani, ed. (Rome: Donzelli Editore, 2010), 15–19.

Waterfront

For years, the city-port project has addressed the relationship between the city and the port, concentrating primarily on brownfield sites abandoned by the port in an attempt to reunite the two territories, long characterized by a profound demarcation line. However, rather than designing the border space, these practices tried to recover the deep-rooted integration that originally characterized port cities: through the property's change of ownership and consequent redevelopment of the port docks, a new waterfront was generated that restored the views of the sea (or river) to the older city, eliminating or transferring the port infrastructure to more distant areas.

At the end of the twentieth century, such practices became such a widespread phenomenon that they gave rise to a codified reconversion plan.[41] The first such instance was the regeneration of the Inner Harbor in Baltimore implemented between the 1950s and 1980s. The complex set of investments put in place in that case, above all in the tourism-cultural sector, led to the formulation of the Baltimore Model, a model of intervention for disused port areas that later spread throughout the world.

The Baltimore experience defined a first generation of projects that, beginning at the end of the eighties, were exported to Europe and applied first in London, Glasgow, Barcelona, and several other port cities affected by decommissioning processes. The transfer, however, threw the basic settings of the model into crisis, highlighting how their application would transform the waterfront into a foreign element removed from local economies and from the historical apparatus of places. In fact, many claim that the practice called "doing a Baltimore" was, more than anything else, a case of real estate speculation that led to the creation of mass-produced spaces and cloned waterfronts that were almost identical in terms of their functional program and urban design.[42] In these solutions, the fronts of the port once dedicated to work were transformed into "cleaned-up places" with respect to the port's past, implementing a form of compensation for the many inconveniences caused by the port.

Subsequently, this way of thinking was proposed even in the absence of large port decommissions: its intervention scheme was crystallized in the conviction that to deal with the spaces between city and port it was essential to remove the "harmful machinery" and deliver a watered-down version of the port infrastructure to the city.

Today, this interpretation highlights the limitations of waterfront projects: port decommissioning reconversions did not actually propose a solution in terms of the city-port relationship and lacked a unified vision,

41
Stephen V. Ward, "Internationalizing Port Regeneration: Models and Emulators", in Helena Porfyriou, Marichela Sepe, eds., *Waterfronts Revisited: European Ports in a Historic and Global Perspective* (London: Routledge, 2017), 95–107.

42
Dirk Schubert, "Three contrasting approaches to urban redevelopment and waterfront transformations", Hamburg: "String of Pearls", HafenCity and IBA (International Building Exhibition), *Review*, no. 10 (2014), 48–60, ISOCARP, The Hague, the Netherlands.

denoting a substantial separation between the city government and that of the port. This approach therefore negated the port identity of places by reducing it to a surrogate that was weakened in meaning and content. The places once occupied by traffic and machinery were deprived of a body, and this pushed the designers to overcome the lack of clear perspectives with spectacular gestures. The decisive character that had exemplified these places for centuries was losing its power, and this required imagining a total "resemantization" of urban spaces and architectural structures; however, they were not always practicable.[43]

43
Paolo Ceccarelli,
"Una nuova frontiera
interna", in *Osser-
vatorio Waterfront
Portuali. GB progetti,
supplement*, no. 8
(Genoa: Editrice Pro-
getti s.r.l., 1991), 2–8.

Surpassing

Although it is really controversial to speak of the success of waterfront projects (some of which, indeed, have brought positive results in the past decades), in some cases it is impossible to talk about success rather than the formation of further borders between city and port, symbolic and figurative ones, but also physical and real. These approaches were symptomatic of the absence of adequate models for intervening in not so much areas that were already abandoned or dismantled (which were regenerated in continuity with the city) but on the heritage of the threshold coinciding with the administrative border and adjacent to an active port.

It is perhaps precisely due to these experiences that today the project of the threshold between city and port is becoming increasingly crucial for investigating new forms of intervention. After all, the end of the great waves of port decommissioning and the intensive expansion and consolidation of operational structures have profoundly influenced the structure and image of the port city, demonstrating the port's increased autonomy in the context of transformations. In this climate, the heritage of the city-port threshold (the decommissioned one, but also the active or underutilized one) is at the center of theoretical and design explorations, functioning as a territorial connector. The threshold loses its original nature as a dividing object and becomes a "design threshold," the supporting framework for the actions of connecting, rationalization, and sharing.

The scientific research of certain significant realities in the European context confirms this trend. For example, in 2010, the ESPO — European Sea Ports Organisation indeed called for the waterfront to be surpassed as a "single development paradigm" in order to explore an alternative approach to border areas. Subsequently, in 2015, AIVP — Le Réseau Mondial des Villes Portuaires strengthened this position by proposing the idea of "planning a city with a port" via a selection of international case

44
For further informa-
tion, see AIVP — Le
Réseau Mondial des
Villes Portuaires,
Plan the City with the
Port: Guide of Good
Practices (2015) (*aivp.
org*), and European
Sea Ports Organisa-
tion — ESPO, Code of
Practice on Societal
Integration of Ports
(2010) (*espo.be*).

studies, a strategy inspired by the natural complementarity and plurality of the city-port threshold.[44]

Coexistence

By surpassing past practices of port delocalization and/or replace-ment, it is hence possible to recognize an alternative approach, one that sees a possible strategy for the city-port threshold in the concept of "coex-istence" between city and port.

The idea of coexistence expresses a relational condition between the two governing entities that can also be investigated as an operational paradigm. Its use is based first of all on the necessary surpassing of the concept of integration that envisaged a return to the origins of the rela-tionship: an anachronistic attempt to reconstruct the old and deteriorated relationship by restoring cohesion through the right combination of spaces and activities.

The contemporary context, however, has already highlighted that this path is no longer feasible, especially due to the evolution of the two enti-ties and the indispensable need for space, structures, and logistic support that they need to function. With this in mind, the idea of integration is a false objective, inappropriate, and in a certain sense also counterproductive. Alternatively, the idea of coexistence captures the duality of port cities and proposes the implementation of a shared existence to be played out on the border, a simultaneous defense of the territories, a compromise in which both parties decide. Thus described, coexistence embodies the preferential approach for the city-port threshold and, translating it into a project strategy and a cooperation model, develops a new form of equilibrium between the two systems. Coexistence, in fact, aims not so much at solving the city-port conflict but at recognizing and managing it.

Consequently, this idea embodies the "standing on the threshold," the simultaneous and ambivalent action that allows one to stay "on the inside" and, at the same time, "on the outside" of a given situation. Taken as an operational strategy, coexistence interprets the indefiniteness and ambiva-lence of the liminal areas: it provides the possibility of characterizing the spa-tial sequences of the threshold using different degrees of definition around which new projects are articulated, but so is the pre-existing urban fabric.

Tools

Obviously, not all city-port contexts are the same, and in each case different kinds of thresholds are encountered that would require a specific modulation in terms of planning and design. Nevertheless, most planning tools do not seem able to address the specificity of port cities and, on the whole, to find a space for regulatory port plans from which their belonging in the overall process is inferred. Indeed, in current plans, the indications gradually blur the closer one gets to the border, and a sectoral approach prevails that once again proposes the port as an element that is foreign to the city.

From these observations emerges the idea of laying the foundations for a new planning tool capable of interpreting city-port territories and of taking on the complexity of the threshold and its heritage; several theories from Rosario Pavia provide an interesting starting point in this direction.[45]

First, Pavia suggested the recognition of different areas between the territory of the city and that of the port that could be useful for differentiating and calibrating the intensity of the interventions. This resulted in a cataloguing of areas, made up of a "port area" in the strict sense (an operational port, the most removed from and incompatible with the city); an "area of overlapping and grafting" between the city and the port; a "field of territorial interconnection" that supports network logics; and a "field of interaction" between the port and the surrounding environmental resources.

While only sketched out and not entirely detailed, Pavia's proposal nonetheless provides an immediate stimulus for the development of a tool dedicated to the threshold between city and port that is capable of recording the wide range of relationships on the border and of restoring the ambivalent nature of the threshold through the project. Moreover, this proposal makes clear the intention to design the port and its dynamics also (or above all) beyond the realm of jurisdiction and legal boundaries, i.e., towards spheres of urban or semi-urban influence.

Finally, this proposal attributes a strategic value to an area of overlaps and grafts between the two territories through which to manage, with a wider selection of tools, the different degrees of openness, intermingling, or conflict that are produced along the city-port axis.

45
Rosario Pavia, "La pianificazione delle aree portuali italiane. Problemi e prospettive", *Portus*, no. 5 (2015), and Rosario Pavia, "Il sistema portuale italiano tra crisi e riforme", *Portus*, no. 31 (2016).

Pendulum Routes

Source: OOCL (Oriented Overseas Container Line Limited)
N.B. Paths are indicative, and the size of the map is altered.

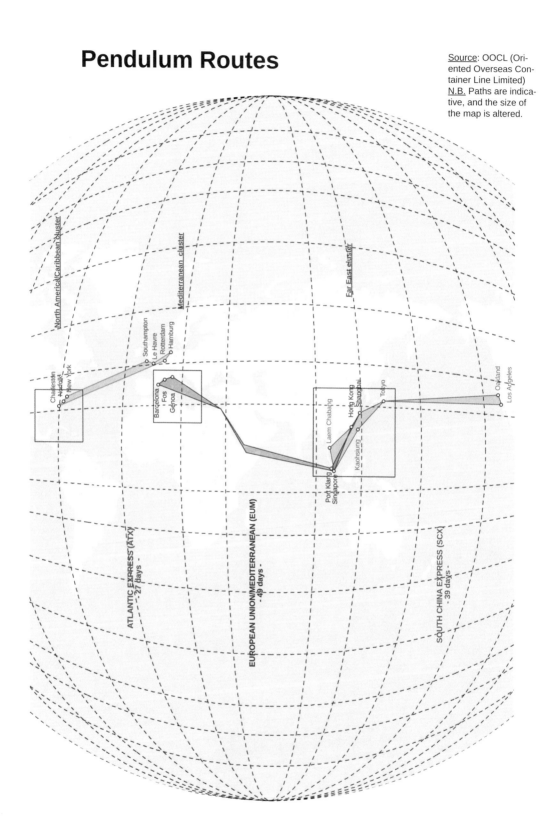

TEN-T Trans European Network

Source: European Commission, Mobility and Transport, REGULATION (EU) No 1316/2013 & 1315/2013 O.J. L348 — 20/12/2013 N.B. Paths are indicative, and the size of the map is altered.

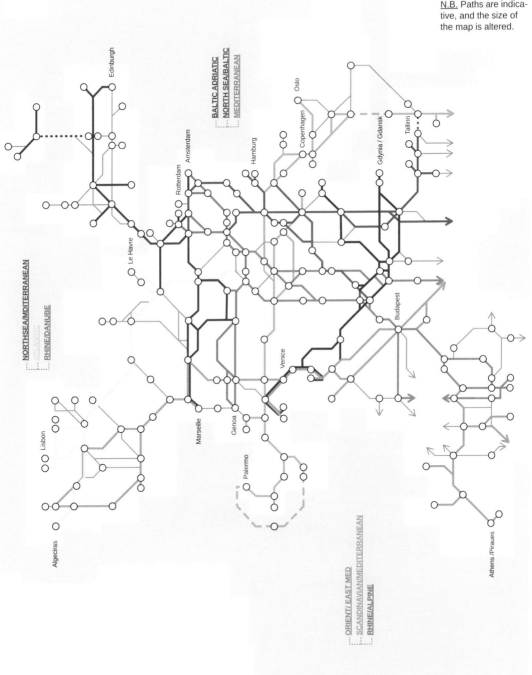

Anyport Model

Source: James Bird, 1963

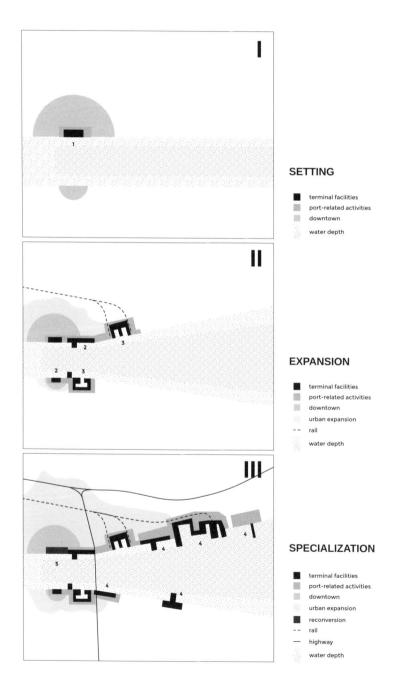

SETTING

- ■ terminal facilities
- ▨ port-related activities
- ▨ downtown
- ⠂ water depth

EXPANSION

- ■ terminal facilities
- ▨ port-related activities
- ▨ downtown
- ▨ urban expansion
- – – rail
- ⠂ water depth

SPECIALIZATION

- ■ terminal facilities
- ▨ port-related activities
- ▨ downtown
- ▨ urban expansion
- ■ reconversion
- – – rail
- — highway
- ⠂ water depth

Port-City Evolution Model
Port Regionalization

Source: Brian S. Hoyle, 1988; Theo Notteboom, Jean-Paul Rodrigue, 2006.

STAGE	SYMBOL ○ city ● port	PERIOD	CHARATERISTICS
I Primitive port/city		Ancient/medieval to 19th century	Close spatial and functional association between city and port
II Expanding port/city		19th – early 20th century	Rapid commercial/industrial growth forces port to develop beyond city confines, with linear quays and break-bulk industries
III Modern industrial port/city		mid-20th century	Industrial growth (especially oil refining) and introduction of containers/ro-ro require separation/space
IV Retreat from the waterfront		1960s – 1980s	Change in maritime technology induces growth of separate maritime industrial development areas
V Redevelopment of waterfront		1970s – 1990s	Large-scale modern port consumes large areas of land/water space; urban renewal of original core
VI Renewal of port/city links		1990s – 2000s	Globalization and intermodalism transform port roles; port-city associations renewed; urban redevelopment enhances port-city integration

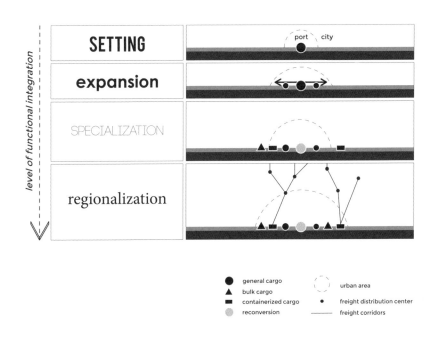

level of functional integration

SETTING

expansion

SPECIALIZATION

regionalization

● general cargo   ⬭ urban area
▲ bulk cargo   • freight distribution center
◼ containerized cargo   — freight corridors
● reconversion

101   Beyond the Port City

Italian Port System

Source: Decree No. 169/2016: "Riorganizzazione, razionalizzazione e semplificazione della disciplina concernente le Autorità Portuali di cui alla legge 28 gennaio 1994, n. 84."

PORT SYSTEM AUTHORITY
Main port
Other ports

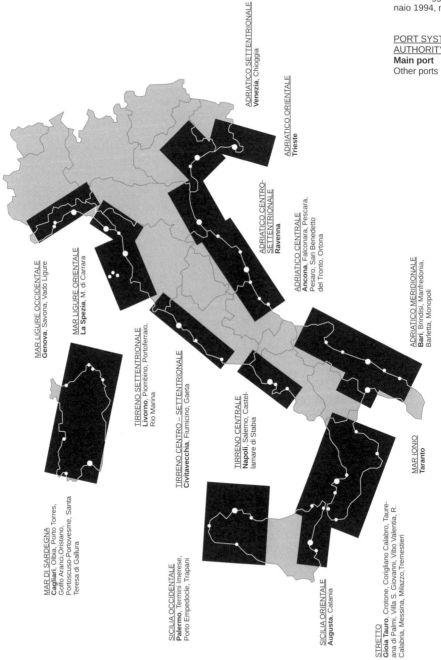

ADRIATICO SETTENTRIONALE
Venezia, Chioggia

ADRIATICO ORIENTALE
Trieste

ADRIATICO CENTRO-SETTENTRIONALE
Ravenna

ADRIATICO CENTRALE
Ancona, Falconara, Pescara, Pesaro, San Benedetto del Tronto, Ortona

ADRIATICO MERIDIONALE
Bari, Brindisi, Manfredonia, Barletta, Monopoli

MAR IONIO
Taranto

MAR LIGURE OCCIDENTALE
Genova, Savona, Vado Ligure

MAR LIGURE ORIENTALE
La Spezia, M. di Carrara

TIRRENO SETTENTRIONALE
Livorno, Piombino, Portoferraio, Rio Marina

TIRRENO CENTRO – SETTENTRIONALE
Civitavecchia, Fiumicino, Gaeta

TIRRENO CENTRALE
Napoli, Salerno, Castellamare di Stabia

MAR DI SARDEGNA
Cagliari, Olbia, Porto Torres, Golfo Aranci, Oristano, Portoscuso-Portovesme, Santa Teresa di Gallura

SICILIA OCCIDENTALE
Palermo, Termini Imerese, Porto Empedocle, Trapani

SICILIA ORIENTALE
Augusta, Catania

STRETTO
Gioia Tauro, Crotone, Corigliano Calabro, Taureana di Palmi, Villa S. Giovanni, Vibo Valentia, R. Calabria, Messina, Milazzo, Tremestieri

Italian Metropolitan Cities

Source: Law No. 56/2014: "Disposizioni sulle città metropolitane, sulle province, sulle unioni e fusioni di comuni."

REGION
Metropolitan cities
Merged provinces/munici-palities

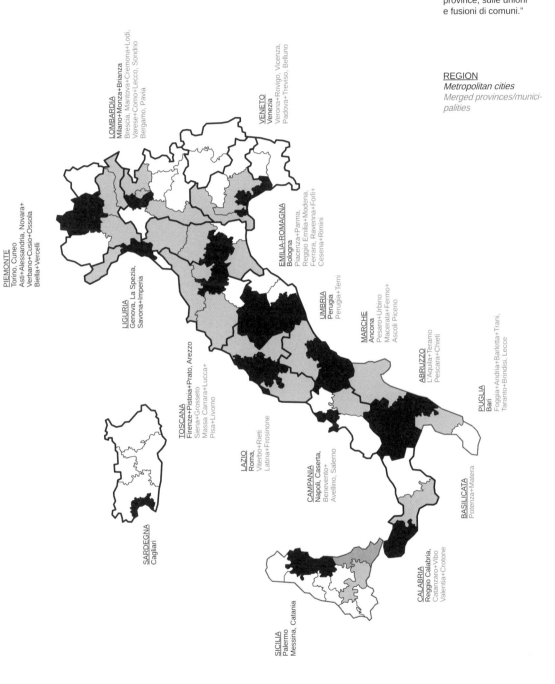

PIEMONTE
Torino, Cuneo
Asti+Alessandria, Novara+
Verbano+Cusio+Ossola
Biella+Vercelli

LOMBARDIA
Milano+Monza+Brianza
Brescia, Mantova+Cremona+Lodi,
Varese+Como+Lecco, Sondrio
Bergamo, Pavia

VENETO
Venezia
Verona+Rovigo, Vicenza,
Padova+Treviso, Belluno

EMILIA-ROMAGNA
Bologna
Piacenza+Parma,
Reggio Emilia+Modena,
Ferrara, Ravenna+Forlì+
Cesena+Rimini

LIGURIA
Genova, La Spezia,
Savona+Imperia

UMBRIA
Perugia
Perugia+Terni

MARCHE
Ancona
Pesaro+Urbino
Macerata+Fermo+
Ascoli Piceno

TOSCANA
Firenze+Pistoia+Prato, Arezzo
Siena+Grosseto
Massa Carrara+Lucca+
Pisa+Livorno

ABRUZZO
L'Aquila+Teramo
Pescara+Chieti

PUGLIA
Bari
Foggia+Andria+Barletta+Trani,
Taranto+Brindisi, Lecce

LAZIO
Roma,
Viterbo+Rieti
Latina+Frosinone

CAMPANIA
Napoli, Caserta,
Benevento+
Avellino, Salerno

BASILICATA
Potenza+Matera

SARDEGNA
Cagliari

CALABRIA
Reggio Calabria,
Catanzaro+Vibo
Valentia+Crotone

SICILIA
Palermo
Messina, Catania

ATLASES

Six Factsheets
Six Maps

<u>Copenhagen</u>
<u>Hamburg</u>
<u>Rotterdam</u>
<u>Genoa</u>
<u>Marseille</u>
<u>Palermo</u>

Case Studies

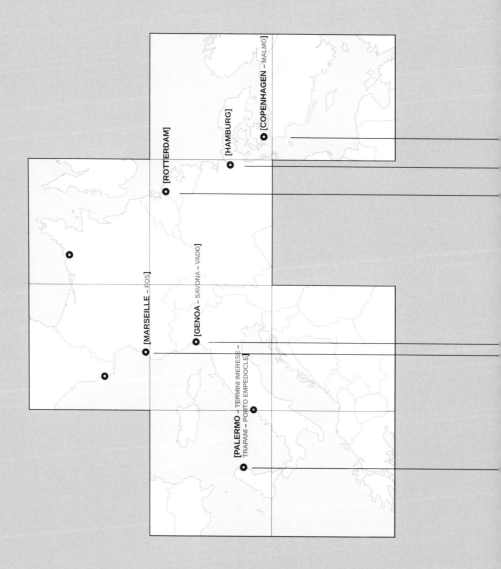

[COPENHAGEN – MALMÖ]

[HAMBURG]

[ROTTERDAM]

[MARSEILLE – FOS]

[GENOA – SAVONA – VADO]

[PALERMO – TERMINI IMERESE – TRAPANI – PORTO EMPEDOCLE]

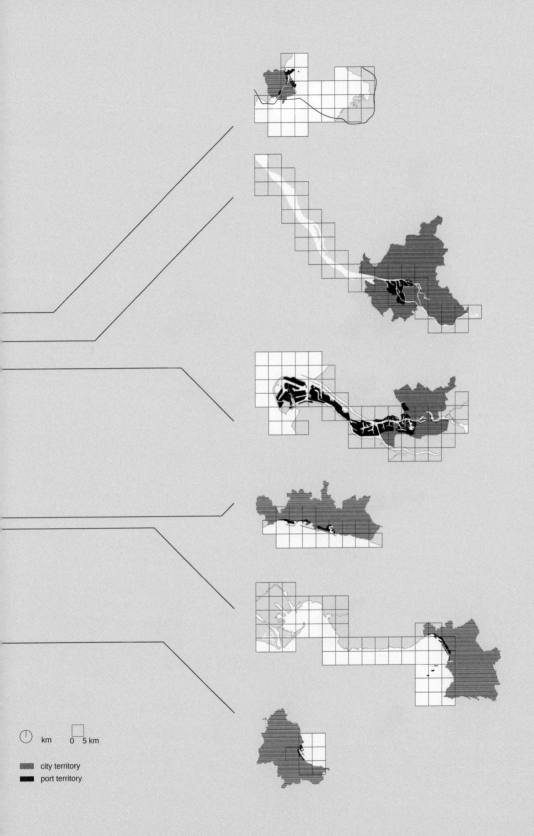

km   0 5 km

city territory
port territory

ATLASES

Taxonomy

			AREA [port]	AREA [city]
[COPENHAGEN] Data referring to the overall port system of the Port of Copenhagen-Malmö.			500 ha 16.5 km (quay length)	8,620 ha
[HAMBURG]			7,200 ha 49 km (quay length)	72,520 ha
[ROTTERDAM]			10,556 ha 40 km (quay lenght)	31,935 ha
[GENOA] Data referring only to the Port of Genoa within the Port System Authority of the Western Ligurian Sea.			1,200 ha 47 km (quay length)	24,030 ha
[MARSEILLE] Data referring to the overall port system of the Grand Maritime Port of Marseille — Fos-sur-Mer.			10,400 ha 60 km (quay length)	24,100 ha
[PALERMO] Data referring only to the Port of Palermo within the Port System Authority of the Western Sicily Sea.			7,670 ha 3,3 km (quay length)	16,059 ha

DRAUGHT	TYPE/SIZE	EUROPEAN RANKING*	VOLUME OF PRODUCTION	WORKERS [port]	INHABITANS [city]	GOVERNANCE MODEL	PLANNING TOOLS
9.2 ÷ 9.5 mt (canal)	River and sea port	beyond the 15th place	0.911764 mil TEUS (2017)	377 (2017)	613,288 (2018)	Copenhagen Malmö Port (2001)	Vision 2030 (2011)
9.4 ÷ 10 mt (canal) 4.9 ÷ 6.1 mt (quays)	Deepwater river port	3rd place	8.9 mil TEUS (2016)	156,000 (2017)	1,763,000 (2015)	Hamburg Port Authority (2011)	Port Development Plan until 2025 (2012)
11 ÷ 12.2 mt (canal) 7.1 ÷ 9.1 mt (terminal)	Deepwater river port	1st place	12.4 mil TEUS (2016)	180,000 (2017)	616,294 (2015)	Port of Rotterdam Ltd. (2004)	Port Vision 2030 (2011)
9 ÷ 15 mt with peaks of 50 mt	Deepwater sea port	12th place	2.62 mil TEUS (2016)	35,000 (2017)	580,000 (2017)	Autorità di Sistema Portuale del Mar Ligure Occidentale (2016)	Piano Regolatore Portuale P.R.P. (2001)
9 ÷ 12 mt	Sea port	beyond the 15th place	1.062 mil TEUS (2012)	45,000 (2011)	858,120 (2014)	Grand Port Maritime de Marseille (2011)	La Charte Ville-Port (2011)
6.8 ÷ 12 mt	Sea Port	beyond the 15th place	0.28633 mil TEUS (2018)	—	666,055 (2018)	Autorità di Sistema Portuale del Mare di Sicilia Occidentale (2016)	Piano Regolatore Portuale P.R.P. (2018)

*Container traffic data (2017). Top 15 container ports in Europe,
Shanghai Maritime University, Prof. Theo Notteboom (porteconomics.eu)*

Copenhagen

Evolution

When Absalon took control of the coastal areas adjacent to his bishopric in the early 12th century, *Havn* was just a small seaside resort. At the behest of the Danish crown, the archbishop conducted a series of operations to strengthen the port to compete with the ports of the North Sea. In 1254, the city received the title of *Køpmannæhafn* (merchant port).

Over the next two centuries, the city and port developed around the channel that separates the islands of Sjælland (to the west) and Amager (to the east), protected by new circular-shaped ramparts. Following two major fires (in 1728 and 1759), more than half of Copenhagen suffered extensive damage. The reconstruction, however, was immediate, so much so that a map of 1761 drawn up by Christian Gedde showed the excellent condition of the buildings already completed or being completed.

At the end of the nineteenth century, the demolition of most of the city walls initiated an expansion of the urban center and corresponded to the first major extensions of the port towards the open sea. At that time, although the coast to the north of Copenhagen was dotted with small landings, commercial maritime activities took place within the area marked by Toldbommen, the customs barrier.

Only in the last decades of the century did port structures begin to spread towards the north, outside of the channel. The first project was the Frihavn (Free Port) in 1894 and, in parallel, the area of Nordbassinet (1880) and Nordhavnen were built, both part of the free port. In the early decades of the twentieth century, the expansion was shaped to include areas with commercial functions within the free port. During the same period, the Refshaleøen peninsula was also developed, a defensive bulwark later transformed into the head-quarters of the Burmeister & Wain shipyards (1871–1996), as was the Prøvestenen peninsula, a military fortress converted into a hub for petroleum and liquid bulk (1922). As a result of these processes, Copenhagen became an important industrial port: the port infrastructures extended beyond the channel where they were originally located and proceeded to occupy, in the form of islands and peninsulas, the coastal territory along the Øresund.

Towards the end of the twentieth century, the dismantling of port structures gave way to a process of reconversion of areas and artifacts. The Copenhagen waterfront, overlooking the channel where the port once stood, gradually transformed into a double linear system in which reconverted historical artefacts and new buildings with a primarily tourist-cultural focus still coexist today.

Within this framework, the logic of the port brought new dynamics into play by joining the Danish and Swedish sides via the Øresund Bridge. Inaugurated in 2000, the connecting route concretized a latent connection between the port cities of Copenhagen and Malmö, mirroring the predisposition to the territorial vision of these places.

Planning Aspects

Underpinning all of the transformations that developed in Copenhagen in the second half of the twentieth century is the *Finger Plan*, the urban development model drawn up in 1947 based on the Green Network Plan of 1936. From the early versions to the most recent formulations, the *Finger Plan* has sought to find an equilibrium for building expansion towards the countryside.

The structure of the *Finger Plan* was divided into a core urban region (the palm of the hand) corresponding to the consolidated city, a peripheral urban region oriented according to preferential directions (the fingers), and finally the green wedges, open spaces dedicated to greenery positioned between one finger and the other. The fingers denoted the lines of urban growth; the wedges, instead, were introduced subsequently and became essential in terms of containing the size of the fingers. Developing the wedges was useful for connecting even very distant parts of the territory with longitudinal and transverse connections, also aligned along the coast.

Already in the seventies, the *Finger Plan* was revised for the first time, then, in 2007 and 2013, new variants enhanced its urban character, introducing the element of green urban wedges, which were large public areas within the core urban region.

Although the *Finger Plan* cannot be catalogued solely as a green development plan, it produced substantial zoning between green and built spaces and between center and periphery. A further gap could be found in the total absence of provisions concerning the coastal areas and, more generally, the industrial and/or port areas: as confirmation of this, the development of the port along the channel and on the peninsulas to the north towards the Sound has progressed in an independent and unconnected way in the decades since the installation of the *Finger Plan*.

In more recent times, the administrative merger with the port of Malmö has introduced a system-oriented logic: a reorganization of the operating spaces of both ports that has prompted the optimization and distribution of functions.

Institutional Aspects

After the transfer of ownership from the Danish Royal Family to government administration, the port passed to the management of the Port of Copenhagen Ltd. in the twentieth century. In 2001, the company became part of a single port authority by formally merging with the port of Malmö.

The Copenhagen Malmö Port – CMP is now the body that manages port operations for both ports, and its origin is linked to the opening of the Øresund Bridge in 2000.[1] CMP is a joint venture that unites two countries: the completion of the bridge in fact meant the end of traditional border traffic and an immediate decrease in freight and passenger traffic in the two ports. At the same time, the Øresund Bridge opened up new transport possibilities by offering a combination of ships–trains–trucking that simplified distribution.

CMP is a limited liability company whose ownership is divided between the CPH City & Port Development Corporation (By & Havn) that owns 50%, the City of Malmö that holds 27%, and private investors that hold 23% of the total shares. CMP does not own the port land but has been granted areas and buildings under concession from CPH City & Port Development and from the City of Malmö.

CPH City & Port Development Corporation (*By & Havn*)[2] is an entity with extensive expertise, particularly in terms of planning and management of intermediate areas between the city and the port. Its origin dates back to the 1980s when the employment crisis and demographic collapse produced a political alliance with private companies which to entrust with the development of urban areas that were abandoned or in need of a new function.

In 1992, the Ørestad Development Corporation was created, taking over the expansion of Ørestad, and in 2007 it merged with the Port of Copenhagen Ltd., creating CPH City & Port Development Corporation (*By & Havn*). CPH was thus born from the merger of two public entities: from a legal point of view, it is owned by the state and by the City of Copenhagen, with 95% and 5% of the total shares, respectively. Operationally, CPH has a board of directors and an executive board that manages the company's activities.

A key element of the entity of CPH is its de-politicized nature, which allows the company to make use of political-legislative structures to finance both large infrastructural projects and the reconversion of underutilized areas or those located within the perimeter of the port.

The success of this management scheme depends above all on the ability to utilize instruments from the private sector for acts of regeneration with public benefits and uses.

1
For further information, see Copenhagen Malmö Port: CMP (www.cmport.com).

2
For further information, see *By & Havn* (www.byoghavn.dk).

Projects

The 2011 Municipal Plan laid out plans for the future of an international metropolis by identifying some sensitive areas where transformation was imminent. In this regard, Nordhavn and Sydhavn constitute two sectors with a strong port character that, albeit via different logics, are modifying their structure and their impact on the surrounding fabric.

Nordhavn is one of the nation's most recent and most extensive redevelopment projects. Built in the early twentieth century as an extension of the Free Port, the peninsula of approximately two square kilometers accommodates a majority of the operational, commercial, industrial, passenger, and recreational functions.

Following the administrative reorganization of the seaport and the dismantling of certain areas and buildings, the area was reconfigured through a competition (2008) for a new urban district in the Inner Nordhavn zone already occupied by the port. The competition asked entrants to imagine an overall development of the peninsula in order to reconvert decommissioned artifacts but above all to create a new piece of the city capable of being fused with the consolidated urban fabric.

The winning project, Nordholmene – Urban Delta, designed by COBE, SLETH, and Rambøll[3], envisaged the formation of a series of islets separated by water channels. The configuration of this large network of waterways mediated the contrasting elements and facilitated the application of a mixed-function program.

Currently, the redevelopment is underway and mainly concerns the part of Nordhavn closest to the consolidated city, i.e., the districts of Nordbassinet, Redmolen, and Sundmolen, areas in which the regeneration of decommissioned artifacts alternates with new projects.[4]

Confirming the hybrid nature of the area, the outermost portions of Nordhavn are still occupied by the port. Indeed, the construction of the urban district proceeds in parallel with the construction of a new landfill of about 100 hectares stretching out towards the open sea. The new operating area will provide the port with a large commercial terminal and a cruise terminal suitable for the docking of larger ships.

At the southern head of the port canal lies the district of Sydhavn, divided into three peninsulas: Sluseholmen, Teglholmen, and Enghave Brygge, where urban and operational port structures continue to coexist. Given its peripheral position, one of the objectives for Sydhavn is the creation of a succession of public spaces and a system of channels on the waterfront that allow for a direct connection with the center, enabling port and industrial activities to continue operating alongside the urban sprawl.

In both Nordhavn and Sydhavn, CPH City & Port Development Corporation is a crucial vehicle for local and national planning. Its plural nature indeed develops solutions capable of grasping the essence of places and of establishing a different relational formula between the two components. Its example represents an alternative approach, since it combines the authoritativeness of institutional actions with the organizational agility of the private sector, generating an exportable model for the transformation of areas in which different owners and development guidelines coexist.

3
For further information, see Cobe (www.cobe.dk).

4
Among the most recent projects, The Silo by Cobe (2017) (www.cobe.dk), the Portland Towers by Design Group Architects A/S – Denmark (2014) (www.dga.dk), and Park'n'Play by JAJA Architects (2016) (www.ja-ja.dk) come to mind.

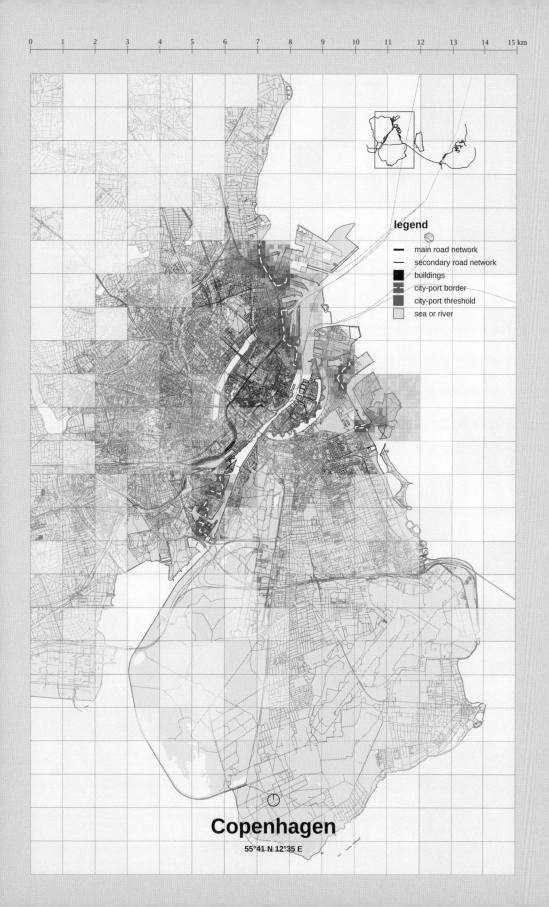

0 1 2 3 4 5 6 7 8 9 10 11 12 13 14 15 km

legend

main road network
secondary road network
buildings
city-port border
city-port threshold
sea or river

Copenhagen

55°41 N 12°35 E

Hamburg

The Hanseatic League was a commercial and defensive confederation of merchant guilds and market towns in Northwestern and Central Europe. Growing from a few northern German towns in the late 1100s, the League came to dominate Baltic maritime trade for three centuries along the coasts of Northern Europe. The Hanseatic cities had their own legal system and operated their own armies for mutual protection and aid. Despite this, the organization was not a state, nor could it be called a confederation of city-states.

2

The duty-free status is the possibility of free trade without paying import, sales, value added, or other taxes.

3

The exemption from customs duties was the main driving force for the port economy, creating many positive effects for the city as well: the goods introduced into the port were stored and processed anywhere to then be exported without undergoing further taxation, favoring the consolidation of sectors related to the port.

4

Ludwig Wendemuth, Walter Böttcher, *The Port of Hamburg* (Hamburg: Meissner & Christiansen, 1932).

Evolution

Apparently, at the beginning of the ninth century, at the confluence of the Elbe, Alster and Bille rivers, a fortification called *Hammaburg* was founded. However, the origin of the port of Hamburg can be traced back to two subsequent events: on May 7, 1189, the founding of the port and the date on which Frederick I Barbarossa guaranteed the privilege of sailing without customs duties, and 1321, the year that marks the entry of Hamburg into the Hanseatic League.[1]

Due to these circumstances, Hamburg inherited commercial duty-free status[2] and the title of *Freie und Hansestadt Hamburg*. These privileges extended the traffic into a vast territorial area, leading to Hamburg acquiring an authoritative position in England, Flanders, and Scandinavia.[3]

Already at the turn of the nineteenth century, the city and the port appeared intimately connected, so much so that much of the building system belonged to both categories: the classic merchant houses (*Bürgerhäuser*) actually combined commercial and residential functions in a single building type.

In the mid-nineteenth century, with the growth of the cargo sector, Hamburg's dock harbor became an open tidal port due to the capacity of the seabed and dock facilities.[4] Through a long planning phase, the port activated the first terminals and ship-to-rail transfers. With the introduction of the steam ship, larger basins were then created, such as Sandtorhafen (1863–1866), which guaranteed docking close to the urban area.

When, in 1871, the city was annexed to the German Reich, the duty-free status was revoked, continuing to exist only in the free port area called *Speicherstadt*, or City of Warehouses (1888). It was the largest warehouse complex in the world: a completely unprecedented warehouse district equipped with the most advanced storage and transshipment technologies that caused profound alterations along the border between the city and the port.

While the First World War didn't cause serious damage to the city-port system, the economic-commercial logic of global trade began to change radically in 1920.

Following the conflict, most of the energy for reconstruction was directed toward the port, which began to take over the south bank of the Elbe River, in particular the largely rural archipelago of the Veddel, Kleiner Grassbrook, Steinwerder, and Waltershof Islands. This expansion generated a separation, one that was not merely functional, between the areas of the port and the city that occupied the two banks of the river in a mirror-like manner. The only exception was the *Speicherstadt* district, which in recent years has been fused with the *HafenCity* quarter: evolving for at least another decade, the broader area of city-port matrix is now becoming a connective element between the operational zone, the urban center, and the southern areas beyond the Elbe River.

Planning Aspects

As in other northern European urban centers, two catastrophes (the Great Fire of 1842 and the aerial bombings of the Second World War) presented an opportunity for Hamburg to radically transform the urban center. The postwar reconstruction was entrusted to Fritz Schumacher (1908–1933), who introduced the results of the research he conducted overseas on public spaces and a building typology capable of responding to work requirements and to the structuring of the modern metropolis.

In 1921, these ideas flowed into the *Federplan*, the "feather plan," which was established as the ordering principle for the development of the metropolitan area for the entire century. The *Federplan* directed development along certain principal urban axes (the feathers) that animated the entire metropolitan area on a large scale. In the decades following the entry into force of the *Federplan*, the network of connections supported the role of Hamburg as a city-state within the Hamburg Metropolitan Region: this aspect, formalized in 1945, required coordinated management of the territories with inter-regional trading networks. In this framework, one of the crucial issues was the expansion of the port infrastructure.

At the end of the twentieth century, the reconquering of the eastern part of its economic region (after the reunification of Germany in 1990) placed the port of Hamburg in a strategic position. This process triggered the occupation of the areas on the south bank of the Elbe and brought to the fore the issue of the reuse of former port areas. In this context, the dismantling of the north bank of the river provided the opportunity to reconstitute the relationship between the city and the river dock. The customs border was removed and, starting in 1985, the series of *Perlenkette* projects was implemented.[5]

The city-port planning of the last century brought radical changes to the city structure and, in this setting, both bodies developed tools to guide future transformations. The Port Development Plan (2005–2007) contained a preliminary version of the Spatial Vision of Hamburg, a programmatic document that addressed the subsequent Structure Plan. The 2005 Port Development Plan was followed by the publication of the Port Development Plan to 2025, drawn up in 2012. This document represents the first program developed by the institution of the port as an independent authority and proposes an approach for the fringe areas between the port and the city.

Institutional Aspects

Hamburg's administrative model reflects its evolution, first as a member of the Hanseatic League and then as a city-state following the unification of Germany in 1871. A representative case of this evolution is the history of *Speicherstadt*, which was created to concentrate the free zone in the port area following the abolition of its duty-free status. After more than 120 years, this privileged status was revoked in 2013 by definitively eliminating the border between port and city and transforming the entire area into a European Customs Seaport.

In line with the territorial organization of the German Federation, Hamburg is today one of the 16 states of the Federation and has dual status as city and state. Undoubtedly, this form of local management with significant regional dependencies also influenced the administrative model of the port. In fact, almost all of Hamburg's port area is managed by the Hamburg Port Authority (HPA), a public institution formalized in 2005, making the previous government department dedicated to port operations autonomous.[6]

The HPA, which reports to the Ministry of Economy, Transport and Innovation, owns most of the real estate in the port area and is responsible for the operational, production, and employment aspects of all of the infrastructure. In terms of planning, the HPA and the Free and Hanseatic City of Hamburg jointly published the Port Development Plan in 2012, an instrument for the development of the urban and port area. At the management level, the port entity has specific competencies in addition to the duties and interests independent of the city; however, urban development in port areas is generally prohibited, and cooperation between the entities is notoriously complex.

Projects

The *Spatial Vision* of 2007 sought to bring unity to large transformation initiatives developed in the same period but animated by different strategies. The *HafenCity* and the *Leap across the Elbe* projects indeed represent two very different approaches in terms of planning between the city and the port. If the *HafenCity* (1997–2030)[7] is a large urban project that replicates the historic city through the transformation of 157 hectares of former port territory, this *Leap across the Elbe*, drawn up in 2004, instead increased the residential

5
Perlenkette – or "Pearl Necklace" – was a project that has given the harbor edge a new character. Its aim was, on the one hand, to revitalize the city's water surface in order to increase the fascination of the city and, on the other hand, to strengthen the establishment of living in Hamburg's core area. Behind the pearl necklace metaphor, there is the desire to connect the contemplative footpaths and promenades. Thus, the pearl necklace is a viable and sophisticated *leitmotif*.

6
Chiara Mazzoleni, "Amburgo, HafenCity. Rinnovamento della città e governo urbano", *Imprese & città, no. 2, Camera di Commercio di Milano*, Monza Brianza, Lodi (2013), 138–156.

7
For further information, see HafenCity (www.hafencity.com).

offer in peri-urban areas in close contact with the port.

The first formal proposal was *Vision HafenCity* (1997), which established a *Special Fund for City and Port* dedicated to the first infrastructure projects on the site, but, above all, financed the new container terminal along the southern part of the river. In 1998, the *HafenCity Hamburg GmbH* company took over the management of operations, and in 2005 an advisory board, made up of representatives of the institutions and members of the academic world, initiated the planning process.

The development of the area proceeded by means of a competition for the drafting of the master plan (1999/2000): the first buildings were realized in 2005, and the first district was completed in 2009. In 2012, the U4 metro line went into operation and, in 2014, the *HafenCity* university campus was opened. At the beginning of 2017, the building, a symbol of the regeneration, was inaugurated: the Elbphilharmonie was erected on the decommissioned Kaispeicher A port depot.

The *HafenCity* is an exemplary project in terms of scale, the involvement of public and private operators, and its experimentation in the field of residential building types that, however, has been carried out to compensate the city for the port. Alternatively, the *Leap across the Elbe* project responded to two underlying needs: to create new housing and to reconnect the two banks of the Elbe.

Through the impact of the exhibitions Internationale Bauausstellung IBA Hamburg and the International Garden Show IGS (2013), a large hub was created on the island of Wilhelmsburg that, surrounded by the imposing Veddel Dam, includes interface zones between port and residential areas and large road junctions.

To consolidate the center-periphery axis, the *Leap* project has created an ideal north-south trajectory leading from the HafenCity via the river and the Veddel to Harburg, home to a river port.

Although really different in many respects, the *HafenCity* and the *Leap across the Elbe* projects share the intent of restoring the balance between port and city through suturing actions on both sides of the river.

The construction of a new part of the city on the water indeed mediates between the oldest neighborhoods in the north and the city-port islands further south; a new system of infrastructures, slow and fast, along with new urban spaces thus fuse the two banks together by integrating them through acts of transformation on a metropolitan scale.

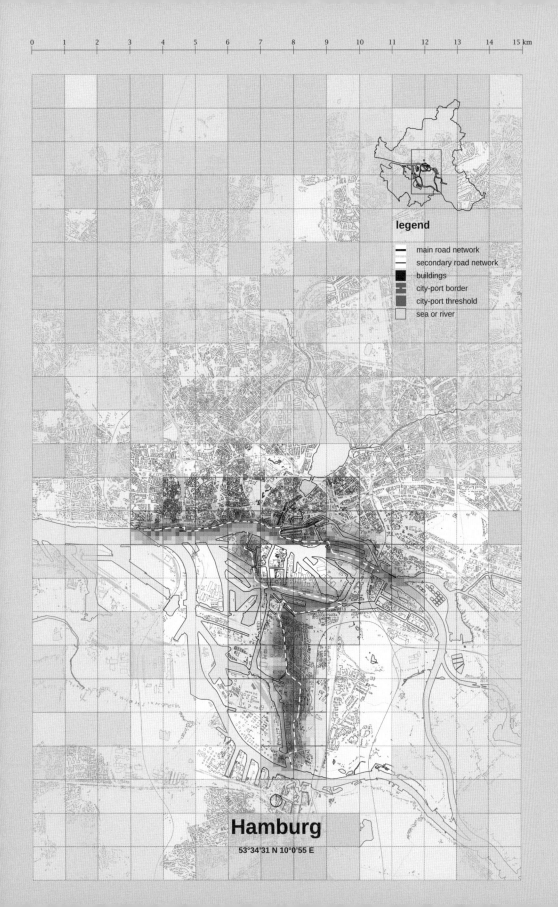

0   1   2   3   4   5   6   7   8   9   10   11   12   13   14   15 km

legend

— main road network
— secondary road network
■ buildings
▨ city-port border
▨ city-port threshold
□ sea or river

Hamburg

53°34'31 N 10°0'55 E

Rotterdam

Evolution

The growth of the Dutch port began with the construction of the *Nieuwe Waterweg* (1872), the new waterway access to the port areas closest to the city center, continuing until the Second World War.

Between the nineteenth and twentieth centuries, investments were mostly concentrated in the transhipment sector, driven by private companies and the involvement of wealthy local families. The presence of the port in the urban fabric initiated integrated housing concepts and *singels*, new residential and work districts overlooking the canals.

Between 1880 and 1895, the port continuously expanded. Following the founding of the Municipal Commercial Establishment and the growing competition between companies for control of the most dynamic sectors, investments in new operating areas multiplied on both sides of the Maas River. In the north, mixed goods transport lines and new grain distribution hubs (Parkhaven, St. Jobshaven, and Schiehaven) were established; in the south, special structures for solid bulk transhipment (Rijnhaven, Maashaven, and Wallhaven) were installed. With the intensification of port construction, extremely diverse landscapes were formed depending on the technologies in use: on the one hand, new fixed structures (silos and warehouses) became part of the productive architectural apparatus, while on the other, the logics of transhipment minimized the impact on the ground as well as the transfer times of goods from ship to ship.

In 1940, when the population of Rotterdam exceeded 600,000 inhabitants, the progression of the port suffered a violent halt when much of the city center was razed to the ground by the *Rotterdam Blitz*. In the port areas, over seven kilometers of docks and at least 40% of the spaces then being used as warehouses were destroyed.[1] Four days after the attack, work began on the drafting of the *Witteveen Plan* in order to rebuild the damaged areas through a total reorganization of the city fabric. Beginning in 1945, the majority of investments were put towards the rehabilitation of damaged structures and towards the technological modernization of the port that reflected the new dynamics in the sea trade sector.

For the rest of the twentieth century, imposing industrial hubs were built that occupied the entire southern bank of the Maas River, up and until a port infrastructure of approximately 40 kilometers in size had been built in the early 2000s.

Planning Aspects

In its current configuration, the Rotterdam port system is a complex infrastructure that produces added strategic value in economic production terms, but above all in terms of spillover effects for the city.

According to the report prepared in 2010 on the topic of the 'strategic value' of the port, such aspects cannot be overlooked since they define the nature of the contemporary city-port relationship.[2]

After the Second World War, Rotterdam undertook an unprecedented era of planning that was based on the progressive migration of operational areas towards the mouth of the Maas River and on reconstruction; investments were directed towards new sectors — for example, the petrochemical sector —, giving rise to the terminals of Botlek and Europoort (1950–1960).

However, the planning in the mid-twentieth century sketched a contrasting picture, proposing, on the one hand, "concentrated deconcentration," that is, the containment of the relentless growth of the port (*Spatial Planning Act*, 1965) and, on the other hand, monumental port projects (*Plan 2000+*, 1969).

Despite the contrasts, the port never ceased its process of expansion, so much so that in 1973, Maas-

1
Marinke Steenhuis, ed., *The Port of Rotterdam – A World Between City and Sea* (Rotterdam: nai010 Publishers, 2015).

2
Rotterdam School of Management (RSM), Erasmus University Rotterdam, ed., *The strategic value of the Port of Rotterdam for the international competitiveness of the Netherlands. A first exploration, Research Report for the Port of Rotterdam Authority,* (INSCOPE Research for Innovation, 2011).

Maasvlakte I is a massive, man-made westward extension of the Europoort and industrial facility that began in the 1970s. The terminal was built by constructing a large belt dam filled with sand, allowing a greater number of container carriers to access the port without entailing risks to movement on the waterways. This project extended the port of Rotterdam by about 2,000 hectares.

4
For further information, see AIR Rotterdam (www.airrotterdam.eu).

5
Maasvlakte II is a container terminal of more than 2,000 hectares, of which at least 1,000 are occupied by port activities. The landfill is protected by a 4-km dam built in the open sea in just two years. Its construction was planned from the early 1960s but was only included in the planning tools in 2011 (Port Vision 2030). Fully automated and electrically powered, this incredible infrastructure has already increased the port's productivity by 20%, even though it is only at the first stage of its definitive development, which is expected to reach full operation in 2033.

6
For further information, see City Work: Co-creation in Urban Development (www.destedenfabriek.nl/en/discussing-waterfronts-rotterdam).

vlakte I, a vast terminal for the new type of standardized trade, was created.[3]

Just as the port reached its maximum expansion, occupying the river estuary at the end of the twentieth century, the progressive decommissioning of the historical docks brought the issue of reconversion to the fore. During this phase, Rotterdam was poised between a dominant port dimension and a subordinate urban component: this required a new narrative capable of recognizing the place's city-port quality, allowing the city to support a productive evolution and the port to instead include an urban logic. It is within this context that the actions of the Architecture International Rotterdam – AIR[4] were framed, which in 1982 announced the competition for the restructuring of Kop van Zuid, but also *Port Vision 2020* (2004), which initiated the construction of the Maasvlakte II terminal, the new platform in the waters of the North Sea.[5]

Institutional Aspects

Underpinning the current management model of the Port of Rotterdam Ltd. (PoR), i.e., the public limited company that has been managing the port since 2004, is the belief that in order to remain competitive, the port must play an active role throughout the entire sequence of transformations and, above all, intervene in the design of areas that exceed its own property and that go beyond its legal border.

Managed by two public stakeholders, the City of Rotterdam (70%) and the Dutch government (30%), the PoR enjoys the status of a government corporation that gives the port a direct position in the market and an involvement in activities that are not strictly internal to its territory. The new political-territorial governance model indeed transformed the port's role by revoking its profile as a sectoral authority; it is the so-called "beyond the landlord role" theorized by Van der Lugt and De Langen (2007).

Clearly, the current management scheme stems from a long evolution. The first autonomous body for the governing of the port, namely the Municipal Port Authority, was formalized in 1932,

generating a state of overall equilibrium between the port and the city that lasted throughout the postwar period, encouraged by the impetus to rebuild, the resumption of traffic, and economic and industrial expansion.

However, the creation of Botlek and Europoort threw the image of the port into serious crisis; in addition, the shift of port activities toward the west produced a further physical and mental distancing of the port from the city: the port was no longer decipherable and was at that point so vast and distant as to make the city-port relationship irreconcilable.

Nonetheless, in the first years of the new century, the attention given to the city-port border areas contributed to establishing an unprecedented role for the port: no longer just a landlord, i.e., owner of the spaces, but a developer, i.e., a direct protagonist in the transformation and management of the shared spaces along the border.

Projects

Underpinning the interests of city and port was the decision to invest in the urban component in order to close the gap vis-à-vis rampant port development. This alliance increased the exchange between the two territories by implying mutual commitments: on the one hand, the city explored new areas so as to optimize the presence of the larger port, on the other, the port secured city's support for activities outside the borders of its property.

The projects were divided into two stages, the first in the late 1980s, and the other, still ongoing, starting in 2002.

The first phase was aimed at including the city in the radical port changes, constructing an identity that portrayed Rotterdam in its entirety: a reality in which the port was never secondary but that for a long time monopolized the perception of the area, obscuring the city. Therefore, the ambition of the *Rotterdam Waterfront Program*[6] was to bring the Maas River back into the heart of the city by removing certain areas of the abandoned port. The program envisaged a predominantly urban regeneration in four areas: Oude Haven, the old seventeenth-century port; Leuvehaven, Wijnhaven, and Zalmhaven, residential and work districts; Scheepvaartkwartier and Parkhaven, residential areas and public spaces; and, finally, Kop van Zuid, an island in the middle of the river on which the city's new business center was established.

The subsequent phase differs both in terms of strategy and approach. The *CityPorts* project is in fact the initiative that the port and the city have been carrying out since 2002 in the city-port interface zones, introducing a radical change of mentality in terms of strategies.

Located in the Stadshavens area of approximately 16,000 hectares, *CityPorts* pursues a different strategy, which has led to the intention to establish alliances with private companies, universities, research centers, and government bodies, in order to generate investments and diversify the urban economy. This was combined with the intention of developing a process capable of adapting to the dynamics of the port's situation. Located on the border between the port and the city, the areas of the RDM Campus and the *M4H* in Merwe-Vierhavens are today the clearest examples of these practices. The RDM Campus, together with the urban district of Heijplaat, is the new hub for industrial manufacturing, applied sciences, and robotics built on the site of the old Rotterdamsche Droogdok Maatschappij (RDM) shipyards, opened in 1902. If the government was initially leaning towards the removal of the shipyards and the demolition of the village, the PoR chose instead to acquire the area and, with municipal support, to include it within the *CityPorts* program.

Inaugurated in 2009, the RDM Campus is now fully operative: its core is the Innovative Dock, an experimental center for companies and students in the marine technology and offshore sectors.

On the north bank of the Maas, on the other hand, the *M4H* district in the Merwe-Vierhavens area is one of the largest hubs of global fruit trade that, due to the migration of the heavy-duty port toward the west, is evolving into an innovative cluster for the medical, foodstuffs, and advanced tertiary sectors. The current process involves a transition from "industrial port" to "knowledge port": since 2007, the former port warehouses have been occupied by companies in the design, communication, and architectural sectors, as well as some commercial macro-functions necessary for providing basic support.

Self-construction laboratories, production facilities, agricultural experimentation centers, and urban gardens have already occupied the old port buildings at the edge of the infrastructure axis for at least two years, with its temporary nature being strongly felt and the intermediate character of ongoing transformation noticeable.

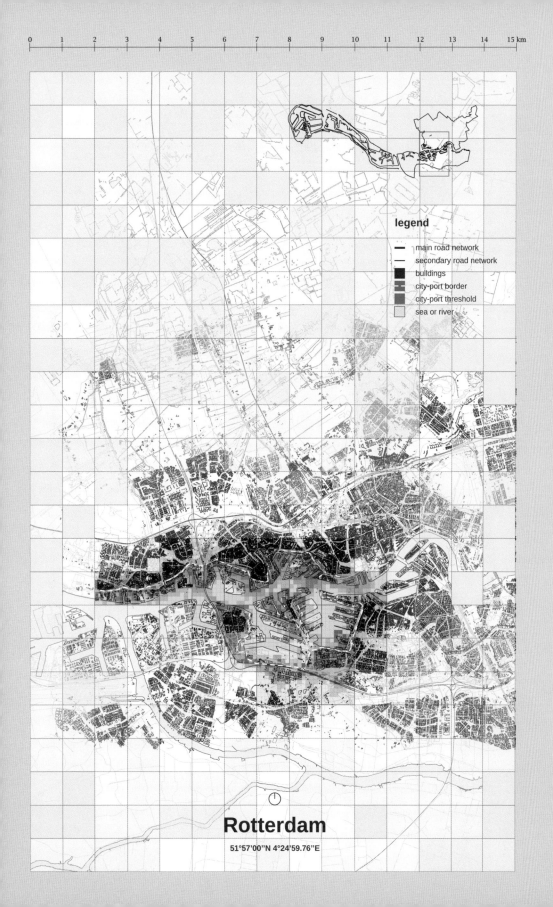

0 1 2 3 4 5 6 7 8 9 10 11 12 13 14 15 km

legend

— main road network
— secondary road network
■ buildings
▦ city-port border
▨ city-port threshold
□ sea or river

Rotterdam

51°57'00"N 4°24'59.76"E

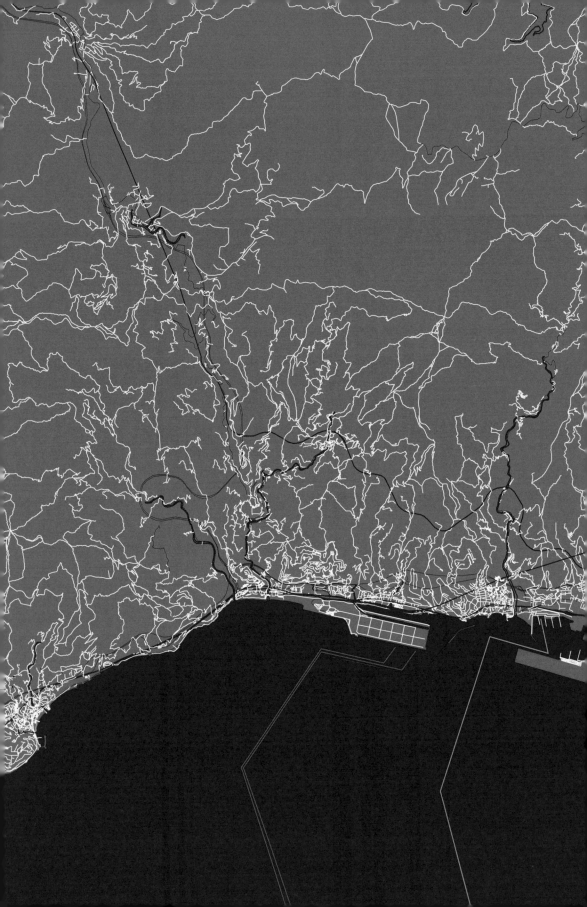

Genoa

Evolution

Looking at the cartographic series *Forma Genuae*[1], it is impossible not to notice the inherited port character associated with the Ligurian capital. From the first charts, the ancient sea protection structures can already be recognized: the Old Pier beneath the castle hill (1130) and the New Pier (1638) that, one to the west and one to the east, enclosed the main basin inside the natural bay.

In the sixteenth century, new walls upended the relationship between port and city, causing a radical fracture. The construction of a closed barrier where commercial activities took place was in fact a mirror of an economic-social division between commerce and business. Subsequently, following the growth in traffic, the situation at the Genoese port reached a critical level and, at the dawn of the nineteenth century, imposed a total rethinking of the port, also motivated by its transition to Savoy rule (1815).

Beginning in the second half of the nineteenth century, the city turned its attention to the development of the port. Early projects envisioned the construction of a new outer harbor capable of reducing maritime agitation and creating new moorings. It was only thanks to the donation of Raffaele De Ferrari, Duke of Galliera, that in 1876 the construction of a new dam began, heralding over a centenary of radical city-port transformations.[2] At the same time as the construction of the Galliera Pier, the port developed regulatory tools for new extensions: the *Parodi Regulatory Plan* (1877) and the *Giaccone Master Plan* (1891) formulated for the first time an all-encompassing port concept, laying the foundations for a significant extension towards the west. This idea had an effect on the urban model of Genoa, replacing the radial system arising from

the natural gulf with a linear system obtained through the formalization of the so-called *Grande Genova* in 1926.[3]

Throughout the first half of the twentieth century, the Autonomous Consortium of the Port of Genoa (CAP) carried out port expansion works with the construction of the Vittorio Emanuele III Basin, built right under the Lanterna, along with a new breakwater and new jetties to accommodate various types of goods. After the First World War, it was evident that industrial expansion had prevailed, and two new plans (Coen Cagli, 1919, and Albertazzi, 1924/1928) encouraged the construction of new berths. On the urban front, the Regulatory Plan of the central city zones (1931/1932) proposed the model of the horizontal city: part of the old center was demolished to make room for the business centers located at hubs far from the urban network.

The Second World War caused considerable damage to the historical fabric of the city and, at the same time, put a halt to the port expansion works, which resumed only after the end of the conflict to build the airport dam (1956/1961). At that time, the rise of heavy industry turned both the city and the port into building sites.

On the port front, the standardized traffic system required non-delayable expansion works to the far west. In 1968, a new plan provided guidelines for the construction of the Voltri-Prà Terminal, a new mechanized landing platform where the goods terminate and are forwarded to the rear port. With this project, combined with the significant development in the shipbuilding and recreational sector in the far eastern part of the coast that had already been underway for several decades, the multi-purpose structure of the port, still in operation, was defined.

Planning Aspects

At the end of the twentieth century, Genoa was an industrial and port hub in serious crisis, with a chaotic economic and demographic structure full of contradictions. According to the guidelines of the *General Regulatory Plan* of 1980, expansion was still the dominant

1
Piero Barbieri, *Forma Genuae* (Genoa: Municipio di Genova, 1938).

2
The legacy of Duke of Galliera Raffaele De Ferrari consisted of a donation of 20 million lire in gold that enabled the construction of the western breakwater, named "Galliera Dam" after him (1876–1890).

3
La Grande Genova (literally, *the Great Genoa*), or the Genoa that extends for over 35 km along the coast from the cliffs of Nervi to the coasts of Voltri, and inland to the valleys of Polcevera and Bisagno, dates back to 1926, when 19 autonomous municipalities were aggregated with the Municipality of Genoa, adding to the six municipalities of the lower Bisagno Valley that had been incorporated in 1874. With this maneuver, the city's population increased from 254,000 to 600,000 inhabitants.

premise at that point, albeit with the idea of substantially reorganizing the existing city. This made certain actions implemented in the name of progress less tolerable and reinforced the idea that the port was a disruptive element for the city.

A few years later, the subject of the port brought together several actors (the Region of Liguria, the Municipality of Genoa, and the Port Consortium) in the formalization of a *Memorandum of Understanding* for the conversion of the historical port to urban uses. The action led to the re-appropriation of the seafront by the city and the subsequent opening of the sector on the occasion of the Expo in 1992.[4] The project, orchestrated by the Commissione Triporto and based on the transfer of the areas from State property to the Municipality, allowed the CAP to free itself of a decommissioned area and for the Municipality to take possession of it with an eye toward a strategic recuperation of the docks and the adjacent historic center.

The axis of cooperation was further reinforced when the Municipality and the Port Authority joined the planning process, proposing a vision beyond the territorial borders of the state-owned property. The *Municipal Urban Plan* (PUC, 2000) designed a system of areas of transformation in state-owned areas, providing recommendations for their restructuring, including activities that were not necessarily port-related. The Port Authority, on the other hand, entrusted the drafting of the *Port Regulatory Plan* (PRP, 2001) to a group of international planners, specifying a set of guidelines and practices that crossed over into the city.

The urban vision of the port was further solidified, driven by the need for the two realities to evolve together. At the Region's initiative, in 2004, the Renzo Piano Building Workshop (RPBW) studio presented *l'Affresco*, a concept for redesigning the port and its border in contact with the city.[5] *L'Affresco* envisaged a waterfront model that advanced into the sea without occupying new stretches of coast, instead redesigning the urban border.

Despite its powerful image, *l'Affresco* was nonetheless incompatible with the guidelines of the urban planning tools in force; for this reason, it remained uncompleted, confirming its excessively visionary nature and the difficulty of its application.

Institutional Aspects

There is a clear divide in Genoa when it comes to the issue of governance, in which the port area ceases to be a matter for the city and becomes an independent territorial entity.

The Autonomous Port Consortium (CAP) was established in 1903 as a self-sufficient entity to which the State delegated a portion of its powers relative to the organization of port spaces. From a legal point of view, the CAP was dependent on the Superior Council of Public Works (Consiglio Superiore dei Lavori Pubblici), but it enjoyed autonomy in terms of works, equipment, investments, working conditions, and the imposition of tariffs.

The administrative figure of the CAP lasted up until 1994, at which point Law No. 84 was enacted, establishing port authorities in the major ports. The transformation of the CAP into a port authority outlined a new framework in which the mayor was an active member of the Port Committee.[6]

The law of 1994 therefore provided clear recommendations on the process of delineating the port area by tracing the border line along the city: the limits of each port authority's circumscribed area were actually established by the minister of transport and navigation, and they defined not only the overall structure of the port but also the area within which the PRP guidelines existed.

In 2016, the Italian institutional framework underwent a further transformation in terms of the port system. This reorganization produced an administrative revolution that, in a good number of contexts, slowed down or even blocked the urban planning processes underway. The reform aimed to rationalize and simplify the port landscape by proposing the amalgamation of several neighboring ports within macro

4
The *International Specialized Exhibition Christopher Columbus: The Ship and the Sea*, or more informally, Expo 1992, was held in Genoa from May 15 to August 15, 1992. The occasion for the organization of the Expo was the five-hundredth anniversary of European colonization of the Americas by the Genoese navigator Christopher Columbus.

5
For further information, see L'Affresco: A Vision for Genoa Harbour, RPBW (www.rpbw.com/ project/78/a-vision-for-genoa-harbour).

6
Reference is to Law No. 84/1994 and further modifications: "Riordino della legislazione in materia portuale".

7
Reference is to
Decree No. 169/2016:
"Riorganizzazione,
razionalizzazione e
semplificazione della
disciplina concer-
nente le Autorità
Portuali di cui alla
legge 28 gennaio
1994, n. 84".

8
Ennio Poleggi,
*Genova. Ritratto di
una città* (Genoa:
Sagep Editori, 1987).

9
For further infor-
mation, see Ports
of Genoa. Planning
Strategy ([www.
portsofgenoa.com/en/
development-strate-
gies/planning-strat-
egy.html](www.portsofgenoa.com/en/development-strategies/planning-strategy.html)).

10
This refers to the
Darsena and Ponte
Parodi areas where
the conversion
of port buildings
took place partially,
leaving numerous
buildings abandoned.
In the case of Ponte
Parodi, the "Ponte
Parodi and the city
of Genoa" competi-
tion of ideas, won in
2001 by UN Studio,
remains unfulfilled.
In the case of the
former Hennebique
granary silo, the
tender launched in
2013 did not produce
any expression of
interest. A new open
call for tenders for
the concession of the
Hennebique building
was published and
completed in 2019.

11
For further informa-
tion, see the Blueprint
Competition ([www.
blueprintcompetition.
it](www.blueprintcompetition.it)).

port systems on a territorial scale as a central innovation. With this reform,[7] Genoa is now the principal port of the Port System Authority of the Western Ligurian Sea, which also includes the Savona-Vado Ligure ports, located 50 km further west.

Projects

At the end of the twentieth century, Genoa lacked an urban image capable of conveying the power and wealth of its past.[8] The buildings that advanced up the hills, the landfill areas for the new port, the intense migratory flow of the population, among other metamor-phoses, altered the layout of the ancient urban structure and prompted most of the subsequent actions aimed at mak-ing up for the loss of identity. Having the opening to the seafront precisely in the center of the city thus constituted the fundamental act of the urban re-evalua-tion process. Other sections of the city-port border followed this example; how-ever, none of these cases produced an equally favorable result.

Over the last twenty years, the administrative evolution of the port authority has consolidated the role of port planner, forcing it to become aware of the city-port architectural heritage in particular. In most recent examples, in fact, the port no longer seems willing to let its areas be converted for urban uses but personally fights to defend its operational nature.

This metamorphosis manifested itself in the urban approaches put together in the *Schema di Piano* (Draft Plan) formulated by the then Port Authority in 2015.[9]

The *Schema di Piano* proposed a subdivision of the port territory into three areas: the "operational port" where the activities predominantly operational in nature were located; the "passenger port," i.e., the hub for ferries and cruise ships; and, finally, the "urban port," which related to the development of the border areas between the port and the city.

The *Schema di Piano* went on to identify the so-called urban grafts: specific features (docks, roads, junctions) or larger stretches of the seafront where a partial opening towards the urban front was envisioned.

On the city front, the current *Municipal Urban Plan* (PUC, 2015) instead includes the port and the shore-line in the Systems of Territorial Con-certation, where an all-encompassing approach capable of overcoming the administrative division is being tried out.

Nevertheless, the delay in port planning constitutes a serious limitation that is preventing a synergistic plan, especially in the fragile border areas. This is certainly the case of the area that includes the former Hennebique granary silo and the Ponte Parodi,[10] but also the area of the *Levante Waterfront*, an extensive stretch of seafront that connects the former Hennebique silo with the mouth of the Bisagno River, traversing the entire historical basin in a single trajectory.

The first version of the RPBW project for this stretch of coast dates back to 2013 and was initially called *Blueprint*. Based on that scheme, in 2016, the Municipality launched the competition of ideas "Blueprint: a draw-ing for Genoa." The competition nomi-nated ten finalists without identifying a winning proposal. The final version of the project was donated to the city by the Genoese studio in 2017 and lays the foundations for the development of the *Levante Waterfront*.

Also, drawn up by the architectural firm Renzo Piano Building Workshop (RPBW), the *Levante Waterfront* proj-ect[11] involves a section of the city-port border that connects the city and some sectors of the operational port occupied by ship repair industries, dry docks, tourism-based and pleasure craft har-bors, sports and nautical clubs, and a large fairground. For long stretches, the project places a navigable water chan-nel alongside the roadway at the level of the dock: through this operation, the border acquires thickness, and the new functions unite with the rich pre-exist-ing architectural heritage, creating a linear urban park capable of streamlin-ing the fairground and naval sectors by increasing their respective functionality and potential for future growth.

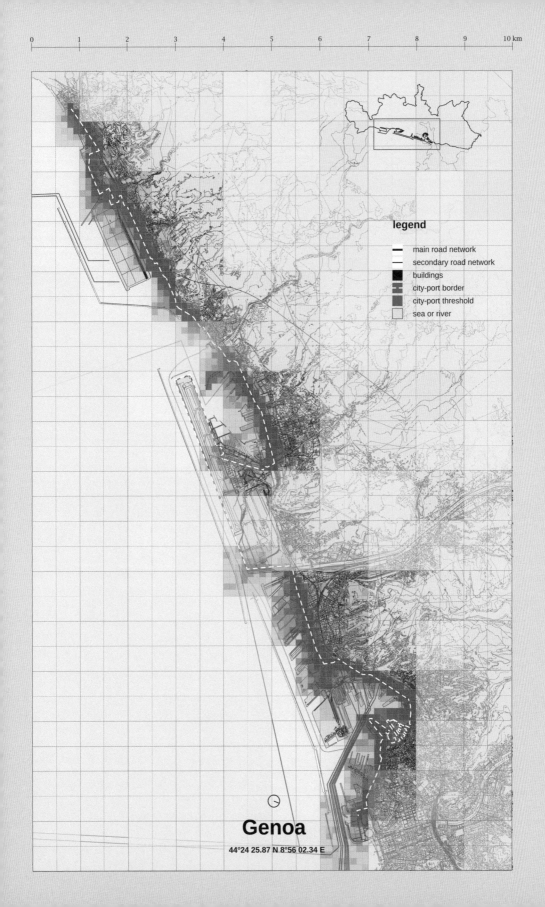

legend

main road network
secondary road network
buildings
city-port border
city-port threshold
sea or river

Genoa

44°24 25.87 N 8°56 02.34 E

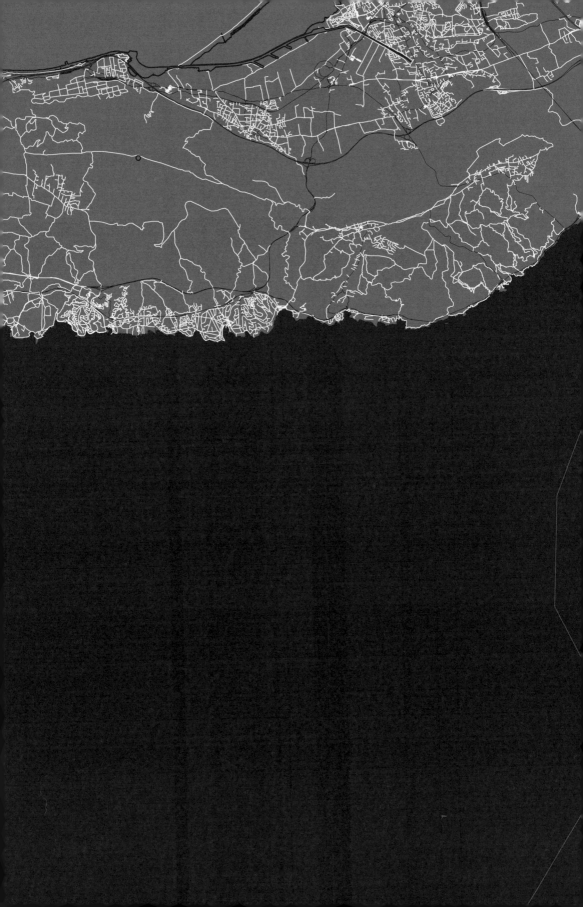

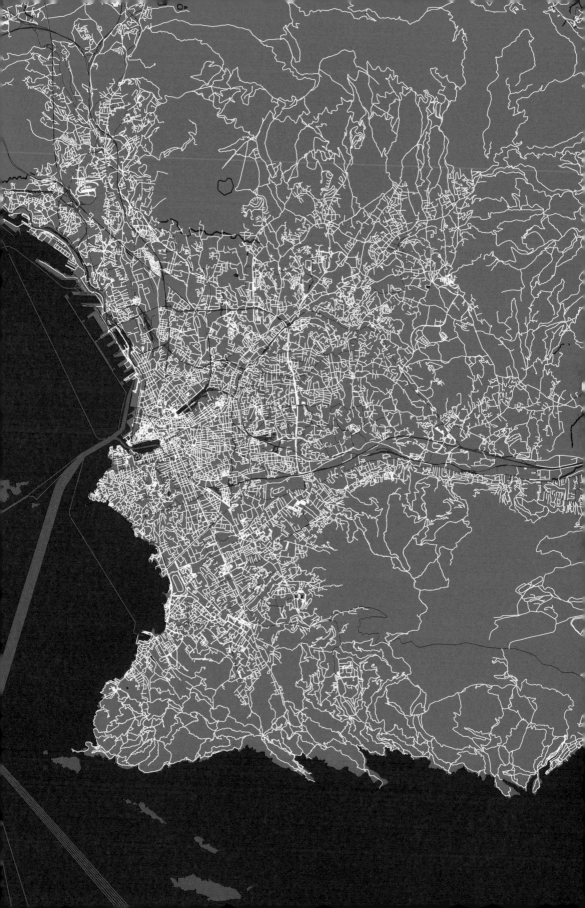

Marseille

Evolution

The original form of *Massalia*, a natural port founded by the Greeks in the northern Mediterranean basin, consisted of a primary fulcrum that, located near Fort Saint Jean, rapidly expanded in Roman times following a linear development on the north bank of the ancient calanque of Lacydon.[1] Along this stretch of coast, the port grew by exploiting the deep natural inlet, becoming an important transit center in the north of the Tyrrhenian Sea.

The morphological articulation of the narrow gulf did not allow for the construction of artificial piers, and thus the shore, the so-called *Carreria Portus*, functioned for decades as a continuous landing site for disembarking and commerce. In the Angevin era, the landing area was extended with a new dock that shifted the urban orientation by bringing the city closer to the sea.

With its annexation to France (1481), Marseille opened toward a vast hinterland, acquiring the role of a territorial port in the Rhone area of influence. To encourage exchanges, a profound urban renewal began on the northern bank of the port: the so-called "lower city," at the time characterized by a tangled fabric that interspersed landing sites, spaces for food markets, industrial areas, and streets reserved for guilds. This arrangement continued until the mid-seventeenth century, when the port was declared a free zone (1669) and the first *Plan d'agrandissement* (1666) was drawn up.[2] Commissioned by Louis XIV, the *Plan* aimed to triple the built areas towards the southeast (from 67 to 200 hectares); the intent was to rely on the investments of merchants to transform the new neighborhood into a prestigious representation of the entire kingdom.

In the following centuries, Marseille became an important port for sorting and processing for manufacturing. During the industrialization in the nineteenth century, maritime traffic made the old port's capacity untenable, also due to the opening of new eastern routes and the founding of the French colonies.

Within a period of thirty years (1821–1851), the population and the built-up area doubled. In this process of unbridled housing development, the state invested in the construction of the Joliette Basin north of Lacydon (1853). Construction of the Lager breakwater began in 1833, and later the basins of Lazaret, d'Arenc, and Napoleon were built. The process of isolating the port outside the ancient inlet was completed around 1935, causing the urban center of gravity to move outside the perimeter of the ancient walls.

Planning Aspects

Already during the nineteenth century, work on the port took on a territorial scale that impacted the Rhone delta. In parallel, new expansions were undertaken in the urban center based on the introduction of wide avenues. Along these lines, the *Plan Général des Coupemens et alignemens de la ville de Marseille* (1812) made the urban fabric accessible by recomposing the texture of the main thoroughfares and giving a face to the port.

In conjunction with the construction of the Bassin Sud in the coastal area of the Joliette, the city exploded outside the eighteenth-century walls, accentuating the dichotomy between the newly built nucleus and the historical one nestled around the Lacydon that became subject to environmental and social criticism. To remedy this condition and to foster a relationship between the historic and commercial ports, the government put into place a program of interventions aimed at reducing the density of the older districts by introducing wide avenues.

The period of major demolitions continued in the following century, becoming a tool for initiating the urban project.[3] The most significant action in city-port terms was the demolition of about two hectares of the Lacydon

1
Maurice Euzennat, "Ancient Marseille in the Light of Recent Excavations", *American Journal of Archaeology*, vol. 84, no. 2 (1980), 133–140.

2
Jean-Lucien Bonillo, René Borruey, Jean-Denis Espinas, Antoine Picon, *Marseille ville et port* (Marseille: Parentheses, 1991).

3
Other plans for the expansion and transformation of the urban center followed between 1930 and 1960. These included the Plan Gréber (1933), the *Plan d'aménagement d'embellissement et d'extension* (PAEE) for three years, the *Plan Beaudouin* (1943) issued by the Republic of Vichy, which revised the previous one, and finally the *Plan d'urbanisme directeur* — PUD (1959) for a large territorial area surrounding the city.

seafront through a systematic cycle of explosions. Named *Operation Sultan*,[4] it was an intervention in an urban section of a maritime-commercial nature that was in particularly critical condition. The area was soon razed to the ground and made available for reconstruction: several teams made proposals, and what prevailed was the grouping by the architect Fernand Poullion. In his project at La Tourette (1943–1953), Poullion applied the currents of rationalism to the historical city fabric by experimenting with the model of collective living space. The residential complex included several large buildings that redesigned the interface between the city and the port. The uniform buildings developed a new relationship with the street level through a continuous arcade: public functions stitched the urban fabric together by reconstituting the ancient artery that originally structured the port's seafront.

By the end of the twentieth century, the relationship between the city and the port had become increasingly distant. As a result, as early as the 1980s, major events were utilized to uplift the neighborhoods adjacent to the seafront that were subject to degradation.

With the *Schéma de cohérence à l'horizon 2015* (1992) and, subsequently, with the *Euroméditerranée* project launched in 1995, interventions were undertaken on the most fragile urban fabrics with the aim of supporting urban identities and, above all, the role of the port. A decade later, a coalition of public bodies signed *La Charte Ville-Port* (2011), a coherence scheme between city and port that planned the evolution of the city-port organism through a subdivision into three mutually synergistic sectors.

To the south, the ancient Gulf of Lacydon became the fulcrum of interaction between city and port; in the center, the industrial port sector functioned as the hub of the vast French logistics platform opening onto the Mediterranean; and finally, the north sector established itself as a tourist-seaside destination through the protection of the coastline of L'Estaque.[5]

4
Operation Sultan took place in the Old Port of Marseille under the Vichy regime during the German occupation of France (1943). Assisted by the French police, the Germans organized a raid to arrest Jews. The idea was to carry out an "architectural purification" of the northern front of the inhabited area overlooking the gulf of the historic port. The Nazis ordered the demolition of about two hectares of seafront, proceeding with a systematic cycle of explosions house by house.

5
République Française, Préfet de la région Provence Alpes Côte d'Azur, Préfet des Bouches-du-Rhône, *La Charte Ville-Port* (2011).

Institutional Aspects

Up until the end of the eighteenth century, the port of Marseille was concentrated within the Gulf of Lacydon, and its transformations were managed independently by the local government.

At the end of the nineteenth century (1881), when the port infrastructure had already long occupied the northern face of the Joliette, the Chamber of Commerce and Industry was appointed the sole operator of the port. In conjunction with the construction of the Marseille Fos hub in the 1960s, the port then became a public entity of an industrial nature called Autonomous Port of Marseille (PAM).

Finally, in 2008, the National Ports Reform established the *Grand Maritime Port of Marseille* (GPMM), a public state body responsible for the operations, management, and promotion of commercial activities. Its jurisdiction extends over both of the operational basins, the east one of Marseille and the west one that includes the hubs of Martigues, Port-de-Bouc, Fos-sur-Mer, and Port-Saint-Louis-du-Rhône.

From this point, the port system throughout France has consisted of ports belonging to the State (the large seaports, GPM, formerly called "autonomous ports," and the large inland waterway ports, that is, the autonomous ports of Paris and Strasbourg) and of ports belonging to territorial authorities. GPM is responsible for the regulation and control of maritime traffic in the port areas, the organization and maintenance of infrastructure, the management and upgrading of the port area, the promotion of the port, the development of port services, rail and inland waterway connections.

With this administrative configuration, the GPMM confirms the importance of managing city-port relationships through cooperation between multiple public institutions. This is evident in the *Euroméditerranée* project, for example, whose origin is due to the public agency *Établissement Public d'Aménagement d'Euroméditerranée* (EPAEM). Composed of state and local authorities, EPAEM is experimenting with forms of cooperation between abandoned territories, logistics areas, city segments, and port docks. In the case of the *Euroméditerranée* project,[6] i.e., the largest urban planning and economic and cultural development project currently underway in Europe, this is an Operation of National Interest (NIO), launched in 1994 with the regeneration of a first area of 310 ha and followed in 2007 with a second phase that enlarged the active area to include another 170 ha.

Projects

With the *Euroméditerranée* project, Marseille envisaged the recovery of the port seafront and the establishment of a new connection to the city. The actions were guided by the recommendations of the *Schéma de Cohérence Ville-Port*, which articulated the importance of keeping port activities in their position to take advantage of their dynamics for the benefit of the city. This reaffirmed the industrial role of the East Basin and laid the foundations for the joint development of the two neighboring entities. A manifestation of this approach can be found in the configuration of the Boulevard du Littoral that, starting from Fort Saint Jean, runs along the port's edge in a south-north direction up to Arenc.

The axis constitutes a linear system hinged on the city-port border and dotted with architectural works serving both fronts. Starting from Pier J4, adjacent to Fort Saint Jean, is the Villa Méditerranée (2013) and the Musée des civilisations de l'Europe et de la Méditerranée — MuCEM (2013). Immediately after that, on Piers J2 and J3, there is the Gare Maritime de la Major (2006), the new maritime station dedicated to international passenger traffic. Continuing along the Boulevard, the J1 Hangar is one of the last reinforced concrete structures still in existence, dating back to the nineteenth-century expansion of the Joliette Basin; it was the subject of the *Osez le J1*[7] international design competition in 2017 for the building and the neighboring piers.

The linear system was then enhanced by the Terrasses du Port, the new maritime terminal (cruise ships, fer-

ries) that runs alongside the docks, acting as an intermodal junction between various strategic hubs (the international airport, TGV station, highway system, interurban lines, metro, and tramway).

Just opposite on the urban side are the Docks de la Joliette. With a length of 400 meters, in the mid-nineteenth century they served the merchant port and the historic districts of the old center of the Panier. Already subject to renovation in 1995, the Docks were reopened in 2015 following the project by the Italian studio 5+1AA. Working with the succession of internal courtyards that structure the original edifice, the Docks now include a rhythmic commercial thoroughfare, a sort of new port seafront, which connects the external public space with the new ecosystems designed for the interior.

At the end of the linear city-port border system is Le Silo d'Arenc, now the CEPAC Silo, a former granary silo built in 1924 and converted into a concert hall in 2011, as part of the second phase of the *Euroméditerranée* project. Placed literally between the operational areas and the residential and tertiary complexes of Arenc, the silo still presents the particularities of the twentieth-century port structures, reinterpreted in the project by Roland Carta and Associates (2011).

The Silo marked the point where the sea touched the shore and, even many decades later, continues to mark the border between the city and the port, embodying in a single work of architecture the formal, functional, and cultural attributes of both.

6
For further information, see Euroméditerranée (www.euromediterranee.fr).

7
For further information, see Osez le J1 (www.osezlej1.fr).

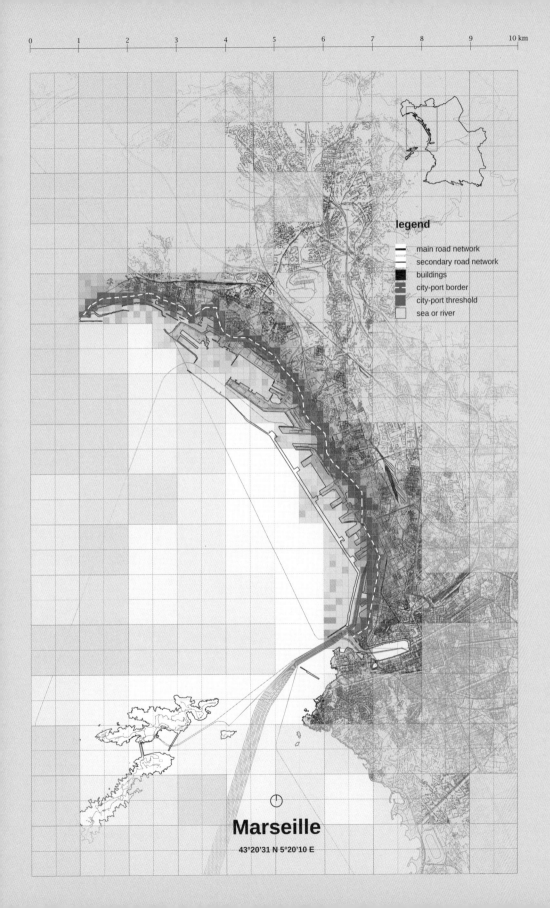

legend

main road network
secondary road network
buildings
city-port border
city-port threshold
sea or river

Marseille

43°20'31 N 5°20'10 E

0   1   2   3   4   5   6   7   8   9   10 km

Palermo

Evolution

The origins of Palermo as a port city already begin to emerge from the toponyms imposed over the years by the different domains. The Phoenicians called it *Zyz* (flower), alluding to the configuration of the settlement with two rivers that drew closer to one another as they proceeded towards the sea. The Greeks coined the name *Pànhormos* (παν — ὅρμος), meaning "all port."[1] With the Arabs and the Normans, the name mutated into *Balarm*, but some historians called the city simply *Madìnah*, which in Arabic means "city" par excellence.

In morphological terms, the Conca d'Oro plain, closed on three sides by the mountains and open to the east towards the sea, demarcates a large natural amphitheater set into the port's seafront. This configuration illustrates a spatial continuity that is the origin of a completed environmental dimension.[2]

Since the Phoenicians, the city's thalassocracy was based on the location of the landing for Mediterranean trade. With the Arab conquest (830 BC), Palermo became the center of traffic to the Middle East, bringing the first major urban transformations, including the construction of the fortified citadel of Kalsa. At the beginning of the eleventh century, with the decline of Islamic power, the monopoly was taken over by foreigners, first of all by the Amalfi, who restructured the urban fabric opposite the Cala, influencing the evolution of the waterfront.[3]

During the fourteenth century, the Arab medina became a Renaissance city with the creation of the vast *Platea Marittima*, a new district that was later connected to the Via Garibaldi axis. The motif of the straight road was taken up again, up through the exemplary venture of Via Toledo, the ancient *Càssaro*, (1567–1581). This perspective empha-

sized the ancient urban spine and connected the governmental structures (palace and cathedral) to the level of the marina, where new structures linked to the port were placed.[4]

In 1597, the urban plan became even more complex with the construction of Strada Nuova, or Via Maqueda, an orthogonal cut with respect to Via Toledo that divided the city into four parts (La Loggia, Il Capo, Kalsa, and the Albergheria). These extra-urban works spurred the development of the port: the construction of the new pier (1567–1590) pushed the operational functions to occupy the north side of the city and created a new district for merchant traffic.

At the turn of the twentieth century, the city expanded further: not only through the proposals of the *Giarrusso Plan* and the construction of the Viale della Libertà but also with the inclusion of elements of a growing modernity, including the railway loop and the station, the Massimo and Politeama theaters, and the breakwater of the port, intended to expand the port during the major development of international maritime traffic. Giarrusso's plan was based on previous solutions that proposed a further multiplication of the major transversal axes and a division of the historical inhabited area into sixteen neighborhoods. In these measures, great space was dedicated to the connection between the new residential areas in the north and the expanding port to the west, considering the edge of the city on the side adjacent to Mount Pellegrino. Although completed in sections and according to the shifting directives of the administration, the *Giarrusso Plan* laid the foundation for modern Palermo, at least until 1940.

Thus shown, the urban growth conducted through massive restructuring of urban neighborhoods and expansions *extra moenia*, highlights a divergence right on the city-port axis. The propensity toward alignments of perspective and geometries suited to urban growth does not actually seem to have been particularly constrained by the presence of the expanding port, which, for its part, followed an autono-

1
The credits for this name are linked to a typical Greek tendency to use the name *Pànhormos* to indicate any city renowned for its port; this gave the term a universal meaning and extended to other important Mediterranean ports of call.

2
Gianni Pirrone, *Palermo* (Genoa: Vitali e Ghianda, 1971).

3
Cesare De Seta, Leonardo Di Mauro, *Le città nella storia d'Italia. Palermo* (Rome and Bari: Editori Laterza, 1980).

4
Rosario La Duca, *Palermo ieri e oggi. La città* (Palermo: Sigma Edizioni, 1994).

5
Pasquale Culotta, "Nine projects for the architecture of the Palermo ring road". *The imagined cities. A trip to Italy. Catalogue of the XVII Triennale di Milano* (Milan: Electa, 1987), 180–208.

6
The PRP was composed of two main areas of intervention, and its drafting was conducted in a shared way through three bodies, the Scientific Committee, the Advisory Committee, and the Port Office, supported by expert advice in the priority areas of intervention. Among these, the Officina del Porto was the main project engine but also a network able to reunify the complexity of the strategic program.

7
Maurizio Carta, "Creative City 3.0. New scenario and projects", *Monograph.it 1* (2009), 160–185; Maurizio Carta, Daniele Ronsivalle, *The Fluid City Paradigm: Waterfront Regeneration as an Urban Renewal Strategy* (Palermo: UNIPA Springer Series, 2016).

mous path, governed by the currents and the protocols of the seabed and the safety of the landings.

Planning Aspects

The first decades of the twentieth century brought new urban issues into focus, including the need to update large-scale systems. In addition to the railway system, it was above all the port that required revitalization through a fundamental expansion.

In 1939, a national competition was launched for the drafting of a regulatory plan for a city of over 700,000 inhabitants. The winning projects proposed the construction of a ring road that would free the city center from heavy traffic. The ring road, foreseen by the PRG 1962, traversed the city, eliminating the continuity between the built environment and the countryside. Just like the straight roads of previous centuries, a large part of the institutional structures were positioned along this infrastructure, transforming it into the new urban border stretching towards the coastline.

In 1988, to mitigate the relationship between city and infrastructure, Pasquale Culotta was commissioned to study nine projects scattered along the twenty kilometers of the ring road. The proposal, renamed *Nove Approdi*, put forward specific solutions for the coast between Acqua dei Corsari and Addaura, identifying significant points of potential interaction and creating a linear spatial system consisting of city gates, bridges, and roundabouts.[5]

The interest in the coastal strip project did not resume until the end of the century, in parallel with the *Strategic Plan* of the City of Palermo (2003–2005), when the then Port Authority began drafting the *Port Regulatory Plan* (PRP).[6] The PRP of Palermo advanced a new concept of a waterfront, according to which the urban waterfront and port areas were to be integral parts of the city. The planning process proposed a master plan, inspired by the Manifesto of the Fluid City, interpreting the fluid metabolism of Palermo and establishing guidelines for the design of the third-generation waterfront.[7]

The PRP identified three types of port areas. In the "liquid" port, immersed into the urban fabric, the areas are used for pleasure craft and associated activities with a high number of interfaces, the advanced tertiary sector, and the Archaeological Park of Castello a Mare. In the "permeable" port, i.e., the area for cruise ships and passenger traffic, the functions are filtered, and the area is characterized by a large transformation zone that holds together the port activities dedicated to passengers and the new cultural and commercial functions linked to the waterfront. In the "rigid" port, i.e., the core of the port machinery, impermeable to urban penetration and protected within its perimeter, the areas are extended to allow for greater efficiency, taking into account the new areas being completed at the Port of Termini Imerese.

Institutional Aspects

In Palermo, similar to other Italian ports, the great expansion of the second half of the twentieth century required governing the use of operational spaces and regulating management aspects. For this reason, the national Law No. 1268 established the autonomous entity of the Port of Palermo in 1961, becoming a publicly regulated institution subject to the supervision of the Ministry of the Merchant Navy. The act formed a governing body for the port, defining its role, function, and nature.

Subsequently, the administrative figure of the autonomous entity or the consortium was replaced by that of the Port Authority when, in 1994, Law No. 84 was adopted. This established a new framework that gave the city an active role within the Port Committee, charged with approving the projects to be carried out in the port. In the 1994 law, the process of demarcating the port area was clarified by establishing the property limits of the port and, consequently, the boundary line with the city.

In 2016, the Italian institutional framework underwent a further transformation with regard to the port system. This reorganization produced an administrative revolution that, in many contexts, slowed down or even blocked the urban planning processes underway. The reform sought to streamline and simplify the port landscape by proposing, as its principal innovation, the regrouping of several ports close to the macro port systems on a territorial scale.

With this reform, Palermo is today the main port of the new Port System Authority (AdSP) of the Western Sicilian Sea that now also includes the ports of Termini Imerese, Trapani, and Porto Empedocle.[8] It is a public entity with its own legal status and administrative, budgetary, and financial autonomy with the duties of guidance, programming, coordination, promotion, and monitoring of port operations and other commercial and industrial activities carried out in the port.

In the current context, the effects of the reform are still difficult to evaluate. Since the law came into force, different administrations have changed their structure and have often abandoned or slowed down the planning process. Nevertheless, in certain cases, and Palermo is one of those, the drafting of the new PRP has not been interrupted, and instead the approval process was concluded in July 2018, although the approved document only concerns the port of Palermo and does not provide plans for the other ports in the cluster.

Projects

The development process of the Palermo PRP (2008–2018) is part of a research framework that is using the city as an experimental laboratory. The work of the Officina del Porto has in fact benefited from international contributions that have expanded the notion of the waterfront: a strategic interface that evolves in parallel with the urban fabric of which it is not only a part but from which it is fed.

Both the city's *Strategic Plan* (2003–2005) and the *Port Regulatory Plan* (2008–2018) were aligned with these concepts. Both documents proposed a robust exchange of intents between the port and the city that has materialized in the creation of a space of convergence that leads the whole city towards the sea. From these arrangements came the new PRP that, finally approved in 2018, is configured as a

structural-type plan configuring two sub-areas: the port and operational area in the strict sense, and the area of the city-port interface. The latter is divided into six zones of intervention with different degrees of intermingling through the use of urban design tools.[9]

With the regular planning process complete in 2018, the port initiated the project phase by announcing a competition for the design of an interface section located along Via Francesco Crispi and extended to the Piave and Sammuzzo Piers. The brief called for the construction of two terminals, one for cruise ships and the other for ro-ro, and a building operating as a hinge between the city and the new port layout. In line with the idea of a permeable port, the winning project proposed two "travel stations" and a "building interface" capable of constituting a new piece of the city.[10] With the aim of reconstructing a two-way dialogue with the city, the building interface is a device that transforms itself into a permeable infrastructure capable of generating a new set of relationships along the shared border.

The renewed city-port connection is also expressed through the new system of public spaces that combine different heights in a continuous path starting at street level. Indeed, through a succession of courtyards, piazzas, and gardens, the building interface creates a new urban plan where pedestrian flows are diverted. Additionally, in this section of the port, the presence of public functions intensifies and is not reserved exclusively for cruise passengers. A new piazza at the height of the city completes the catalogue of new public spaces, positioning itself in continuity with the system of trajectories that extend from the city to the S. Lucia Pier.

The building interface and the new passenger stations are then fused with the pre-existing structures (the Castello a Mare and the archaeological area, for example) that, in this way, assume new value from the perspective of the system as a whole. They become invariants of the contemporary project, permanent features of the border, and ingredients of a new form of city-port landscape.

8
Reference is to Decree No. 169/2016: "Riorganizzazione, razionalizzazione e semplificazione della disciplina concernente le Autorità Portuali di cui alla legge 28 gennaio 1994, n. 84".

9
For further information, see Palermo Port Master Plan, Document of Synthesis 2008–2018 (www.portpalermo.it).

10
The winning project of the competition announced by the Port System Authority of the Sea of Western Sicily was developed by a temporary planning group coordinated by the company Valle 3.0 srl of Rome. Architects: Emanuela Valle, Maria Camilla Valle, Silvano Valle with Carlo Prati. Consultants: Francesco Karrer and Levino Petrosemolo. Team: Isabella Grippo, Astrid Manara, Andrea Piattella, Veronica Regoli, Giulia Spagnuolo, Davide Pellegrini, and Andrea Rossi. Engineering: SIO-PROGETTI srl, ETS srl, HYPRO srl.

legend

main road network
secondary road network
buildings
city-port border
city-port threshold
sea or river

Palermo

38°6'43"56 N 13°20'11"76 E

BEYOND THE PORT CITY

**Models
Strategies
Features
Recurrences**

BEYOND THE PORT CITY

Models
Strategies
Features
Recurrences

Interpretive and Design Tools

The contemporary port city is a plural urban form that is dealt with using solutions that are at times partial and, at other times, extreme. In many circumstances, the port is still seen today as serving the city and remains excluded from its transformations. For this reason, the dual nature — semi-urban and semi-maritime — that by definition animates port cities is neither incorporated in nor utilized by plans of transformation; consequently, the intrinsic vitality of the port is rarely put to use for urban purposes. This prevents a different assessment of the port component as an integral part of the city from being formulated and from having it take on a new standing, showing its design potential.

According to the effects of the primary global phenomena, then, even the most recent — among all, for example, the port clustering phenomenon — confirms this attitude: it exponentially increases the framework of possibilities (introducing the notion of a port system and attributing value to the connective space between ports), but it addresses changes exclusively in the logistical-commercial sphere without thinking about the impact on the city.

However, as emerges in this study a number of times, there are city-port contexts in which it has been possible to identify new approaches, namely, those capable of overcoming past design situations and providing new perspectives on the city-port relationship, intervening in a prioritized manner on the common border. In these contexts, the capacity of port systems to engage with the city and, while still maintaining their operational aspect, to mitigate the effects of the demarcation and isolation generated by property borders can be seen. What further emerges in these examples is the way the city-port project can be implemented without relocating the port, instead putting into play the idea of coexistence.

In other words, in the following pages a renewed version of the city-port relationship is outlined in which the idea of portuality can be seen in the various configurations of the threshold. Thanks to this, it becomes possible to respond to the specific global phenomena that are pushing the two entities farther apart and accentuating the port city's loss of identity.

In order to specify these statements also in terms of design, this investigation develops a number of tools aimed at going beyond the previous approaches and favoring a repositioning of the cataloguing of the port city. These interpretive and design tools that propose interpretations aimed not so much at deriving an alternative concept of a port city, but rather at extending its original meaning, increasing the spectrum of its applicative potential and refining the techniques of its treatment. These tools are derived via an induction process (a logical process by which the ascertainment of particular facts rises to general statements or formulations) that is divided into two coordinated parts. The first focuses on the city-port threshold by obtaining *Models* and *Strategies*, while the second outlines the contours of portuality by identifying *Features* and *Recurrences*. While the Models and the Strategies focus primarily on operational-strategic aspects of the threshold, Features and Recurrences, on the other hand, are of a more theoretical-conceptual nature, which broadens the perspective of the descriptive attributes of portuality.

Models, Strategies, Features, and Recurrences are tools that favor a morphological interpretation, which gives priority to the genesis and evolution of organisms and their forms. In this sense, the filter of urban morphology makes it possible to grasp city-port structures as a whole, that is, as real beings in continuous evolution.

Models, Strategies, Features, and Recurrences are tools that contribute to transcending the idea of the waterfront as the only design paradigm and to moving "beyond" the approaches of the late twentieth century, i.e., "beyond" the idea of a more consolidated port city.

The definition of these tools therefore serves to grasp concepts thus far scarcely used and that are instead representative of the mutable nature of the administrative border. Ambivalence, indefiniteness, coexistence, transience, and varying evolutionary temporalities, to name but a few, are components that strongly characterize the city-port condition, transferring the qualities of the liminal regime to its spaces.

Tools of this kind make it possible to understand the attributes of the threshold and the contours of the conditions of portuality, generating a complete picture but not a rigid one. The six port cities investigated are indeed only intended as a first selection of examples that can produce an updatable method that can be applied to a larger sample of port cities.

Models and Strategies

The Models are interpretive tools dedicated to the morphological variations of the city-port threshold. Each Model produces a conceptual synthesis of the threshold through which it captures a tendency and evokes a quality. It interprets the geometries that shape it, defining the articulations of the connective element and the embodiments of the city-port duality. Each Model is deduced from the single study context through a process of abstraction.

Operationally, the Models are products of an investigation that employs the tool of the Aspect/Model Matrix. The Matrix activates a selection and a conceptualization of certain guidelines (Aspects) in order to give a form to the threshold configurations present in the six study contexts (Models). The Matrix is based on the identification of three Aspects: physical, institutional, and functional.

The physical Aspect concerns the analysis of morphology, particularly of factors such as spatial continuity, differences in dimensions, and the presence of natural or artificial disruptions. The institutional Aspect concerns the investigation of the management model, i.e., the administrative role of the port in terms of planning and interactions with other local and non-local bodies. Finally, the functional Aspect focuses on the distribution of activities and consequently of functions, according to the guidelines of the planning tools. Specifically, a distinction is made between permeable or impermeable activities, that is, those that make accessibility and sharing along border areas compatible (or not).

The Strategies, on the other hand, are potential design approaches dedicated to the city-port threshold. The Strategies are inextricably linked to the Models, since the geometric shape of the threshold is modeled on the application of design strategies. Each Strategy is derived by emphasizing the predominant approach found in the study context. In this process, the threshold is considered in strategic terms and evolves from a field of theoretical speculation to a design threshold.

Features and Recurrences

The Features are tools for a critical reading of portuality. These are emerging attributes and representations of the intermediate dimension that characterizes the areas along the city-port border. Even if they emerge from a specific observation of the six port cities, they are of a much larger, almost universal, symbolic-figurative nature, which makes it possible to orient the critical reading of portuality and, at the same time, to employ it as an ingredient for developing project design.

The Features capture some of the most expressive particularities of the city-port dimension: the scale of the elements, the permanence or voluntariness of city-port connections, the varying evolutionary temporalities of its spaces, and their composition from the perspective of uses, habits, and gestures, the specific languages produced by the relationship itself.

The Recurrences, on the other hand, are interpretive tools that generate comparable categories found with different degrees of intensity and frequency. Exploring them with the same interpretative filter, the Recurrences define new perspectives: what recurs several times generates replicated but above all replicable scenarios. This constructs a common ground made up of permanent elements and future scenarios for design. After all, the changes in the border space between urban areas and the operational area have the characteristic of "resembling" one another. In fact, their non-specific nature is capable of describing events and sympathies, metamorphoses, and modulations of many port cities, far apart in latitude, but close in evolution.

With this in mind, both the Features and the Recurrences bring to the fore particular aspects and representative places that generally escape the traditional definition offered by the plans. They provide an alternative language through which to approach the project of the border and potentially contribute to reducing the shortcomings in urban planning with regard to ports.

Matrix

ASPECTS

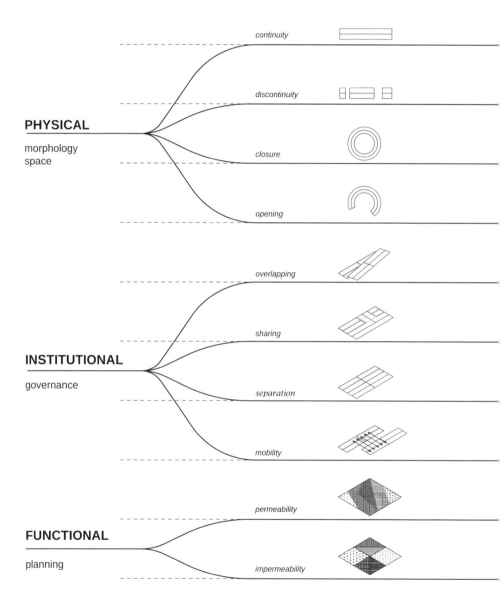

PHYSICAL

morphology
space

continuity

discontinuity

closure

opening

INSTITUTIONAL

governance

overlapping

sharing

separation

mobility

FUNCTIONAL

planning

permeability

impermeability

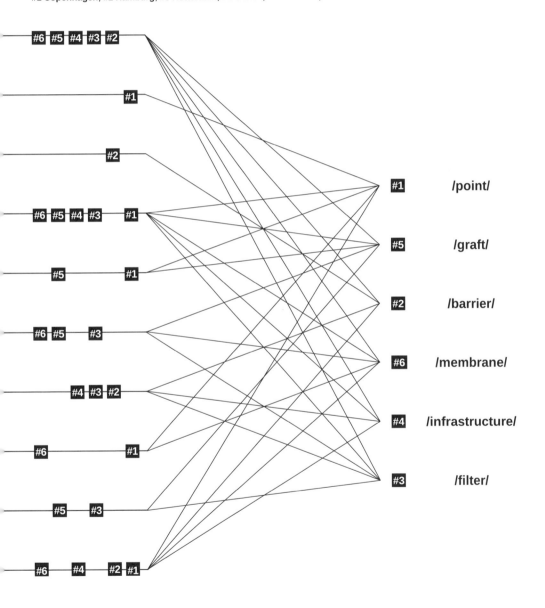

MODELS

CASE STUDIES
#1 Copenhagen; #2 Hamburg; #3 Rotterdam; #4 Genoa; #5 Marseille; #6 Palermo

#6 #5 #4 #3 #2

#1

#2

#6 #5 #4 #3 #1

#5 #1

#6 #5 #3

#4 #3 #2

#6 #1

#5 #3

#6 #4 #2 #1

#1 /point/

#5 /graft/

#2 /barrier/

#6 /membrane/

#4 /infrastructure/

#3 /filter/

Models

/point/
/barrier/
/filter/
/infrastructure/
/graft/
/membrane/

point
/ˈpȯint/

_____

"A small and reduced segment, a section of extremely limited dimensions"

0   1 km

[FUNCTIONAL]
impermeability

[INSTITUTIONAL]
mobility
overlapping

[PHYSICAL]
discontinuity
opening

This city-port threshold model is localized in a punctiform and univocal way, not extended to the connection between the urban territory and the port, i.e., largely at the mouth of the infrastructures that connect the various peninsulas to the mainland. Depending on the morphological shape and the features of the transport route, this threshold is discontinuous and open and presents limited development in terms of size.

Its management is mobile and generates overlaps of competencies between the different actors involved. In functional terms, there is a persistent impermeability of activities that seem to be fenced in.

Looking at the ensemble of Copenhagen peninsulas and the positioning of the operational sectors with respect to the city, the threshold appears as an intermittent element: not a continuous and uniform figure, but a broken border that is both precise and detailed.

barrier
/ber-ē-ər/

———————

"A compact and clear sign that controls and at times inhibits exchange and transitions. A two-dimensional but also volumetric organism"

This threshold model is a solid element that, through acts of hardening, draws different types of borders. In this sense, the Veddel Dam, built to contain flooding, clearly separates the city from the adjacent port basins. Its path is raised above the level of the road and acts as a shield between the two territories: although it is a demarcation, the dam is also a cycling path and an urban promenade. This structure conveys continuity and closure from a morphological standpoint.

The island of the *HafenCity* can also be considered as a solidification of the threshold. Very large in terms of size, it acts as a separation for the passage of water, raising the level of the public space and protecting it from river flooding. At the same time, it represents a compact transition area between the city to the north and the port to the south.

Finally, the functional impermeability corresponds to a separation on the management level between the port authority and the urban one.

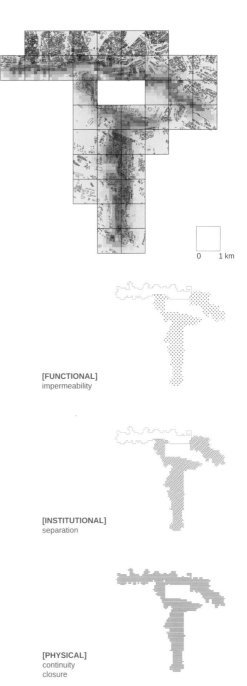

0   1 km

[FUNCTIONAL]
impermeability

[INSTITUTIONAL]
separation

[PHYSICAL]
continuity
closure

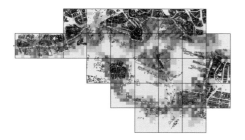

filter
/fil-tər/

_____

"Adjustment device able to balance and govern the degree of interaction between two syntactically different areas"

This threshold model rarely solidifies into a finite form and dimension: instead, it is configured as a vast and difficult to circumscribe area, in which extremely different activities coexist. This contributes to its functional permeability and, at the same time, to a continuity and opening from a morphological standpoint.

Despite the fact that heterogeneity is undoubtedly one of the dominant features, for sure in Stadshavens planning approaches and realized schemes, it denotes an overall compactness that is achieved through a set of progressive and calibrated actions.

In this sense, the Rotterdam threshold encourages sharing and mobility. It works to establish the degree of permeability: by balancing antithetic pressures (public or private, port and city, definitive or temporary), by working to maintain a clear functional separation (where necessary for specific activities) or, on the contrary, to allow for passageways and hybridization.

0   1 km

[FUNCTIONAL]
permeability

[INSTITUTIONAL]
sharing
mobility

[PHYSICAL]
continuity
opening

infrastructure
/in-frə-ˌstrək-chər/

––––––––––––

"Equipped axis placed among other elements from which it stands out due to its form, consistency, and use. Organism of exchange that revolutionizes the places it passes through"

This threshold model resolves and rationalizes friction points by installing itself on the borders and providing them with the necessary equipment. This threshold model is articulated into different configurations: it is an axis for mobility or a channel suitable for navigation or water sports. In both cases, waterways and water function as an infrastructure: they divide but create a potential for interaction thanks to the creation of two banks. Morphologically, the infrastructural axis creates an opening at the threshold but also discontinuities that have an impact in terms of management: the infrastructure is interrupted and separated by the presence of marinas and the airport, located right in the center of the coastal stretch. This contributes to the development of impermeable functional areas between them. Exemplary cases of this model are the elevated streets and the infrastructures of the Prà channel and the one in the Waterfront of Levante.

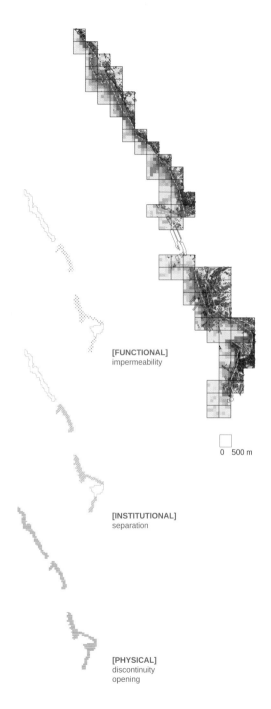

[FUNCTIONAL]
impermeability

0   500 m

[INSTITUTIONAL]
separation

[PHYSICAL]
discontinuity
opening

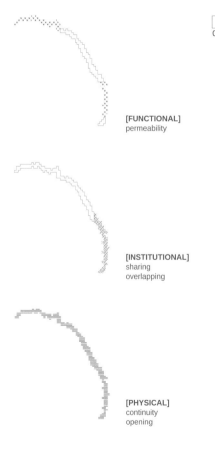

0   500 m

[FUNCTIONAL]
permeability

[INSTITUTIONAL]
sharing
overlapping

[PHYSICAL]
continuity
opening

graft
/graft/

_____

"Device for establishing a connection between several parts of a system. Insertion tool for an element in a heterogeneous whole"

This threshold model works on individual artifacts aligned along the city-port border, proposing reconversion, redevelopment, or re-use, depending on the situation. The interventions are developed on an architectural scale on port buildings (docks, silos, hangars) that, through design, become wide-ranging territorial centralities. This process takes place initially at a functional level since the inserted activities complement each other, producing a balanced and permeable pattern of uses.

The grafts are conjunctions that structure a morphologically continuous and open system, anchored along the infrastructural axis of the Boulevard du Littoral.

This system is the product of a cohesive management: *Euroméditerranée* is indeed based on a substantial sharing of intents and the overlapping of tasks between public and private entities and city-port management.

membrane
/mem-ˌbrān/

———————

"Formation of a varied nature characterized by the prevalence of surface over thickness and having the function of containing and covering"

This threshold model has features that allow for expansion, especially depth-wise into the city; it dilutes and, at times, erases the feeling of a border. A membrane has a variable section that engages with different boundaries imposed by the surrounding tissue and the interaction between mixed uses.

Through these attributes, the membrane brings to life a figure of an architectural and urban scale capable of fluidly encompassing extended urban areas and even those far from the border between city and port. Articulated into different levels, the membrane puts different degrees of connection into play between the port and the surrounding territory, to which correspond different levels of autonomy and compatibility with urban activities.

This confers on the threshold an open and continuous morphology that envelops the entire port arc. From a functional point of view, this corresponds to a diffuse and permeable quality managed with mobile and shared methods.

0   500 m

[FUNCTIONAL]
permeability

[INSTITUTIONAL]
sharing
mobility

[PHYSICAL]
continuity
opening

Strategies

[isolating the areas]
[solidifying the borders]
[planning incompletely]
[equipping the borders]
[designing liminal architectures]
[softening the edges]

[isolating the areas]

The Danish territory that surrounds the capital has developed according to a hierarchy controlled by the *Finger Plan* of 1947 and its subsequent versions, which have guided urban growth along preferential guidelines by proportioning the combination of private and public space and the natural component according to specific needs.

However, this model did not contain specific guidelines for the design of the port, i.e., it completely lacked instructions related to the organization of the operational infrastructure and, what's more, of the port border with the city. It is perhaps also for this reason that Copenhagen's principal port functions sprang from layers of artificial land gradually positioned in the water, almost as if to draw a mirrored figure diametrically opposed to the corridors that stretched inland along which the city was organized. This configuration attests to both a clear separation between port and urban areas, also due to the shift of some heavy-duty activities to Malmö, and a persistent port quality inherent in the oldest urban fabric, especially along the canal that runs through the historic center.

Today, a large part of Copenhagen's harbor occupies a complex of peninsulas originating from the northern coast. During the second half of the twentieth century, important maritime-commercial transformations influenced the morphology of the three main peninsulas in which very different scales of relationships and approaches to the city-port project can be found.

Among the larger peninsulas, Prøvestenen is the easternmost one. Founded as an artificial island with a military fortress, it has been modified several times over the centuries, becoming the headquarters of the oil and liquid bulk port in 1922. Since then, it has been connected to the mainland by a road that unites it with the Amager coast. Due to the functions it holds, Prøvestenen is far from the urban center. Nevertheless, the perception of its operational landscape is devoid of particular interpositions: the axis that connects it to the mainland includes a bike path, and the eastern profile of the island is impacted by the design of a recreational dock and a public park.

A little further west is Refshaleøen, the oldest of the port peninsulas. Originally, it was a bulwark at the entrance to the port, then, at the end of the nineteenth century, it became the headquarters of the Burmeister & Wain shipyards that modified the profile of the dock to set up several dry docks. After the closure of the yards (1996), Refshaleøen was the subject of a vast conversion, but the action did not eliminate the site's original port character; on the contrary, it was combined with the new structures, generating an intermediate and heterogeneous dimension. In addition to the HOFOR industrial plant and the incinerator built by the Bjarke Ingels Group (waste-to-energy plant inaugurated in 2017), the shipyards have left space for activities with a greater public and urban component. An educational institution, commercial services, a theater, and several retailers have relocated to the former port warehouses, regenerating most of the area. More recently, new functions related to the sea, including ship repairs, yacht clubs, and nautical support services, have again occupied the largest and most external areas of the peninsula.

Further west lies the largest port peninsula, Nordhavn. Today, the majority of port functions of the Danish port are concentrated on the Nordhavn peninsula, as are the most significant transformations in terms of the conversion of port buildings for urban uses. In addition, Nordhavn is the site of the largest port expansion currently being completed: a new commercial dock that will accommodate new cruise lines and a maritime station.

Taken together, each of these peninsulas represents a variation of the city-port relationship. While in Prøvestenen the presence of the port is predominant, in Nordhavn the two entities coexist in parallel, seeking an equilibrium still being defined today. Alternatively, the situation in Refshaleøen is more indecipherable: despite the fact that the port function is no longer active in most areas, the reconversion was based on a refunctionalization of the sites.

The three peninsulas are emblematic examples of the predominant design strategies with regard to city-port borders. The most obvious is that of "isolating the operational areas," not so much locating them away from the city but rather detaching them from the urban fabric by introducing compact elements that act as a concise and precise interruption. Isolating the operational functions from the urban ones, while keeping them within the city landscape, allows a compact and pervasive system to be created between port and city.

[solidifying the borders]

What unites the two main projects underway in Hamburg between city and port (*HafenCity* and *Leap Across the Elbe*) is the pressing demand for new housing and the need to identify new areas for urban expansion. These actions aim to increase the quality of public spaces, but above all they seek to reestablish the relationship with the Elbe River that has been compromised over time. What distinguishes the two experiences, though, is the starting point and the process developed as a result.

The *HafenCity* is a project based on a decommissioning-replacement-reconstruction mechanism orchestrated by strong urban management that first acquired the areas by demolishing a large part of the existing port structures and subsequently drafted a reconstruction plan from scratch. From a management standpoint, it is a highly complex coordinated project, conducted by the municipality with rigor and consistency; however, the effects that the vast transformation has produced on the relationship between the city and the port, both physically and in terms of identity, remain unclear.

The *HafenCity* (literally *The Port City*) is actually much more a city than a port: indeed, in its positioning, the decision to clearly separate the two areas is evident, bringing life to a new piece of the city. Nevertheless, the contribution of the *HafenCity* project remains exemplary in terms of the management process and a replicable post-industrial regeneration model.

The *Leap Across the Elbe*, on the other hand, is a project aiming to use new volume to saturate and densify an area extending to the periphery of the consolidated city. In this sense, the project demonstrates a significant evolution in the local planning guidelines. If the basic strategy for the *HafenCity* has been anchored above all in twentieth-century regeneration models, the actions in the implementation process for the core project of the *Leap Across the Elbe* extend to the entire city, and the architectural project is a contemporary and appropriate intervention tool.

Moreover, the transformation of Wilhelmsburg, for years a residential neighborhood, seeks to develop an incorporated building-urban model that makes it possible to restructure the interface spaces between city and port and lend them a new quality.

HafenCity and *Leap Across the Elbe* are two generational projects, seemingly far apart but linked by a common trajectory that makes it possible to consider one as the evolution of the other. In both a prevailing approach of "solidifying the edges" emerges through the project, that is to say, literally constructing the border spaces by giving them thickness and consistency.

Thus, the solidification of the border element produces a detachment but also a gradual transition between two different realities due to which a new urbanity is generated, one that stretches across the border between city and port. Following a route that ideally connects the consolidated city with the opposite bank of the Elbe, the *HafenCity* appears as a natural extension of the old Hamburg that is fused with the port component located on the opposite bank; this creates a large-scale city-port threshold.

Perhaps this is why, despite the sometimes artificial and still maturing atmosphere, in the *HafenCity* one can recognize a composite, semi-urban, and semi-maritime identity and can see the intertwining of the city with the landscape and the scale of the port.

[planning incompletely]

In Rotterdam, the two waves of projects that changed the city-port relationship in the last thirty years were based on two distant and antithetical approaches. On the one hand, the Rotterdam *Waterfront Program* of the 1980s was an urban planning affair that replaced port functions with city-oriented districts; on the other, the *CityPorts* project at Stadshavens, which is still underway, is seeking a new version of the city-port connection, founded on sharing the area's design but also on a new management formula.

The *CityPorts* project explores a city-port dimension in which the two entities coexist and the pre-existing fabric is regenerated through a mixture of uses that highlights the importance of the spaces of the city-port threshold in particular.

In 2012, Aarts, Daamen, Huijs, and de Vries asserted: "Where the city and the port grew apart from each other in the twentieth century, the city and port are now positioning the *CityPorts* project as the place where new connections are being made. And naturally, one cannot do that all by oneself. [...] In this area, where the city and the port meet, space has been created to develop new activities which are important to both the city and the port."

Today, Rotterdam is a port that handles more than 12 million containers a year and, in the middle of the economic crisis, invested in an expansion towards the North Sea by completing the Maasvlakte II Terminal.

With this in mind, it is difficult to trace a parabola capable of framing all the different lines of development. Nevertheless, it is possible to recognize coordinating logics that motivate both the *CityPorts* project and the realization of Maasvlakte II. In fact, the terminal was not only conceived as a commercial platform and an industrial hub but also as a large natural infrastructure. In addition to the port functions, Maasvlakte II hosts an equipped marine park, a sort of mixed-zone landscape in which port areas and spaces for the community, such as the large beach, coexist to create a new form of logistics landscape of an alien nature but which evolves in a coordinated manner. Thus, one of the strengths of the Stadshavens project is the gradual nature of the interventions and the step-by-step procedure that provides tools for calibrating the work, taking into account the dissimilarities of the city-port areas.

Putting aside the significant contrasts (between city and port and city and nature) and the more extreme situations (above all, the coexistence of operational structures and public spaces), a prevailing attitude is taking shape in Rotterdam that responds to the strategy of "planning in an incomplete or undefined way."

This recalls the theory of "planning in uncertainty or incompletely" articulated by Peter V. Hall in 2016: "Port-city interfaces are continuously shifting, arising in new locations within metropolitan space.

This incompleteness can be positive in a planning sense, because it means that we are not locked into the existing set of port-city relations. Indeed, let's get over the idea that the waterfront should (and can) ever really be continuous or complete.

The waterfront and other points of port-city interface are at their most vibrant and innovative when they are diverse, open and changing. We should not try to make the waterfront too neat, too tidy, too safe, or too finished [...]." Through this approach, characteristics such as the undefined and the incomplete find concrete expression, so that the urban border with the port can be molded with greater flexibility.

They become the ingredients of a flexible process rather than a static and immobile project.

[equipping the borders]

Comparing the conversion of the Porto Antico (completed) and the *Affresco* proposal (which remained a suggestion), it emerges that in the last twenty years Genoa has had privileged extemporaneous approaches, i.e., ones that rarely originated from the guidelines of applicable urban plans but instead stemmed from solutions endowed with a strong visionary power. Often the exceptional nature of these projects guaranteed them great visibility but not as much viability.

This approach is confirmed by the most recent episode of the new *Levante Waterfront* (2017/2018) that started off with the suggestion initially called *Blueprint* (2013), donated to the city by the Renzo Piano Building Workshop during a collaboration between the Region of Liguria, the Municipality of Genoa and the then Port Authority. In this case too, as in the 2004 *Affresco* project, the impulse for the project came from an external source, advancing a hypothesis for developing the port and city together in a concentrated form along a stretch of the city-port border. Subsequently, the public authorities in support of the project allowed its integration into the planning process of both entities.

In terms of the project, the *Levante Waterfront* proposes a coastal territorial system aimed at creating a connection between parts of the sea front converted for urban uses (the area of the Old Port and the Dock) and a part of the coast that is instead still occupied by active port functions. The system of mobility, i.e., the new multi-level roadway and the navigable water channel, are thus devices for separating the two areas but, at the same time, for creating a dialogue between the two fronts.

As a whole, the project demonstrates a decisive surpassing of the strategies that guided interventions in the city-port area at the end of the 20th century. In fact, at the *Levante Waterfront*, the port is not decommissioned and delocalized to make room for the city, instead remaining active, strengthening its work areas, and streamlining the access system. The city front, on the other hand, reestablishes its relationship with the water and the employability of a new continuous coastal path. In this way, the city and the port coexist, attributing a strategic role to the border between the two territories, which becomes the design framework that activates the whole operation.

In other sections of Genoa's city-port threshold, though, decommissioning is the first step of the project. These are areas with a different degree of integration in the urban context, which in some cases are in close contact with the city (the former Hennebique grain silo), while others have just completed the production cycle and remain inside the port. This is the case of the thermoelectric plant located on Calata Concenter at the foot of the lighthouse. Closed in 2017, the building (which was listed in 2019) will return to being available to the port authorities.

Because of its unique position between the sea, the lighthouse fortress, and imposing portions of the port, and not least due to its historic value, the Centrale is a candidate to become a particularly interesting junction in the near future.

What these spatial and symbolic connectors between city and port have in common is a trend rooted in the Genoese context that tends to overcome insurmountable spatial enigmas, generating a catalogue of exceptional landscapes in which spatial discontinuities, such as borders, take on a crucial role.

Today, this propensity is towards the prevailing strategy of "equipping the borders," transforming them into infrastructural spaces, functional axes that work between the strips of contact between two or more territories. Thus, where the lack of space and morphological fragility are at their extreme, borders become devices capable of equipping areas between city and port, guaranteeing permeability, exchange, and transition.

[designing liminal architectures]

For several decades now, the port of Marseille has been structured around a number of hubs across which various operational functions are distributed. Even in the vicinity of the consolidated city, there is a portion of the active port that is used for commercial and cruise ship functions.

In effect, the process of reconversion at the end of the twentieth century remained limited to the Vieux Port, which from once being an ancient commercial landing site has evolved into a vast public space at the water's edge. Then, starting from 1995, the *Euroméditerranée* initiatives have focused on the sections of the city that are in conflict with the port, proposing a redevelopment of the abandoned heritage sites that is motivated by an idea of coexistence of the two entities and the two territories.

Both with the first phase and even more so with the second, initiated in 2007 and still in progress, *Euroméditerranée* has envisaged the reconstruction of the ancient alignment, not only in terms of infrastructure, but also between port and city areas and structures. Indeed, like the original *Carreria Portus*, which served as a port-like urban fabric in the absence of a real dock, the Boulevard du Littoral has been inserted between the districts of the Joliette along the *Cité de la Méditerranée* longitudinally, reaching as far as the northernmost Arenc district. Moving from south to north, this linear system connects two opposing fronts along which different spaces and architectural works are set, whose redevelopment in a coordinated fashion produces an intervention strategy that is particular to the city-port threshold.

The predisposition to "designing liminal architecture" is therefore a clear approach in this context: the intervention on single artifacts indeed makes it take on extraordinary value not only in terms of their position *on the border* but above all of their *borderline* quality.

This strategy guides the most of the urban redevelopment and is reflected in several specific solutions. The project for the Docks de la Joliette, aligned with the Boulevard, is in fact based precisely on the concept of narrative sequence. The opening of the internal courtyards and all of the building's side portals makes the ground floor accessible and proposes a new way of using the volume in a transverse direction. A pedestrian promenade runs through the center of the volume, replicating the patterns of the urban scheme. With this maneuver, the Docks lend weight to the threshold, embodying the spatial progression between the city and the port.

Intervening on single works of architecture with strategies of this type solidifies a different sense of heritage, in which buildings are not isolated cases but fragments in a complex system that exists on the unstable territory of the threshold and that is shaped according to a dynamic conception of space.

With this strategy, the design of the threshold is carried out gradually, intervening on the structures as they become available for change. This ultimately transforms the works of architecture into literal products of the liminal dimension.

[softening the edges]

If it is true that the evolution of Palermo has gone in directions not always influenced by the growth of the port, it is equally true that in the contemporary context the project for the coastline is a central issue contributing to the development of a new idea of the urban border and the waterfront. By introducing the concept of the "interface," widely used by current city-port programs, the port unleashes its characteristics as an osmotic infrastructure, functional in terms of the performance of logistical and commercial activities and a determining factor in urban development.

Thus, when the city wraps around the entire front of the port, creating a continuous curtain along the edge of the property border, the city-port relationship is concretized through some linkages and gaps in the more permeable fabrics that are closer to the city. These are areas named "liquid port" or "permeable port," for which port activities are more compatible with urban ones and, although part of the port territory from a legal point of view, which function as new urban centers.

Following this approach, the winning project of the competition launched by the AdSP in the Sea of Western Sicily in 2018 designed the section of the seafront enclosed between Sammuzzo Pier and Piave Pier, proposing the creation of a building interface that embodies the characteristics of the border thanks to its volumetric configuration and the heterogeneity of its functions.

In the project proposal, the interface device offers a response to the theme of port architecture by lending weight to a particular variation of the threshold placed halfway between nature and architecture. This is an actual demarcation that, nonetheless, also works to reduce the perception of a physical and symbolic barrier. In this way, the project suggests a fundamental strategy: an action that aims to "soften the edges," i.e., to reduce its intensity through a particular threshold configuration that in a certain sense dilutes its concentration and thins out its effects. Thus, the border fades, and more than disappearing, it expands and extends towards the city according to an animating logic: it transfers its natural role of limitation and containment on multiple levels that overlap and intersect in a process of extension that moves at different depths from the port to the city.

The softening of the borders between city and port transcends the sectoral logic and produces a mixture of dissimilar parts. This helps to increase the biodiversity of the context and, above all, prompts a search for a new combination of forces in place, a new state of coexistence. This mixture then develops the ability of the place to incorporate differences as generative forces.

Therefore, the city is the result of a contamination that has brought together very diverse elements in form, nature, and use. Just like in the painting by Francesco Lojacono, *View of Palermo* (1875), where none of the botanical species represented is indigenous but is the legacy of a variety of domination by others, Palermo is a paradigmatic image of a plural city capable of appearing at the same time compact and multiform, collective and personal.

Features

«incomparability»
«heterogeneity»
«impermanence»
«duality»
«alterity»
«ambiguity»
«inevitability»
«rituality»

incomparability

«An absolute lack or insufficiency of a common measure or term of reference for the purpose of an appropriate quantitative definition»

The port poses a problem of scale. It provokes a sense of disorientation resulting from finding oneself in a place that does not seem to have been conceived for humans. The feeling of walking in a "city" made for others raises the (sometimes implicit) question of what to refer to when determining dimensions and providing oneself with instruments of comparison.

The port presupposes contrasting dimensional relationships, strong contradictions, and the impossibility of a univocal interpretation. It creates a misunderstanding, an estrangement that actually generates the opportunity to experience a difference. It pushes the boundaries of classifications and makes it possible to go from a condition of foreignness to a state of total citizenship.

The port is a space that is measured in oceanic magnitudes. Its scale exceeds that of the dock, the pier, the dam, and even that of the ship; it is confronted with the size of the sea, the sky, and the horizon line.

The shift from urban spaces to port spaces produces a widening and juxtaposition between dimensions that are very far apart.

The port is an area of transition where relationships intersect and intertwine, where the city loses its scale in order to become a landscape. In its dimensions, it experiences a multiscalarity, that is, a condition that holds different orders of magnitude together.

For this reason, the port connects the territorial scale with the urban one through the genesis of extraordinary architectural works: warehouses, silos, bunkers, lighthouses, depots, hangars, and dock facilities that enhance the port's role as an attractor of the entire urban ecosystem.

heterogeneity

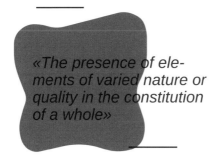

«The presence of elements of varied nature or quality in the constitution of a whole»

The world of the port represents innumerable settings, as many as there are observation points: these are scenes that form a theater whose stage can be trodden upon, but that can also be observed from a distance, from the ship or from buildings, from the ground or from the sea. This contributes to the production of spaces of various or complex varieties in which, putting aside an apparent confusion of languages, each element experiences a concrete interaction.

Port and city diverge and converge along and across a border, a limit defined in functional and institutional terms.

In the age of the simultaneous, of the juxtaposition, of the near and the far, of the side by side and of the dispersed, the border is the place where discrepancies are fully revealed. As Pietro Zanini (2000) writes, the border is a space that "more easily accepts the possibility of being modified, something that holds within itself two or more different ideas, none of which exclude the other." A space that possesses "the curious property of being in relation with all the others, but in such a way as to suspend, neutralize, or invert the totality of the relationships that they themselves designate, reflect, or mirror [...]."

A space that cannot be thought of as a homogeneous reality: purporting to want to make it such would inevitably mean causing its explosion and sacrificing its enormous richness.

Thus, the border persists in that particular area where different groups find themselves in a state of interaction, often oppositional and competitive.

impermanence

«*The nature of what is temporary and provisional which implies or provides for the transition to another state*»

The dynamics of the port are affected by the passing of time, by the pauses and accelerations of exchanges, by technical performance, by the rhythm of the infrastructures. They deal with the overlapping of moments and with the stratification of actions, with the accumulation of matter, with the fast-paced stuffing, and, of course, with waiting.

In this oscillation between two everlasting truths seen as fixed (suspension and movement), the gaze gravitates towards the sea, towards something that is about to arrive, towards an illusory and temporary stability.

In fact, it is thanks to trade, to its rules, habits, and needs, that ports have been created. Maurizio Maggiani (2000) relates that ports are established "by virtue of the fact that merchandise is made of things and of men in movement and has an absolute need for places to stop just a moment to take a breath and reflect on how to become always more beautiful and precious before resuming the journey and proceed-ing to where it will stop permanently. Before ceasing to be merchandise and becoming another thing: becoming things that are consumed."

Thus, as in the Sofronia described by Italo Calvino (1972), the city-port organism is transient and elusive because it is made up of two half cities: "One of the half-cities is permanent, the other is temporary, and when the period of its sojourn is over, they uproot it, dismantle it, and take it off, transplanting it to the vacant lots of another half-city."

duality

«*The quality of what is composed of two elements or principles. A dual relationship, common to both, interchangeability*»

The essence, reason, and genesis of port sites are based on the contrast between two states of matter. Two states that generate two natures, the foundation of the world of the port. The fluid nature refers to movement, to the movement of resources; it is infrastructure. The solid nature, on the other hand, is used for storage, for stops; it is the landing. Fluid and solid, material and immaterial, lightness and heaviness.

Thus, the port is a great number of ephemeral places, leading to the eradication of the multitude of its experiences.

However massive, city-port architecture is part of a continuous process in an incessant state of becoming. Consisting of provisional and mobile structures, it presents functional equipment for use and circumstances that shift the overall physiognomy of the port panorama, even if only for a short interval. It contributes to an intermingling and a transfer of codes that generate a particular form of a double and dual identity.

The city-port organism is at once semi-urban and semi-maritime: it incorporates technical innovations into urban culture, especially those coming from ships and from the sea, along with the engineering and naval component.

After all, as Giancarlo De Carlo wrote regarding Genoa (1992), "The modes and images of traveling have influenced the architectural warps, the infrastructural apparatuses, the equipment for the movement of goods, even the distribution systems of the buildings, the composition of their internal spaces, their relationships with external spaces, the split of their constructive and decorative parts."

alterity

———

«The characteristic of what is or presents itself as something else, that is different, not identical, sometimes opposite»

———

Universally, the city-port relationship presupposes a contrast between distinct and distant figures: in this sense, the action that defines an alternative and "other" nature is the opposition.

Orsini and Palermo (1994) write that, "A new beauty is born. [...] Born from the remnants of what we thought we knew, from the consolidation of a suburb that is not urban, but oceanic [...]. It is another world, a new city, a new beauty. An elsewhere where the buildings are machines, and among them some are monuments that stand out for their isolation, their uniqueness, their functional significance, and their symbolic presence. [...] This elsewhere gravitates toward taking on readings and interpretative canons that once again have the old city as the background and figure of comparison: our mechanical application of urban categories regulates the first contact with these strange territories. [...]

This city has squares of concrete and water, continuous and separated by a step; their dimensions are determined by the length and draft of the ship and the size of its cargo."

The presence of the port produces a condition governed by spatial, construction-related, perspective and functional "foreign" rules: a grammar, but above all a syntax alien, foreign, apart.

ambiguity

*«A condition of ambiva-
lence that implies the
possibility of a co-pres-
ence or double interpre-
tation»*

It is not uncommon in the world of the port to have the sensation of being on an edge, a unique moment in which two realities meet. According to Orsini and Palermo (1994), an ideal scene originates on this border where the harmony of the world and the unity of elements can be reconstituted.

The edge is by definition the line of differences, the place of identification by contrast, of the contact between two presences. The edge is that inevitably clear moment in the decreeing of the end and the beginning, the union and the separation.

In this state of unstable transition, the border becomes "a threshold: inhabiting or crossing it means recognizing a third place where the rigid rule of the border no longer applies," argues Piero Zanini (2000).

The presence of a threshold, that is, a gap between two different territories, implies a state of suspension in which a thing is no longer what it was and is not yet what it could become.

The threshold is a space where the status of someone or something changes. An ephemeral statute but one of great semantic value that serves to hold incompatible conditions together, becoming a terrain of confrontation and conflict.

So, this ambiguous state describes a liminality in which the project is implied and elusive. The act of crossing over it introduces a horizon without rules, in which a change of state takes place: as in chemistry, it represents that minimum value at which a stimulus is of sufficient intensity to start producing a tangible effect.

inevitability

«A condition that cannot be evaded, avoided. A relationship from which one cannot withdraw, which one cannot escape»

The relationship that develops and solidifies between the territories of the city and the port, sometimes harmful and sometimes fruitful, is nonetheless inevitable.

Historically united, cohesive, and overlapping for centuries in spaces and intentions, today the two entities are structurally distant, "thinned out" for mutual survival.

Inevitability describes the city-port connection that is constrained into a sort of impracticability or impossibility of changing. It is a condition analogous to persistence, to doggedness: it does not allow any possibility of yielding, of accommodation, or of conciliation.

It is a dimension that cannot be reduced, wherein the unavoidable or unescapable is the confrontation, from which often arises a symbiosis or subordination that freezes the city-port relationship in an obstinate state of adjacency.

Investigating deeply the contours of this connection, the port is not just the usual background: however far and inaccessible, it remains an essential element of the urban system. Despite centuries of change, this inexorable dialogue produces a state of coexistence, in which endurance and intimacy remain constant.

rituality

«An ensemble of habit-ual, repeated, and codi-fied behaviors. A tenden-cy to repeat gestures, movements, and pos-tures according to a rite»

The port is an intermediate site where only some parts of the overall process take place. Yet, even if only in these fragments, there is a rhythm that transforms actions into a celebration. In this endless cadence, man perceives his transitory nature.

The port is governed by habits, expectations, and promises. Its territory is constructed on a foundation of repetitiveness, tested movements, assigned roles, and mechanisms learned by heart.

Whether it's the cranes that await the docking of the ship on the wharf, the evolutionary maneuvers of a container ship, or the stuffing/emptying phases of a dry dock, this ritual, celebrated in its slowness, produces a progressive modification of the places.

No longer sea and not yet land, the space of water that separates the ship from the landing is shaped by both lines that, narrowing in the approach process, cancel each other out in their overlapping.

Recurrences

Heritage, decommissioning, conversion, and demolition.

Architecture on the threshold between impermanence and sedimentation.

Port panoramas and new infra-structural forms.

Models of government, states of coexistence, and cities of clusters.

Heritage, decommissioning, conversion, and demolition.

Born out of a constant and unstoppable process of modification and overlapping, port cities are characterized by a strong and secular economic, physical, and cultural connection between the parts; this is testified to, in the first instance, by the presence of a disposed piece of architectural and industrial heritage in the current structure, often very extensive and varied.

The set of artifacts anchored along the outline of the city-port threshold is a special type of heritage, explored for its characteristics of being a unique and unitary system. Already on its own, its identification on the sutured border between city and port offers a first and explicit field of transversal investigation.

The genetic vitality of the port thus changes the concept of heritage being referred to: not a system formed by sterile accumulation, but the result of a perpetual process of renewal, replacement, and updating that alters the entire structure. After all, as Carmen Andriani (2018) argues, "Heritage is not only what is inherited but it is also what we manage to make it become in our present time, giving it value.

It is the ensemble of signs, behaviors, and habits in which we recognize ourselves and to which we belong. It is the ability to construct narratives as sites of a collective mythology with which each of us can identify."

In some Nordic contexts in particular, the wartime destruction affected the state of the artifacts, transforming the heritage of the threshold between the city and the port into a collection of urban architectural works in different states of conservation. The wars created a new "degree zero" by resetting the pre-existing equilibria and producing unpredictable horizons of development.

However, the heritage of the threshold was also modified by the large waves of port decommissioning at the end of the twentieth century. If this phenomenon occurred in all the ports covered by this study, the recovery measures, on the other hand, intensively involved only certain zones of the port, operating in a way that was not always coordinated and simultaneous.

Moreover, the methods of intervention as a result of the alterations of the decommissioned architectural and industrial heritage were very dissimilar depending on the contexts. In some cases, in fact, the action employed the functional reconversion of the decommissioned artifact; in others, it instead adopted the tool of demolition. Extended to entire neighborhoods (for example, in the ports of Marseille, Hamburg, and Rotterdam), or limited to individual buildings (such as in Genoa and Palermo), the action canceled out a fundamental layer of the overall palimpsest of port cities by offering a new foundation on which to write.

Architecture on the threshold between impermanence and sedimentation.

The process of updating the twentieth-century port, often more episodic than systematic, profoundly altered the landscape in which the contemporary project intervened. This encouraged the plural nature of the artifacts positioned on the city-port threshold: architectural works that resulted from processes of contamination and hybridization that made them heterogeneous from a functional but also compositional point of view. The position they occupy on the border therefore grows and favors this heterogeneity, providing them with liminal characteristics. For these reasons, these are not simply edifices generated through a combination of uses but custodians of an architectural typology in its own right, one that not only inhabits the border but interprets and embodies it.

In contemporary times, the architectural works along the border present a functional program oriented increasingly less towards leisure and tourism and, instead, more towards the support of activities and the world of the port in general.

This phenomenon generates completely new uses of a pure port — or rather "city-port" — nature. Often located in urban property areas, thus public and accessible, the architecture of the threshold is significantly engaged with the operational activities, the economy, and the spatial and social dynamics generated by the port. It finds legitimacy in the definition of a space that hosts it, at once intermediate and ambiguous. This reverses the perspective: it is the places, those of the border in this case, that generate the functions and activities that are situated there.

In general, the production of these spatialities originates from a broad overcoming of the regeneration models of the late twentieth century and gives rise to a different strategic approach with regard to the city-port project.

The end of the great events, mostly major commemorations or celebrations in fact led to a more lasting model of intervention on city-port heritage, and this had important repercussions on the nature of the new fabrics being constructed. While waterfront projects were the result of occasional and temporary events, such as celebrations or festivals, and used the wave of investments as a vehicle for change, city-port renovation projects in the contemporary context favor instead long-term approaches developed in stages, in which exhibition halls become architectural works that, whether reconverted or built from scratch, remain even after the end of the event.

Port panoramas and new infrastructural forms.

Port cities are genetically marked by recurring features. The ancient foundation, the progressive stratification over time and, more recently, the dematerialization of traffic all generate undeniable similarities: each port has a list of similar elements that, when combined with urban morphology, make it a place that is simultaneously particular and generic.

The interaction of city-port attributes creates a specific identity that remains uniquely recognizable, and this transforms the landscape of the port city into a collective representation with a communal value.

The view of a port city itself, inclined at varying angles to the horizon one had in ancient times when coming from the sea, was for a long time the frame chosen to represent and, consequently, to understand a port. Countless were the maps or paintings that, like romanticized postcards, put art and geometry together in order to immortalize in a single shot the natural gulf, the river inlet, the ships in motion, and the maritime structures.

Already in those days, this practice contributed to the construction of a panorama, a privileged point of view. A synthetic image that could not be verified or falsified because it existed in itself; and even today, whether it is a perspectival view or a perfectly horizontal map, it reestablishes the complexity of the port infrastructure

as a perpetual recurrence. With the evolution of ports, however, the figurative unity of port cities was frequently compromised. The image of the seaport was altered by being mixed with the technical apparatus of the city.

Nevertheless, a certain structuring element, having actually assumed new strength recently, has remained evident. In this sense and beyond the most simplistic interpretations, the presence of water as a form of infrastructure for connection and movement is an undisputed recurrence among port contexts. Water channels and bodies of water connect and, at the same time, generate a clear division between areas that need separation and autonomy. Water functions as an infrastructural material, and the intentional insertion of this component leads to two (or more) opposing but dialoguing sides.

Such a configuration occurs in the river ports of northern Europe especially; for example, in Hamburg it is particularly evident. Here, the heavy-duty activities are located on the opposite side of the city and maintain a spatial and functional detachment from it. Nonetheless, they continue to see the port landscape in its overall picture; indeed, they offer an advantageous point of view on the operational water's edge. As confirmation of the strength of the element of water, recent strategies (those described for the future of the Genoese

Models of government, states of coexistence, and cities of clusters.

Levante, for example) propose resolving the issue of a lack of space by opening a stretch of sea located along the coastal edge. In this case, the duplication of the banks distributes urban and port uses and at the same time establishes a clear equilibrium between the two hubs by multiplying the possibilities of encounters.

The establishment of autonomous entities governing ports during the twentieth century went through several phases: a first period of substantial port independence related to transformative interventions was followed by generalized regulations in which the figure of the port authorities emerged. As already mentioned, today's most recent phase leans towards the clustering of ports, bringing several ports together within the same system and implicitly orienting the port toward a regional scale.

Although each context highlights non-negligible evolutionary variations, it is clear that the port governance model has influenced both the morphological-spatial configuration of the city-port threshold and the design approach by cities and ports with regard to shared areas.

Where the management of the port, and more specifically the entity's administrative structure, generally follows a privatized scheme, the transformation of spaces is based on strategies for an innovative integration between the port and the city, based on the formulation of subsequent phases and on the conceptualization of a development process rather than a static and definitive project. This situation occurs above all in some northern European ports (Copenhagen, Rotterdam, and Hamburg) where the port entity is a joint stock company managed by public stakeholders, generally the municipality and the state.

Conversely, in Mediterranean ports, the management model provides for port system authorities or large territorial ports acting as public entities with a legal status and having a more qualified decision-making role, especially in terms of finances.

From this administrative model, an outlook is then established in terms of planning and design. Public management is indeed often weighed down by particularly complex processes that hinder the initiation of shared actions (for example, with private investors) and, more generally, make the design process extremely complex in the interface areas.

Through these analogies, seen in the contexts covered by this study but also visible in other European port cities, the threshold takes on diverse forms and systems of relations. Along its path, more or less stable equilibria are generated that contribute to the formation of not only various threshold models but also of different states of coexistence that are more or less provisional or permanent.

Again, from a managerial standpoint, the port clustering process is undoubtedly an element of comparison between contexts, even at very distant latitudes. In reality, the formation of consortium ports is not a recent phenomenon but has been found in certain situations since the second half of the twentieth century. Depending on the period of formation of port systems, different configurations then appeared, since the rationales and starting points were different.

In the case of Marseille, the polycentric configuration of the port had already been established in the 1950s with the construction of the Fos-sur-Mer hub, intended for industries, and the so-called heavy-duty port. This sector, which grew further in the following decades, has always been part of the administrative structure of the port of Marseille but has never gotten close to the urban center, located more than 70 km to the east. This delocalization is therefore an "a priori" choice and not the result of a removal or even less of a decommissioning or reconversion of areas adjacent to the city freed from operational functions.

The phenomenon of port clustering is thus very different when looking at the cases of Copenhagen (2001) or the Italian ports (2016). In both situations, the merging of ports actually follows from a political decision on a national scale (supranational in the Danish case) that recognizes definite economic and productive advantages in the cooperative structure. This time, it is therefore a clustering implemented "downstream" through a mechanism whereby the new bureaucratic and urban planning apparatus replaces the existing one.

If the clustered model occurs in multiple contexts, the idea of coordination in terms of the port project and the streamlining of functions between the various ports proceeds instead in a misaligned manner.

Whereas in the port of Copenhagen-Malmö, port activities were already organized and distributed in an alternative way as early as 2000 by perfecting the balance between the two hubs, the reorganisation of Italian ports initiated in 2016 had to be measured against past decisions and against the completion of previously approved and often still ongoing plans and projects.

From the contemporary framework, it therefore emerges that clustering is the most fundamental recurrence, especially in strategic and design terms. The effects produced by this phenomenon indeed show a long trajectory of action aimed at functional optimization, but not only that.

The merging actually generates potential cluster cities, polycentric, linear or diffuse coastal conurbations in which the city-port project assumes a crucial role: that of attaching value to the intermediate landscape derived from the creation of the cluster.

A liminal and logistical landscape that brings together multiple ports, multiple cities, and multiple border spaces separating but, mainly, connecting them through a rinnovated and strong formula.

A landscape that is at once particular and global, where every single entity exists not only to share expenses but to build an increasingly plural idea of a port.

NEW HORIZONS

Port Clustering and Governance Patterns

The Emergence of the Port City of the Cluster

Port Clustering

In contemporary ports, one of the most interesting phenomena is represented by the clustering of ports, a growing process that is unifying different harbors into a single administrative and spatial entity, namely the "cluster."

Port clustering consists of the administrative union of two or more ports not necessarily belonging to the same region or state but active in the same economic, political, and infrastructural context. Due to financial and management benefits as well as logistics, it is a recurrent scenario that has already been experienced in some European contexts since the end of the twentieth century. Among the clearest examples is the hub of Copenhagen and Malmö, which has constituted a single port authority in the Baltic region since 2000, and the alliance formed in 2012 between Paris, Rouen, and Le Havre (HAROPA), which provides an Atlantic access to the logistics activities located along the path of the Seine River. In both cases, the formalization of the new governance model anticipated spatial transformations that require several decades to manifest themselves.

In Italy, the concept of port systems, together with the need to involve the hinterland territories in their overall development, was already included in the first port law enacted in 1994. Law 84/1994 considered the port a system capable of affecting areas outside the state-owned property area functionally connected to maritime traffic. However, it was only with the *2016 Port Reform* that the 24 Port Authorities were finally merged into 15 Port System Authorities.[1]

Port clustering in Italy has been also coordinated with the formalization of metropolitan areas in 2014 that eliminated the figure of provinces by merging more cities and territories.[2]

Although the consequences of the two laws are not yet tangible due to their recent approval, it is clear that they contribute to introducing new scenarios not only for ports, but also (or above all) for cities involved in these changes.

Governance Patterns

The phenomenon of port clustering is a contemporary recurrence that is creating a correlation between very distant port contexts all over the world. Such processes increase the framework of the relational possibilities even if they are exclusively addressed to the logistic-commercial field, focusing much less attention on the effects derived for the city. Indeed, there is no doubt that even today the port often remains an outsider in urban transformation: this precludes a different evaluation of the port as a driver and developer of spatial transformations.

Nevertheless, the formation of port consortia has introduced new governance patterns and new horizons in the field of city-port studies.

1
The Port Reform in Italy was introduced by Legislative Decree no. 169/2016, "Riorganizzazione, razionalizzazione e semplificazione della disciplina concernente le Autorità Portuali di cui alla legge 28 gennaio 1994, n. 84". The Port Reform is part of the National Strategic Plan for Ports and Logistics approved by the Council of Ministers in 2015 as part of the wider law named "Sblocca Italia" (literally "Unlock Italy") aimed at urgently unlocking public works on the national territory.

2
The Metropolitanization of Cities in Italy was introduced by Law no. 56/2014, "Disposizioni sulle città metropolitane, sulle province, sulle unioni e fusioni di comuni".

Truth be told, port clustering is not a recent dynamic but could already be seen in some contexts in the second half of the twentieth century. Thus, depending on the period of establishment of the cluster, different spatial configurations and governance models were created.

In the port city of Marseille, e.g., the polycentric configuration of the harbor was first conceived in the 1950s with the realization of the Fos-sur-Mer infrastructure, occupied by the so-called "heavy port." This sector, further developed in the following decades, is located more than 70 km to the east but has always been part of the administrative structure of the port of Marseille. This delocalization therefore was a choice made at the outset and not the result of a subsequent removal, dismantling, or reconversion.

In Copenhagen or Italy, by contrast, port clustering is a sequential phenomenon. In these contexts, the port association was derived from a political decision on a national scale (supranational in the Danish case) which expected that cooperation would undoubtedly bring advantages in economic and productive terms. So, in these circumstances, the clustering process was a choice made afterwards, and the bureaucratic and planning apparatus of the cluster completely replaced the existing one.

Governance and Planning

Governance and planning are two closely related topics, especially along the border between city and port. Government patterns influence the planning actions of the public/private bodies involved in the transformation of spaces often located along the city-port threshold, where the effect of planning tools is generally weaker and more blurred.

However, the coordination introduced by the clustered model does not seem to have immediate repercussions on the planning strategies adopted by the ports. While, in some cases, clustered ports are experimenting with solutions to organize their activities in a more balanced and complementary way, in other contexts (Italy, definitely) the Port Authority Systems are still substantially separated, dealing with the implementation of local projects.

Through the study of some European — clustered — cases, it is possible to build a reference framework and, at least partially, understand and evaluate the effects of the port clustering process.

During the eighteenth century, the port of Marseille was located entirely within the Gulf of Lacydon, and its transformations were managed autonomously. At the end of the nineteenth century (1881) — when the infrastructures had already occupied the northern front of the Joliette — the Chamber of Industry and Commerce was appointed as the exclusive port operator. Alongside the construction of the Fos-sur-Mer harbor in the 1960s, the port became a public entity and took the name of Autonomous Port of Marseille (PAM).

Finally, in 2008, the National Port Reform established the *Grand Maritime Port of Marseilles* (*GPMM*), a public body of the State responsible for operations, management, and promotion. Its jurisdiction extends over two basins: the east one in Marseille and the west one composed by Martigues, Port-de-Bouc, Fos-sur-Mer, and Port-Saint-Louis-du-Rhône.

The *Euroméditerranée* project,[3] active since 1995, confirms the importance of managing city-port relations through shared actions conducted jointly with the institutions. Its origin is due to the public agency *Établissement Public d'Amènagement d'Euroméditerranée* (*EPAEM*) which is experimenting with various formulas of cooperation, including the regeneration of disused urban districts and the implementation of logistics areas and operative docks. Practically speaking, Euroméditerranée worked on the reconstruction of an ancient alignment between port and city.

The redevelopment of the 400 meters of the Docks de la Joliette (2015–2016) is based on the concept of narrative sequence: with this strategy the design of the threshold is accomplished gradually increasing its breadth by inter-

vening on spaces and artifacts as they become available for change.

Otherwise, in Copenhagen — after passing the ownership from the Danish Royal Family to a state administration — in the twentieth century, the port was managed by the Port of Copenhagen Ltd. In 2001, the company became part of a single Port Authority formally joining the Port of Malmö. Today, Copenhagen Malmö Port (CMP) manages port operations in both harbors: its origin is clearly linked to the opening of the Øresund Bridge between Denmark and Sweden in 2000.

CMP is a joint venture that unites two cities and two ports, and, most of all, two nations: from a management standpoint, this makes it a unique case in the European port landscape. Bureaucratically, CMP is a limited liability company whose ownership is divided between different entities: CPH City & Port Development Corporation (By & Havn) that owns 50%, the City of Malmö that holds 27%, and private investors with 23% of total shares. CMP does not own the land but takes over areas and artifacts from CPH City & Port Development and the City of Malmö.[4]

CPH arises from the fusion of two public entities: one dedicated to urban development and the other in charge of port governance.

A key element of the CPH figure is its "de-politicized" nature, which allows the company to operate in a position of substantial independence from national and local political interference. The company uses the political-legislative structures to finance large infrastructure

3
For further information, see Euroméditerranée (www.euro-mediterranee.fr, www.marseille-port.fr).

4
For further information, see By & Havn (www.byoghavn.dk).

projects and, at the same time, under-utilized reconversions of areas included in the perimeter of the port.

In planning terms, CPH is guiding important transformations that are influencing the morphology of the three peninsulas on which most of the port is located. This has generated different degrees of interaction and approaches to the city-port project. If the presence of the port is absolutely predominant in Prøvestenen, in Nordhavn the two entities coexist, seeking an equilibrium still being defined through mixed-function projects. Even if the port is no longer active in most areas, in Refshaleøen, however, the reconversion was based on a more modulated re-functionalization that has not removed the operative character of the district.

The Port City of the Cluster

As illustrated, port clustering processes highlight a latent potential of the heterogeneous territories included in the cluster.

Pushing the reasoning further, the administrative aggregation implicitly gives rise to a new city-port reality extended along the coast and towards the hinterland. This is a polycentric conurbation that we can conceptually call the *City of the Cluster*: a multi-coastal-city that, composed of different

ports, cities, and coasts, emerges to be responsible for new relational opportunities in the decades to come.

In Italy, the planning of this new city-port reality was undertaken via a new document drawn up in 2017 by the Superior Council of Public Works.[5] Replacing those issued by the same national body in 2004, the new *Linee Guida per la Redazione dei Piani Regolatori di Sistema Portuale* (Guidelines for the Drafting of the Port System Regulatory Plans) deal with logistics and infrastructure connections but above all reflect on a new definition of a "port." A definition that recognizes that the scope of port planning may not coincide with the territorial jurisdiction of the Port System Authority: in fact, some maritime state-owned areas can be excluded from this area, as they are considered non-strategic for port purposes. On the contrary, some non-state-owned areas may be included, since they are functionally linked to the port. Therefore, through the agreement, the Municipality can accept that some non-state areas, functionally interconnected with the port, are governed by the port planning tool.

At the same time, the new Guidelines make a fundamental distinction between "operating port" and areas of "city-port interaction." With this maneuver, the attempt to speed up the process is evident, easing the planning of the operational areas of the port from interference with local administrations, while still remaining attentive to the urban requalification of waterfront spaces.

A division of tasks seems to emerge: the planning of the oper-

5
For further information, see Linee guida per la redazione dei Piani Regolatori di Sistema Portuale (www.mit.gov.it).

ating port is assigned to the Port Authority and that of the city-port interaction areas to the Municipality. The process remains strongly anchored in a principle of shared decision-making.

What is clear from all of this is the central importance of a collaborative relationship between the Port System Authority and the Municipality, especially with regard to the areas of interaction between the city and the port, which are not easy to define. Indeed, if we reviewed the port plans approved under the first Guidelines (2004), we would find a variety of different situations that cannot be neglected.

Liguria and Genoa

Investigating the particular case of Liguria, a region located along the northwestern coast of Italy, it is possible to discern a singular combination of nature, city, and infrastructure. Liguria is a region that, more than others, has had to face obstacles such as steepness of terrain, lack of flat spaces, and the fragility of ecosystems, generating a set of complex landscapes. In this context, Genoa represents an expressive fragment of this diversity, a place where each intervention has produced an alternation of weak and strong signs and an inimitable relationship between morphology, technical machinery, and urban plot. Thus, the Ligurian example — and the Genoese in particular — is a case of a logistics landscape that, starting from the coastal edge, curves along the riverbanks and towards the hinterland, giving rise to an inner port linked with the logistics platforms of Northern Italy and Europe.

There is a clear point of rupture in the Genoese port governance, a specific moment when the port ceased to be an urban affair and became a separate and independent territorial entity. This point occurred in 1903, when the Autonomous Consortium of the Port (CAP) was established as a self-sufficient body to which the State delegated part of its powers relative to the organization of port spaces.

From a legal point of view, the CAP depended on the Superior Council of Public Works, but it possessed broad independence in terms of works, installations, investments, working conditions, and imposition of tariffs. During its administration, the CAP operated autonomously in the state-owned areas given by the State and carrying out construction works without the need for an agreement with the Municipality. However, at the planning level, the contents and the approval process of the Port Master Plan remained unclear for a long time. In parallel, the Municipal Urban Plan dealt with its own territory, ignoring what happened beyond the customs barrier.

As anticipated (see *Atlases* and *Factsheets*), in 2016, the Italian institutional framework experienced a further transformation.

Due to this reform, Genoa became the main port of the Port System Authority of the Western Ligurian Sea, which also includes the Savona-Vado Ligure harbors, located about 45 km further west. Although recently finalized, the new governance model has imposed a substantial (and still ongoing) internal reorganization and a new concept of cooperation in order to overcome the previous fragmentation and sectoriality.

The cluster creates similar complications for the ports that it unifies, but it does not take into account the particularities of the cities of these ports, also united in a new territorial system. These cities are different in size, scale, impact on the territory, city-port heritage, relations with the hinterland, etc. The reform doesn't give indications about the formulas through which these diverse components have to deal with each other: how their individualities have to be enriched by the system, and what role has to be attributed to mobility to encourage their cooperation. This is particularly evident in the Ligurian context, e.g., when confronted with major emergencies such as the consequences of the collapse of the Morandi Bridge in Genoa (August 2018).

From these standpoints, the relational, social, economic, and urban potentials of the port cluster of western Liguria now emerge. Conceived as a whole, the City of the Cluster in the Western Ligurian Sea has an extension of 45 km, roughly the current extension of the Port of Rotterdam calculated from the Schiedam docks to the commercial terminals of Maasvlakte II (almost completed in the North Sea). This *City of the Cluster* is the mirror of a reform that, so far, does not seem to have had the strength to create synergy between all the territories and the authorities involved.

However, these assessments show that port clustering is still a decisive element for planning and project matters as well. The effects produced by this phenomenon foresee a long trajectory committed to concretizing, among other things, the objective of functional optimization theorized by the laws.
On this, the Port System Master Plans — which have not yet been drafted — will provide an overall view of the future development projects, taking into account the particularities of the merged harbors.

Lastly, the unification confirms that in these polycentric coastal conurbations, the project of the city-port threshold plays a crucial role. It brings value to the intermediate landscape derived from the creation of the cluster.

In fact, the space between the port and the city — but furthermore the one between one port and another port — is an infrastructural landscape where every entity exists not only to share the costs but also to build a plural idea of the contemporary port within the integrated project of the coastline.

AFTERWORD

Designing Thresholds in the Port Cityscapes

Carola Hein

Carola Hein is professor and head of the History of Architecture and Urban Planning Department at Delft University of Technology (the Netherlands). She has published widely and received a Guggenheim and an Alexander von Humboldt fellowship as well as other major grants. Her books include *Adaptive Strategies for Water Heritage* (2019), *The Routledge Planning History Handbook* (2017), *Uzō Nishiyama, Reflections on Urban, Regional and National Space* (2017), *Port Cities* (2011), *The Capital of Europe* (2004), *Rebuilding Urban Japan after 1945* (2003), and *Cities, Autonomy and Decentralisation in Japan* (2006), and *Hauptstadt Berlin 1957–58* (1991). Hein is head of the Leiden-Delft-Erasmus (LDE) PortCityFutures research program, vice president of the International Planning History Society, editor of PORTUSplus, the journal of RETE, and of the IPHS Section of Planning Perspectives.

Port cities are built and managed to facilitate flows of goods, people, and ideas between a maritime foreland and what is often a transnational hinterland. These flows depend on carefully controlled tangible and intangible boundaries used to delineate spaces that facilitate movement. Planners reinforce coasts and riversides to separate the spaces between water and land and to facilitate shipping and sea/land transfers. Their interventions create physical boundaries, such as security fences or infrastructures, but also intangible ones, such as governance and legal systems or land-use patterns. Boundaries relevant to port city planning are also embedded in statistics and quantifications: assessing population or economic growth patterns are limited by existing municipal borders and their collection systems. Such borders can also be imaginary: the industrial spaces of the port create a different imaginary environment than the sailors or pleasure districts on the borders of the city.

Port-related flows of goods, people and ideas cross these spatial, institutional, and imaginary boundaries and create complex, vague territories without strong, mutually supportive governance frameworks, legal systems, and planning guidelines. Multi-scalar markets and global value chains leave their imprint on the spaces of the port, and on neighboring urban and rural territories. Stakeholders in these areas are diverse and pursue different goals and functions. The result is a port cityscape, a networked space that extends from land to sea, including ships and pipelines, port facilities and warehouses, industrial and logistic structures, headquarters and retail buildings, but also housing and leisure facilities. This port cityscape is administered, planned, imagined, and represented by multiple institutions, but rarely as part of a shared vision. The separate consideration and planning of the various entities leads to a segregated planning approach to waterfront revitalization or river and coastline development, even though water connects all of these spaces. (Figure 1)

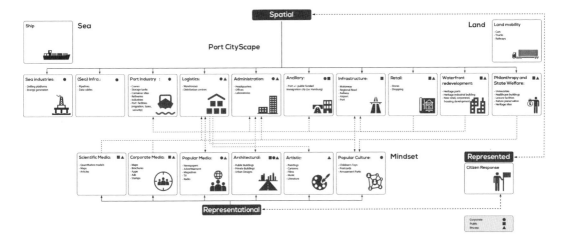

Fig. 1
Port Cityscape,
Carola Hein, 2019.

Contemporary ports are giant infrastructures with little human presence, very different from the mixed-use areas where traders and seamen worked and lived in the past. Port spaces today are hugely different from those of the neighboring cities and function with different temporalities.

Meanwhile, cities develop their own spaces and functions, often without any link to maritime and shipping practices. As ports and cities have grown apart, the boundary between them has solidified to separate different types of spaces and temporalities with controlled gates and entrances. Liminal spaces that once accommodated functions that depended on the port, complemented it or facilitated interaction between port and city have largely disappeared.

Policy makers and designers need to identify and conceptualize the spaces where port and city intersect and recognize challenges and opportunities. They need to understand who controls these spaces and how spatial design can provide solutions.

Conceptualizing the spaces where port and city intersect, identifying challenges and opportunities, developing methodologies, and designing innovative spatial features, Beatrice Moretti takes an important step towards a method that will help accomplish those tasks. What principles should guide the development of spaces and institutions at a time when port city territories are undergoing profound change? Territories are fragmenting, governance systems are overlapping, flexible coalitions of actors in different positions of power are emerging. We need to pay attention to port city flows and the ways in which they shape port city's urban spaces. Moretti proposes the concept of portuality and identifies it as a concept that represents "a new urbanity capable of embodying the inescapable bond that often places an entity (city or port) in co-dependence or in opposition to the other. This is a condition that presupposes the existence of an otherness with respect to the city and the port as simply understood. It outlines the contours of a hybrid and heterogeneous dimension that, as the result of diverse and juxtaposed components, embodies the complexity of the current city-port relationship." (p. 51)

Spatial interventions are most effective if and when they are part of a larger vision and comprehensive investigation at the scale of the landscape. This is especially the case with interventions that affect the port-

city relationship. Designers must conceptualize and spatialize these relationships and develop a new approach towards them. Bringing in new design-based perspectives requires a thorough reading of a vast range of documents from a multitude of fields with different methodologies and approaches. Economists, geographers, sociologists, and historians all have particular understandings of port-city regions and their long-term development. Each uses their own language and method. Connecting them is often a challenge. Single terms and approaches may become dominant because they correspond to particular interests.

To conduct the complex investigation she proposes, Moretti appropriately first takes the reader through a diverse body of literature that explores questions of port and city relations through the lens of boundaries. She specifically uses the concept of threshold as a zone of intersection with gradually changing spatial conditions.

Fig. 2
A historic crane appearing at the end of a street in Trieste, linking port and city,
Carola Hein, 2013.

The concept of threshold helps to identify the particularity of approaches towards the city and of visual and physical proximities. The appearance of a crane at the end of an urban street (as the one in Trieste shown in Figure 2) becomes part of people's mental maps. It serves the development of a maritime mindset or a port city culture that links port and city.

The concept of the threshold is key to the understanding and also the design of port cities. It replaces the notion of a hard border with one that is more continuous. Moretti explains this appropriately when she writes "The softening of the borders between city and port transcends the sectoral logic and produces a mixture of dissimilar parts. This helps to increase the biodiversity of the context and, above all, prompts a search for a new combination of forces in place, a new state of coexistence. This mixture then develops the ability of the place to incorporate differences as generative forces." (p. 171) Architectural projects that reflect the hybrid nature of the city-port threshold can enrich and enliven port and city interactions. Architectural interventions are not only needed in former, historic port areas; as the book shows, designs are also needed for urban or undeveloped areas on a landscape scale. Conceptualized in this way, the threshold can host a diverse range of functions, contemporary port-related and city-based uses, as well as energy generation or agriculture. They could be used on a temporary basis or facilitate the emergence of new practices — think of entrepreneurial districts.

The book focuses on six European case studies with different geographical particularities, historical developments (captured in the Factsheets (*ATLASES*), and appearances, which have experienced the same macro-transformations. The parallel investigation of these case studies shows the importance of the geographical location, topographical formation, and the impact of institutional interventions over time. An overview of the historical development of the cities shows the importance of longitudinal development. The mapping-based methodology at the heart of the thesis demonstrates the power of mapping as a gap-finder.[1] It highlights the importance of connecting spatial analysis with institutional investigation in line with Moretti's statement that these maps serve as "non-neutral images [that] give voice to the discontinuity of territories." (p. 80)

This mapping-based approach allows for a comparative understanding of the role of "Architecture on the threshold between impermanence and sedimentation," as Moretti aptly points out. The city-port threshold is here understood as an "architectural figure" (p. 76) that includes different morphologies and functions, planning tools and institutions. Identifying the port-city threshold as a condition in space and time allows architects and planners to develop a long-term strategy.

1
Carola Hein, Yvonne van Mil, "Mapping as Gap-Finder: Geddes, Tyrwhitt, and the Comparative Spatial Analysis of Port City Regions", *Urban Planning*, vol. 5, no. 2 (Lisbon, Portugal: COGITATIO Press, 2020), 1–15.

Moretti writes: "With this strategy, the design of the threshold is carried out gradually, intervening on the structures as they become available for change. This ultimately transforms the works of architecture into literal products of the liminal dimension." (p. 170) Capturing the analysis in easy to read convincing visuals serves the need of architects and planners to talk to and be heard by decision-makers at all levels of government as well as the general public. Such maps can provide the much-needed focus to identify frictions and opportunities that otherwise may remain hidden.

This book is a very welcome piece of thought that calls for a thorough, systematic, and comparative analysis of port-city relations from a spatial perspective. The vignettes of port cities studied here call for a more comprehensive investigation in terms of theory, methodology, and design. The field is too large for a single book to cover. A growing number of doctoral theses and books investigate not just ports and cities but engage with the relationship between them and the role that architecture and planning can play. Together they form a body of knowledge that can help us develop a more comprehensive, landscape-scale approach to design in the port-city threshold and provide a foundation for designers to make creative solutions based on shared values and for the benefit of ports, cities, and regions.

Ports are regional, sometimes national, economic powerhouses, and as such they can offer benefits to their urban neighbors. Their development is interlinked with national and regional policy-making, but that means that outside authorities can occasionally overrule the interests and decision-making powers of cities. Their temporalities are different from those of the city and its citizens, posing yet another challenge for cohabitation in the same space.[2]

Port authorities need to engage with ever more diverse stakeholders as well as political pressures, market forces, and legislation. Simultaneously, many cities and regions that exist alongside ports have come to host multiple non-maritime urban functions that occasionally compete with port interests, or even suffer from the presence of port industries and shipping. City governments have limited control over the port authorities but need to facilitate port functions. Urban growth extends beyond existing administrative borders and often competes with the land use and expansion needs of port installations in the wider region. Choices about the form and function of ports and cities as well as the reuse of historic port areas often depend on the constellations of local actors.

We need to develop types of intervention that align with the different spaces of port and city within the sea/land continuum. There needs to be

2
Carola Hein, "Temporalities of the Port, Waterfront and the City", in *City on Water*, Günter Warsewa, eds. (Wroclaw: Association of European Schools of Planning, 2016), 36–45.

a clear attempt to consolidate planning needs and approaches for all partners. While ports are often the drivers of regional development through port clustering such as in Italy, I would add that this is a call not only to port authorities but also to all other public and private institutions. The field of port city research has long been dominated by a focus on economics, logistics, and quantitative approaches. A spatial rethinking of the port city is still missing. The concept of the port-city threshold can be further expanded to address the whole port cityscape, that is the entire sea/land continuum alongside which port and city functions, institutions, and tools intersect. (Figure 3)

3
Neil Brenner, Christian Schmid, "Planetary Urbanization", in *Urban Constellations*, Matthew Gandy, ed. (2012), 10–13

Conceptualizing port cities as hubs and major agents in the larger framework of planetary urbanization,[3] will help better understand the complex patterns that shape ports, cities, and their forelands and hinterlands. The collective governance of these extensive landscapes, the logistics of the multiple flows, and the multi-layered use of space of these regions require careful analysis and development. The spaces of port functions and those related to port functions are sometimes shared with those used by the city. We urgently need new approaches that emphasize flows across borders.

We need to get past the notion of the waterfront as the main point of intersection between port and city. We need a paradigm change in terms of architecture and planning. This new territorial and institutional scale needs to be theorized and studied in a methodological manner with a focus on the implications of governance systems that can contribute to a redefinition of port-city-region relationships. Such a reconceptualization is urgently needed as port city regions around the world face a number of complex problems that require integrated spatial and social planning and design measures for the use of this limited space so that the port and city (and region) can evolve together.

Buy-in from local stakeholders is necessary. That will facilitate the construction of the hard infrastructures necessary for the functioning of the port, for acceptance of the side effects of ports (noise, security, emissions), but also the development of the skillsets and technologies needed for the port and port city of the future.

4
PORTUSplus — Special Issue: *Governance in Port City Regions*, vol. 8 (Venice: RETE Publisher, 2019).

The approach requires a rethinking of the governance of port city regions[4] and of the role and scale of architecture and planning. Studying how the "city-port threshold materializes in the space along the margin between the two authorities" (p. 6), as Beatrice Moretti does, is one (important) way to look at the port.

Fig. 3
Singapore waterfront,
Carola Hein, 2019.

AFTERWORD

Bibliography

landscape urbanism

Allen S. (1997), "From object to field". In: Architectural Design, no. 5–6, pp. 24–31;

Allen S. (1999), "Infrastructural urbanism". In: Points + Lines: Diagrams and Projects for the City, Princeton Architectural Press, New York, pp. 46–59;

Andriani C. (2014), "Ripensare l'infrastruttura. Note sul sistema ferroviario dismesso". In: La freccia del tempo, Cozza C., Valente I. (eds.), Pearson Italia Edizioni, Turin, pp. 32–34;

Andriani C. (2015), "Patrimonio materia attiva". In: Il progetto sostenibile, ricerca e tecnologie per l'ambiente costruito, no. 36–37. Edicom Edizioni, Monfalcone (GO);

Andriani C. (2016), "Reti minori ed Entroterra". In: Re-Cycle Italy. Atlante, Bocchi R., Fabian L., Munarin S. (eds.), letteraventidue Edizioni, Siracusa, pp. 56–59;

Andriani C. (ed.) (2010), Il patrimonio e l'abitare. Donzelli editore, Rome;

Ashraf K.K. (2017), "Fluid Spaces". In: The Architectural Review, no. 1442;

Bélanger P. (2009), "Landscape as Infrastructure". In: Landscape Journal, vol. 28, no. 1, University of Wisconsin Press, pp. 79–95;

Berger A. (2007), Drosscape: Wasting Land in Urban America, Princeton Architectural Press, New York;

Boeri S. (2001), "Eclectic Atlases". In: Stefano Boeri et.al., Mutations, Actar, Barcelona;

Burdett R., Sudjic D. (2011), The Endless City. An authoritative and visually rich survey of the contemporary city, PHAIDON Press, London;

Calvino I. (1972), Le città invisibili, Arnoldo Mondadori Edizioni, Milan (1993);

Carta M. (2015), Reimagining Urbanism: Vision, Paradigms, Challenges and Actions for Better Future, Series BABEL, LISt Lab, Trento;

Castells M. (2008), La nascita della società in rete, UBE Paperback, Milan, pp. 435–491;

Clément G. (2005), Manifesto del terzo paesaggio, Quodlibet, Macerata;

Corner J. (2006), "Terra fluxus". In: The Landscape Urbanism Reader, Waldheim C. (ed.), Princeton Architectural Press, New York, pp. 21–33;

Desimini J., Waldheim C. (2016), Cartographic Grounds. Projecting the Landscape Imaginary, Princeton Architectural Press, New York;

Doherty G., Waldheim C. (eds.) (2015), Is Landscape…? Essays on the Identity of Landscape, Routledge, Oxford;

Farinelli F. (1991), "L'arguzia del paesaggio". In: Casabella, no. 575–576, pp. 10–12;

Farinelli F. (2003), Geografia. Un'introduzione ai modelli del mondo. Piccola Biblioteca Einaudi, Bologna;

Farinelli F. (2009), La crisi della ragione cartografica, Piccola Biblioteca Einaudi, Bologna;

Foucault M. (2007), Security, Territory, Population. Lectures at the Collége de France, 1977–1978, New York;

Foucault M., Vaccaro S. (ed.) (1985), Spazi altri. I luoghi delle eterotopie, Mimesis Edizioni, Milan;

Guallart V., Gausa M., Muller W. (2000), Diccionario Metapolis Arquitectura Avanzada, Actar, Barcellona;

Jakob M. (2017), Dall'alto della città. 04 costellazioni, letteraventidue edizioni, Siracusa;

Jakob M. (2009), Il paesaggio. Universale paperbacks Il Mulino, Bologna;

Kipar A. (2010), "Infrastrutture e paesaggio". In: Ce.S.E.T., Atti del XXXIX Incontro di Studio, Firenze University Press, pp. 47–53;

Koolhaas R. (2001), Mastrigli G. (ed.), Junkspace. Quodlibet, Macerata;

Kuo J. (ed.) (2016), Space of Production: Projects and Essays on Rationality, Atmosphere, and Expression in the Industrial Building, Park Books, Zurich;

La Cecla F. (1988), Perdersi. L'uomo senza ambiente, Laterza, Rome, Bari;

La Cecla F., Zanini P. (2004), Lo stretto indispensabile. Le terre divise da un piccolo pezzo di terra, Bruno Mondadori, Milan;

Lynch K. (1964), Ceccarelli P. (ed.), L'immagine della città. Marsilio Editore, Milan;

Quaini M. (1991), "Per un'archeologia dello sguardo topografico". In: Casabella, no. 575–576, pp. 13–17;

Rankin W. (2016), After the Map: Cartography, Navigation, and the Transformation of Territory in the Twentieth Century, The University of Chicago Press;

Sassen S. (2005), "The Global City: Introducing a Concept". In: Brown Journal of World Affairs, JSTOR, vol. XI;

Snyder S. N., Wall A. (1998), "Emerging landscapes of movement and logistics". In: Architectural Design Profile, no. 134, pp. 16–21;

Valery P. (1921), Eupalino o Dell'Architettura, Edizioni biblioteca dell'Immagine, Pordenone (1988), p. 38–39;

Venturi R., Scott Brown D., Izenour S. (1977), Imparare da Las Vegas, Quodlibet ABITARE Edizioni, Macerata (2010);

Waldheim C. (ed.) (2006), The Landscape Urbanism Reader, Princeton Architectural Press, New York;

Waldheim C., Berger A. (2008), "Logistic Landscape". In: Landscape Journal, vol. 27, no. 2, Harvard Graduate School;

Waldheim C. (2016), Landscape as Urbanism. A General Theory, Princeton University Press, Princeton and Oxford;

Waldheim C. (2016), "Four: Post-Fordist Economies and Logistics Landscape". In: Landscape as Urbanism. A General Theory, Princeton University Press, Oxford, pp. 69–85;

Zukin S. (1991), Landscape of Power. University of California Press, Berkeley.

port

Acciaro M. (2013), "A Critical Review of Port Pricing Literature: What Role for Academic Research?" In: The Asian Journal of Shipping and Logistics, vol. 29, pp. 207–228;

AIVP — Le Réseau Mondial des Villes Portuaires (2015), Plan the City with the Port. Guide of good practices;

Basilico G. (1992), Bord de mer, Art&, Udine;

Benvenuto E. (1991), La ricerca d'identità. In: Osservatorio: Waterfront Portuali. "GB progetti" supplement to no. 8, EDITRICE PROGETTI s.r.l., pp. 8–12;

Bobbio R. (2005), "Complessità di rapporti e iniziative di integrazione fra la città e il porto di Genova". In: Portus, no. 10, RETE Publisher, Venice, pp. 35–41;

Braudel F. (2002), Il Mediterraneo. Lo spazio e la storia, gli uomini e la tradizione. Newton&Compton Editori, Rome;

Broeze F. (1985), "Port cities: the search for an identity". In: Journal of Urban History, vol. 11, pp. 209–225;

Broeze F. (1989), "Introduction: Brides of the sea". In: Brides of the sea: port cities of Asia from the 16th–20th centuries, NSWU — New South Wales University Press, pp. 1–29;

Broeze F. (1997), "Gateways of Asia: port cities of Asia in the 13th–20th centuries". In: Asian Studies Association of Australia, Comparative Asian Studies Series, vol. 2, Kegan Paul International, London and New York, pp. 1–17;

Bruttomesso R. (n.d.), "A New Port Landscape". In: Portus, no. 18, RETE Publisher, Venice;

Bruttomesso R. (1993), Waterfronts, a new frontier for cities on water. Centro Internazionale Città d'Acqua, Venice;

Bruttomesso R. (1999), The maturity of the waterfront. Marsilio Editore, Padua;

Bruttomesso R., Alemany J. (2011), The Port City of the XXIst Century. New Challenges in the Relationship Between Port and City. RETE Publisher, Venice;

Bruttomesso R. (2011), "Port and City: from integration to coexistence". In: Bruttomesso R., Alemany J. (eds.), The Port City of the XXIst Century. New Challenges in the Relationship between Port and City. RETE Publisher, Venice;

Carta M., Ronsivalle D. (2016), The Fluid City Paradigm. Waterfront Regeneration as an Urban Renewal Strategy. UNIPA Springer Series;

Ceccarelli P. (1991), "Una nuove frontiera interna". In: Osservatorio: Waterfront Portuali. "GB progetti". Supplement to no. 8, EDITRICE PROGETTI s.r.l., pp. 2–8;

Costa P., Maresca M. (2013), Il futuro europeo della portualità italiana. Marsilio Editore;

De Carlo G. (1992), La Città e il Porto. Marietti Editore;

Della Pergola G. (1999), "Il Mediterraneo, l'Europa, la Storia". In: DOMUS, no. 813, pp. 2–3;

Delponte I. (2007), "Porto-città-retroporto logistico". In: Portus, no. 15, RETE Publisher, Venice;

Ducruet C. (2004), Les villes-ports, laboratoires de la mondialisation. Gèographie. Université du Havre;

Ducruet C. (2011), "The port city in multidisciplinary analysis". In: Bruttomesso R., Alemany J. (eds.), The Port City of the XXIst Century. New Challenges in the Relationship between Port and City. RETE Publisher, Venice, pp. 32–48;

Ducruet C., Jacobs W., Monios J., Notteboom T., Rodrigue J.P., Slack B., Tam K.C., Wilmsmeier G. (2014), "Port geography at the crossroads with human geography: between flows and spaces". In: Journal of Transport Geography, no. 41, pp. 84–96;

Gabrielli B. (1992), La città nel porto, Nuova ERI, Turin;

Gallanti G. (1998), "Relazioni porto-città e ruolo delle città portuali". In: Urbanistica Informazioni, no. 159, p. 5;

Hein C. (2015), "Temporalities of the Port, the Waterfront and the Port City". In: Portus, no. 29, RETE Publisher, Venice;

Hein C. (ed.) (2011), Port Cities: Dynamic Landscapes and Global Networks, Routledge, London;

Hein C. (2016), "Writing Port City". In: Portus, no. 31, RETE Publisher, Venice;

Hoyle B.S., Pinder D.A., Husain M.S. (1994), Aree portuali e trasformazioni urbane. Le dimensioni internazionali della ristrutturazione del waterfront. Ugo Mursia Editore, collana Biblioteca del Mare;

Hoyle B.S. (2000), "Global and Local Change on the Port-City Waterfront". In: Geographical Review, vol. 90, no. 3, pp. 395–417;

Hoyle B.S. (2011), "Tomorrow's World? Divergence and Reconvergence at the Port-City Interface". In: Bruttomesso R., Alemany J. (eds.), The Port City of the XXIst Century. New Challenges in the Relationship between Port and City. RETE Publisher, Venice, pp. 14–29;

Jodice F., Perrella C. (eds.) (2018), Nuova Terraferma. Sagep Editori, Genoa;

Khosravi H., Bacchin T.K., LaFleur F. (2019), Aesthetics and Politics of Logistics. Humboldt Books, Venice and Rotterdam;

Kokot W. (2008), "Port Cities as Areas of Transition — Comparative Ethnographic Research". In: Kokot W., Gandelsman-Trier M., Wonneberger A. (eds.), Port Cities as Areas of Transition: Ethnographic Perspectives. Transcript Verlag, Bielefeld;

Laxe F.G. (2011), "Redefining the new Port-City Equilibrium". In: Bruttomesso R., Alemany J. (eds.), The Port City of the XXIst Century. New Challenges in the Relationship between Port and City. RETE Publisher, Venice;

Ministero Italiano delle Infrastrutture e dei Trasporti (2016), Riorganizzazione, Razionalizzazione e Semplificazione delle Autorità Portuali (D. Lgs 21/01/2016);

Moretti M. (n.d.), "Aree portuali tra conservazione e trasformazione". In: Portus, no. 5, RETE Publisher, Venice;

Murphey R. (1989), "On the evolution of the port city". In: Broeze F., Brides of the sea: port cities of Asia from the 16th–20th centuries, NSWU — New South Wales University Press, pp. 223–247;

Musso E., Ghiara H. (2007), Ancorare il porto al territorio, Dai traffici alla marittimizzazione. Mc-Graw Hill;

Notteboom T., Rodrigue J.-P. (2005), "Port Regionalization: Towards a New Phase in Port Development". In: Maritime Policy and Management, vol. 32, no. 3, pp. 297–313;

Pavia R. (2016), "Il sistema portuale italiano tra crisi e riforme". In: Portus, no. 31, RETE Publisher, Venice;

Pavia R. (2006), "La pianificazione delle aree portuali italiane. Problemi e prospettive". In: Portus, no. 5, RETE Publisher, Venice;

Pavia R., Di Venosa M. (2012), Waterfront, dal conflitto all'integrazione, Series BABEL, LISt Lab, Trento;

Pilan C., Nonveiller M. (2012), Logistica e territorio: la rete dei nodi complessi di interscambio. Le nuove piattaforme logistiche distrettuali. Edizioni IUAV, Venice;

Pinho P., Malafaya F., Mendes L. (2002), "Urban Planning and Port Management: The Changing Nature of City-Port Interactions". In: Littoral 2002, The Changing Coast. EUROCOAST/EUCC, Porto – Portugal Ed. EUROCOAST – Portugal, pp. 567–575.

Prelorenzo C. (2009), "The Cultures of Port Landscapes. Differences and Similarities between Port and City". In: Portus, no. 18, RETE Publisher, Venice;

Reeves P. (1989), "Studying the Asian Port City". In: Broeze F., Brides of the sea: port cities of Asia from the 16th–20th centuries, NSWU — New South Wales University Press, pp. 29–30;

Rosselli A. (2005), "Il porto come struttura e significato". In: Portus, no. 10, RETE Publisher, Venice;

Russo M. (2016), "Harbourscape: Between Specialization and Public Space". In: Carta M., Ronsivalle D. (2016), The Fluid City Paradigm. Waterfront Regeneration as an Urban Renewal Strategy. UNIPA Springer Series, pp. 31–44;

Schubert D. (2011), "Seaport cities: phases of spatial restructuring and types and dimensions of redevelopment". In: Hein C. (ed.) Port Cities: Dynamic Landscapes and Global Networks. Routledge, London, pp. 54–69;

Staniscia S. (2011), Islands. LISt Lab, Trento;

Vallega A. (1997), Geografia delle strategie marittime: dal mondo dei mercanti alla società transindustriale. Ugo Mursia Editore, Milan;

van den Lugt L., de Langen P., Hagdorn L. (2013), "Beyond the landlord: Typologies of port authorities strategies". In: International Association of Maritime Economists (IAME) Conference, Marseilles, France, 3–5 July 2013;

Verhetsel A., Sel S. (2009), "World maritime cities: From which cities do container shipping companies make decisions?". In: Transport Policy, no. 16, ELSEVIER, pp. 240–250;

Viola P., Grimaldi F., Olivieri M., Rigoni A. (n.d.), "I Piani regolatori Portuali in Italia". In: Portus, no. 13, RETE Publisher, Venice;

Viola P., Grimaldi F. (n.d.), "Waterfront fra piano (quale?) e progetto". In: Portus, no. 10, RETE Publisher, Venice.

border, interface, threshold

AA.VV. (2012), La soglia, Firenze Architettura, Dipartimento di Architettura di Firenze (ed.), vol. 2;

Balibar E. (1998), "The borders of Europe". In: Cheah P., Robbins B. (eds.), Cosmopolitics. University of Minnesota Press, Minneapolis;

Brambilla C, Laine J., Bocchi G. (2015), Borderscaping: Imaginations and Practices of Border Making. Routledge, London;

Brambilla C. (2015), "Il confine come borderscape". In: inTRASFORMAZIONE, no. 4, Palermo, pp. 5–9;

Boeri S. (1984), "Il vuoto e il margine: i progetti per il waterfront di San Francisco". In: Casabella, no. 503, pp. 22–25;

Bunschoten R. (2010), "Liminal Bodies and Urban Incubators". In: Schoonderbeek M., Border Conditions, Architectura & Natura, first edition, Amsterdam, pp. 278–282;

Crotti S. (2000), Figure architettoniche: soglia. Edizioni Unicopli, Milan;

Daamen T. (2007), "Sustainable Development of the European Port-City Interface". In: Paper ENHR Conference, Sustainable Urban Areas, Rotterdam;

Daamen T., Vries I. (2012), "Governing the European port–city interface: institutional impacts on spatial projects between city and port". In: Journal of Transport Geography, no. 27, ELSEVIER, pp. 4–13;

Di Venosa M. (n.d.), "L'interfaccia porto-città". In: Portus, no. 10, RETE Publisher, Venice;

Ferrara P. (2011), "Limes. Il confine nell'era postglobale". In: Sophia, vol. 3, no. 2, pp. 183–194;

Hall P. (1992), "Aree portuali: nuovi approdi del progetto", In: Casabella, no. 589, pp. 30–45;

Hayuth Y. (1982), "The Port-Urban Interface: An Area in Transition". In: The Royal Geographical Society Stable, vol. 14, no. 3, pp. 219–224;

Harbers A. (2005), "Borderscapes, The influence of national borders on spatial planning". In: Broesi R., Jannink P., Veldhuis W., Nio I. (eds.), Euroscapes – Forum 2003. MUST Publishers and AetA, Amstredam, pp. 143–166;

Hoyle B.S., Pinder D.A., Husain M.S. (1994), Aree portuali e trasformazioni urbane. Le dimensioni internazionali della ristrutturazione del waterfront. Ugo Mursia Editore, collana Biblioteca del Mare;

Hoyle B.S. (2006), "Identity and Interdependence. Transport and Tranformation at the Port-City Interface". In: The 4th Project Meeting of the Ionian and Adriatic Cities and Ports Joint Cooperation (IONAS);

Koolhaas R. (2014), "Doors". In: Elements of Architecture. Marsilio, Venice;

Land R., Rattray J., Vivian P. (2014), "Learning in the liminal space: a semiotic approach to threshold concepts". In: Higher Education, vol. 67, no. 2, Special Issue: Knowledge, Curriculum and Student Understanding in Higher Education, Springer, pp. 199–217;

Paasi A. (1996), "A Border Theory: An unattainable dream or a realistic aim for border scholars?". In: Wastl-Walter D. (ed.), The Ashgate Research Companion to Border Studies. Ashgate, London;

Rajaram P.K., Grundy-Warr C. (eds.) (2007), Borderscapes: Hidden Geographies and Politics at Territory's Edge (Borderlines series), University of Minnesota Press;

Rumford C. (2006), "Theorizing Borders". In: European Journal of Social Theory, no. 9, Sage Publications, London, pp. 155–169;

Schoonderbeek M. (2010), Border Conditions, Architectura & Natura, first edition, Amsterdam;

Schoonderbeek M. (2015), "Complexity and Simultaneity. The border as spatial condition". In: Territorio, no. 72, pp. 95–100;

Schoonderbeek M. (2013), "The border as threshold space of simultaneities". In: Archimaera, no. 5, pp. 151–165;

Sidaway J. (2007), "The Poetry of Boundaries". In: Rajaram P.K., Grundy-Warr C. (eds.), Borderscapes: Hidden Geographies and Politics at Territory's Edge (Borderlines series), University of Minnesota Press, pp. 161–181;

Simmel G. (1994), "Bridge and Door". In: Theory, Culture & Society Journal, vol. 11.1, Sage Publications, London, pp. 5–10;

Unwin S. (2007), Doorway. Routledge, Oxon;

Zanini P. (2000), Significati del confine. I limiti naturali, storici, mentali. Bruno Mondadori Editore, Milan.

case studies

Copenhagen

Bruzzese A. (2014), "Opportunità, risorse e limiti di progetti sul confine: Milano, Parigi e Copenaghen". In: Territorio, no. 67, Franco Angeli, Milan, pp. 44–52;

Ministry of the Environment, Denmark 2015), The Finger Plan. A Strategy for the Development of the Greater Copenhagen Area;

Vejre H., Primdahl J., Brandt J. (2007), "The Copenhagen Finger Plan: Keeping a green space structure by a simple planning metaphor".

In: Pedroli B., van Doorn A., de Blust G., Paracchini M.L., Wascher D., Bunce F. (eds.), Europe's living landscapes: Essays exploring our identity in the countryside. Zeist: Koninklijke Nederlandse Natuurhistorische Vereniging, Stichting Uitgeverij, pp. 310–328.

Hamburg

Fuchs C. (2014), "More city in the city. A dialogue with Wihelm Schultz and Jörn Walter". In: Area, no. 126;

Hamburg Port Authority (2012), Hamburg is staying on Course. The Port Development Plan to 2025. Free and Hanseatic City of Hamburg – State Ministry of Economic Affairs, Transport and Innovation;

Hein C. (2011), "Hamburg's port cityscape. Large-scale urban transformation and the exchange of planning ideas". In: Port Cities: Dynamic Landscapes and Global Networks. Routledge, London, pp. 177–197;

Hellweg U. (2013), "Building the City Anew: the International Building Exhibition in Hamburg". In: Portus, no. 26, RETE Publisher, Venice;

Mazzoleni C. (2013), "Amburgo, HafenCity. Rinnovamento della città e governo urbano". In: Imprese & città, no. 2, Camera di Commercio di Milano, Monza, Brianza, Lodi;

Schubert D. (2014), "Three contrasting approaches to urban redevelopment and waterfront transformations in Hamburg: 'string of pearls', HafenCity and IBA". In: ISOCARP, Review 10, pp. 48–60;

Schubert D. (2014), Contemporary Perspectives on Jane Jacobs. Reassessing the Impacts of an Urban Visionary. Routledge, London;

Schultz J., Sieweke J. (2008), ATLAS IBA HAMBURG Wilhelmsburg neu vermessen. BRAUN editor;

Wendemuth L., Bottcher W. (1932), The Port of Hamburg, Meissner & Christiansen, Hamburg.

Rotterdam

AA.VV. (2007), "Rotterdam. Porto di architettura". In: Rassegna, no. 88;

Aarts M, Daamen T, Huijs M, De Vries W. (2012), "Port-city development in Rotterdam: a true love story". In: UPM Departamento de urbanística y ordenación del territorio revista digital — territorio, urbanismo, sostenibilidad, paisaje, diseño urbano;

Daamen T.A. (2010), Strategy as Force. Towards Effective Strategies for Urban Development Projects: The Case of Rotterdam City-Ports. IOS Press, Amsterdam;

Daamen T.A., Van Gils M. (2006), "Development Challenges in the Evolving Port-City Interface. Defining Complex Development Problems in the European Main Seaport-City Interface: Rotterdam and Hamburg". In: 10th International Conference Cities and Ports, International Association of Cities and Ports;

Daamen T.A., Louw E. (2016), "The Challenge of the Dutch Port-City Interface". In: WINDOW ON THE NETHERLANDS, Royal Dutch Geographical Society KNAG;

De Martino P., Garofalo F., Hein C. (2017), "Arcipelago di Conoscenza. Da ricerca a progetto". In: Eco Web Town, no. 16, vol. 2, Edizioni SUT — Sustainable Urban Transformation, Università degli Studi di Chieti-Pescara;

Kuipers B., Manshanden W., Huijs M. (2012), Rotterdam: port city, port with a city or city with a port?, pp. 1–16;

Hall P. (2016), "How can joint urban and port planning facilitate the next economy — flexible frameworks of port and city?". In: AIVP World Conference 2016 Proceedings;

Meadows D., Meadows D.L., Randers W.J., Behrens W. (1972), The Limits to Growth. A report for the CLUB OF ROME'S project on the Predicament of Mankind. Universe Books;

Merk O., Notteboom, T. (2013), "The Competitiveness of Global Port-Cities: the Case of Rotterdam, Amsterdam – the Netherlands". In: OECD Regional Development Working Papers, 2013/08, OECD Publishing;

Reinhardt H. (1955), The story of Rotterdam: the city of today and tomorrow. ROTTERDAM Municipal Printing Office;

Steenhuis M. (ed.) (2015), The Port of Rotterdam – A world

between city and sea. nai010 publishers, Rotterdam;

Vries I. (2014), "From Shipyard to Brainyard. The redevelopment of RDM as an example of a contemporary port-city relationship". In: 3th Sefacil Pubblication, "Port-City Governance", part 2: Sharing Intenational Experiences, pp. 107–126.

Genoa

Airaldi G. (2012), Breve storia di Genova. Pacini Editore, Pisa;

AA.VV. (1987), Dossier Genova. In Spazio e Società, no. 37;

AA.VV. (1967), GENOVA LIBRO BIANCO. Sagep, Genoa;

Barbieri P. (1938), Forma Genuae. Municipio di Genova;

Borzani G. (1978), Porto e aeroporto di Genova. Cento anni di pianificazioni e costruzioni marittime al porto di Genova 1877–1977, Mensile del Consorzio Autonomo del Porto di Genova, no. 6, Sagep, Genoa;

Cabona D., Gallino M.G. (1993), Consorzio Autonomo del Porto di Genova, Archivio Storico, vol. 2, 1903–1945, part 1, L'autorità Portuale, Sagep, Genoa;

De Carlo G. (1992), La Città e il Porto. Marietti Editore, Bologna;

Forno G. (1985), "Gênes: ville-port". In: Villes-ports de la méditerranée occidentale, Actes du Colloque International de Marseille, 1984, "Renaissance Urbaine en Europe", Conseil de l'Europe, Strasbourg, pp. 75–84;

GB progetti no. 8 (1991), Cronache di progetto: Il Porto di Genova 1992, EDITRICE PROGETTI s.r.l.;

Molinari L. (ed.) (2002), Piano porto città. L'esperienza di Genova. Skira, Milan;

Moriconi M., Rosadini F. (2004), "Genova 900. L'architettura del Movimento Moderno". In: Universale di architettura, no. 154, Testo&Immagine, Rome, pp. 5–18;

Paone F. (n.d.), "Quartieri portuali in Italia: i casi di Genova e Trieste". In: Portus, no. 3, RETE Publisher, Venice;

Pellicci G., Bottari M. (1992), Genova nuova. Edizioni Colombo, Genoa;

Poleggi E., Cevini P. (2003), Genova. Edizioni Laterza, collana Grandi Opere;

Solimano S. (ed.) (2005), Attraversare Genova. Percorsi e linguaggi internazionali del contemporaneo. Anni '60–'70. Skira, Milan.

Marseille

Bonillo J.L., Borruey R., Espinas J.D., Picon A. (1991), Marseille ville et port. Parentheses;

Carrino A., Salvemini B. (2012), "Come si costruisce uno spazio mercantile: il Tirreno nel Settecento". In: Studi Storici, year 53, no. 1, Fondazione Istituto Gramsci, pp. 47–73;

Crane S. (2004), "Digging up the Present in Marseille's Old Port: Toward an Archaeology of Reconstruction". In: Journal of the Society of Architectural Historians, vol. 63, no. 3, University of California Press, pp. 296–319;

Euzennat M. (1980), "Ancient Marseille in the Light of Recent Excavations". In: American Journal of Archaeology, vol. 84, no. 2, Archaeological Institute of America, pp. 133–140;

Hénin B. (1986), "L'agrandissement de Marseille (1666–1690): Un compromis entre les aspirations monarchiques et les habitudes locales". In: Annales du Midi: Marseille et les marseillais, XVIIe–XXe siècles, no. 173, privat, pp. 7–22;

Merk O., Billaud L. (2012), The Competitiveness of Global Port-Cities: The case of Marseille-Fos — France, OECD Regional Development Working Papers, OECD Publishing;

Puget J. (2014), "Marseille merchants and the urban factory, between real estate disinterest and political involvement (1666–1789), In: Rives Méditerranéennes, no. 49, pp. 141–158.

Palermo

Carta M., Ronsivalle D. (2016), The Fluid City Paradigm. Waterfront Regeneration as an Urban Renewal Strategy. UNIPA Springer Series;

Bruttomesso R. (2006), "Palermo, Mediterraneo". In: Città-Porto, X Mostra Internazionale di Architettura, la Biennale di Venezia, Marsilio Editore, pp. 223–236;

Culotta P. (1987), "Nove progetti per l'Architettura della circonvallazione di Palermo". In: Le città immaginate. Un viaggio in Italia. Catalogo della XVII Triennale di Milano, Electa, pp. 180–208;

Carta M. (2015), Reimagining Urbanism: Vision, Paradigms, Challenges and Actions for Better Future. LISt Lab, BABEL, Trento, pp. 191–213;

De Seta C., Di Mauro L. (1980), Le città nella storia d'Italia. Palermo. Editori Laterza, Rome, Bari;

Office for Metropolitan Architecture — OMA (2018), Manifesta 12. Palermo Atlas. Humboldt books, Milan;

Pirrone G. (1971), Palermo. Vitali e Ghianda, Genoa;

La Duca R. (1994), Palermo ieri e oggi. La città. Sigma Edizioni, Palermo;

Raso A., Raso M., Poncellini L., Testa S. (2010), "Grande Sud-Palermo-Mediterraneo". In: Città-Porto, X Mostra Internazionale di Architettura, la Biennale di Venezia, Marsilio Editore, pp. 177–180.

Websites

Assoporti — Associazione dei porti italiani (assoporti.it)

Autorità di Sistema Portuale del Mar Ligure Occidentale (portsofgenoa.com)

Autorità di Sistema Portuale del Mar Tirreno Centrale (adsptirrenocentrale.it)

Autorità di Sistema Portuale del Mare di Sicilia Occidentale (portpalermo.it)

Baltic Port Organisation (bpoports.com)

Copenhagen-Malmö Port — CMP (cmport.com)

CPH City & Port (byoghavn.dk)

Delta Urbanism Research Group — TU Delft (deltaurbanismtudelft.org)

Euroméditerranée (euromediterranee.fr)

HafenCity Hamburg (hafencity.com)

HAROPA Ports (haropaports.com)

Human Settlements on the Coast (oceansatlas.org)

IAPH — International Association of Ports and Harbors (iaphworldports.org)

IBA Hamburg (iba-hamburg.de)

ISOCARP — Knowledge for better cities (isocarp.org)

Ministero delle Infrastrutture e dei Trasporti (mit.gov.it)

Networker Italy — Porti commerciali (networkeritaly.com)

OECD Port-Cities Programme (oecd.org)

Port Economics (porteconomics.eu)

Port of Barcelona (portdebarcelona.cat)

Port of Hamburg (hafen-hamburg.de)

Port of Marsiglia-Fos (marseille-port.fr)

Port of Rotterdam (portofrotterdam.com)

PORTUS — The online magazine of RETE (portusonline.org)

Reinventer La Seine Paris-Rouen-Le Havre (reinventerlaseine.fr)

Stadshavens, Rotterdam (stadshavensrotterdam.nl)

The European Sea Ports Organization — ESPO (espo.be)

The Meditelegraph Shipping & Intermodal Transport (themeditelegraph.com)

UrbanAge LSE Cities (urbanage.lsecities.net)

Alexander von Humboldt and Aimé Bonpland at the "Chimborazo" volcano.

Friedrich Georg Weitsch, 1806, oil painting

This book is the result of years of research and of physical and imaginary travels around and through port cities. Years that would not have been possible without the fundamental support of people to whom I would like to express my gratitude:

Carmen Andriani, who guided me enthusiastically and dedicated many resources to my personal and professional development.

Manuel Gausa, who offered me important opportunities for discussion, learning, and involvement;

Susanne Komossa and Nicola Marzot, to whom I owe the international research experience at TU Delft in the Netherlands;

Carola Hein for the significant afterword she wrote for this occasion;

Acknowledgments

Davide Servente for his always very apt advice;

Francesco Bacci for the day-before reviews and the everyday afternoons;

Clara Vite and Guido Rossi for the sea voyages and the big and small thoughts;

the unbreakable friendships and those I had not expected but that were able to change me, thank you;

my parents and grandparents, with all my heart.

This book is dedicated to Fabrizio for the strength with which he pushed me to always do what I desired.

Image Credits

p. 2 *XXXIX. Universalior Cogniti Orbis Tabula ... ex. ed. Geographiae Ptolemaei, Romae 1508,* in Voyage aux régions équinoxiales du Nouveau Continent fait en 1799, 1800, 1801, 1802, 1803 et 1804, J. Smith Publisher, Paris, 1831.
Alexander von Humboldt, Aimé Bonpland
© David Rumsey Collection (davidrumsey.com)
pp. 8–9 *Port of Rotterdam (the Netherlands), 2016*
Frans Berkelaar (the Netherlands)
© Flickr, Attribution 2.0 Generic (CC BY 2.0) license
pp. 12–13 *Port of Valparaiso (Chile), 2007*
Luigi Bosca, own work (Italy)
© Creative Commons Attribution-Share Alike 3.0 Unported license
p. 15 *Elevator 5 B1, Montréal (Canada), 2017*
Pymouss, own work (Canada)
© Creative Commons Attribution-Share Alike 4.0 International
p. 18 *Former Hennebique grain silo in Genoa (Italy), 2016*
Gian Luca Porcile (Italy)
© Gian Luca Porcile, free of rights
p. 20 *Port of Genoa (Italy), 2015*
Roberto Merlo (Italy)
© Port System Authority of the Western Ligurian Sea
pp. 22–23 *Port of Hamburg (Germany), 2010*
Reinhard Kraasch (Germany)
© Creative Commons Attribution-Share Alike 3.0 Unported license
pp. 38–39 *Port of Marseille (France), 2016*
Beatrice Moretti (Italy)
© Beatrice Moretti, free of rights
pp. 66–67 *Port of Genoa (Italy), 2015*
Roberto Merlo (Italy)
© Port System Authority of the Western Ligurian Sea
pp. 94–95 *Port of Algeciras (Spain), 2010*
Alex Proimos (Sydney, Australia)
© Creative Commons Attribution 2.0 license
pp. 96–97 *Port of Copenhagen (Denmark), 2009*
Politikaner (Denmark)
© GNU Free Documentation License, GFDL
pp. 198–199 *Port of Barcelona (Spain), 2015*
Marc McBey (Spain)
© Flickr, Attribution 2.0 Generic (CC BY 2.0)
p. 202 *A crane in the port of Trieste (Italy)*
Carola Hein (the Netherlands)
© Carola Hein, free of rights
pp. 206–207 *Singapore waterfront (Republic of Singapore)*
Carola Hein (the Netherlands)
© Carola Hein, free of rights
pp. 208–209 *Port of Shanghai — Yangshan Port (China), 2013*
Bruno Corpet, own work
© Creative Commons Attribution-Share Alike 3.0 Unported license
p. 214 *Alexander von Humboldt and Aimé Bonpland at the "Chimborazo" volcano, 1806.*
Friedrich Georg Weitsch
© Creative Commons Public Domain, uploaded to German in June 2005 by de:Benutzer:APPER

Imprint

© 2020 by jovis Verlag GmbH
Texts by kind permission of the author.
Pictures by kind permission of the photographers/holders of the picture rights.

All rights reserved.

Cover: Beatrice Moretti

Project Management: Nina Kathalin Bergeest
Translation to English: Stephanie Carwin
Design and Setting: Beatrice Moretti
Lithography: Bild1Druck, Berlin
Printed in the European Union.

Bibliographic information published by the Deutsche Nationalbibliothek.
The Deutsche Nationalbibliothek lists this publication in the Deutsche Nationalbibliografie.
Detailed bibliographic data are available on the Internet at http://dnb.d-nb.de.

jovis Verlag GmbH
Lützowstraße 33
10785 Berlin

www.jovis.de

jovis books are available worldwide in select bookstores. Please contact your nearest bookseller or visit www.jovis.de for information concerning your local distribution.

ISBN 978-3-86859-613-7